Thorns on the Tudor Rose

Thorns
on the Tudor Rose
Monks, Rogues, Vagabonds, and Sturdy Beggars

J. THOMAS KELLY

University Press of Mississippi
Jackson

Copyright © 1977 by the
University Press of Mississippi
Manufactured in the United States of America
Printed by Vail-Ballou Press, Inc., Binghamton, New York

THIS VOLUME IS AUTHORIZED
AND SPONSORED BY
JACKSON STATE UNIVERSITY

Library of Congress Cataloging in Publication Data

Kelly, J   Thomas.
  Thorns on the Tudor rose.

  Bibliography: p.
  Includes index.
    1. Monasteries—England. 2. Secularization—
England. 3. Great Britain—Politics and governments—
1485-1603. 4. Poor laws—Great Britain—History.
5. Poor—England—History. I. Title.
BX2592.K44   271'.00942   76-58547
ISBN 0-87805-029-9

DR. CARL B. CONE

was of invaluable assistance in the production of this manuscript; therefore, I take this opportunity to thank him for the advice and suggestions that he so generously contributed.

Contents

Introduction

There are many works on Henry VIII's dissolution of the monasteries and the function of Tudor poor laws, but I found few statements concerning the impact of the Dissolution on contemporary poverty problems. Most authors have dismissed this aspect of the issue by taking either a pro-Roman Catholic position that the Dissolution was a catastrophe for the poor or a pro-Protestant position that the monasteries were decadent and actually increased the problems of the poor. This study will, I hope, throw additional light on the foggy interpretative relationship made by historians between the Dissolution and the poverty and vagrancy during Tudor times.

It is not possible to write a statistical monograph comparing monastic disbursement of funds for poverty with those disbursed under the Tudors after the Dissolution. However, there are other approaches to the problem of poverty. For example, one object of this study is to prove that late medieval and early modern British poverty care formed a continuum in the manner of collecting and administering money for the poor. The Dissolution and the Tudor poor laws actually altered traditional practices very little, except that the Dissolution removed one source of poor relief. If this is an acceptable statement, then the need for a comparison will have been eliminated, and recognition of the very sameness of the poverty care before and after the Dissolution merely proves the point.

There then emerges a need for considering Tudor purpose, or lack of it, in provisions for poor relief after the Dissolution. The Tudors either intended to provide adequate assistance to the rogues, vagabonds, sturdy beggars, and impotent poor, or they planned to use the pretense of providing such assistance as an excuse for passing restrictive measures of social control. Evidence indicates the latter to be true.

The Pilgrimage of Grace set an important precedent for the future social history of England, especially during the reign of Queen Elizabeth. By her time the fear and distrust felt toward the common mob—greatly increased from the time of her father's supression of the Northern Rebellion and the establishment of the Council of the North—had solidified and become a chronic ailment of state. The people had had a taste of rebellion, and their appetites desired more of the same as a means of expressing dissatisfaction with a society built upon poverty and oppression. In addition, northern England had emerged from the Reformation and the Dissolution as the major area of discontent. Control of the North became an obsession with the dynasty. The crown kept on guard by passing an additional number of repressive statutes and demanding the enforcement of older ones in its vain attempt to retain control over rebellious subjects in all parts of the realm.

The manner of alms-giving and care of the poor after the Dissolution remained, as before, antiquated and inadequate. This study concludes that there is little foundation for trying to compare monastic care with post-Dissolution care on other than a basis of intent. The reasons for the Dissolution had little to do with poverty problems, and the Tudors developed no subsequent program directed toward building an effective poverty-care structure upon new foundations and in terms of the real needs of the people concerned. Instead, the old system continued with the burden for relief still upon the Church's framework. The monastic and secular churches had shared much of the obligation before the Dissolution; thereafter, however, the secular church had to carry the same load while under the constant aggravation of the Tudor poor-law statutes. Therefore, Tudor efforts not only failed to control the unrest of the common mob but also failed to ameliorate the problems of poverty. It was indeed an age of "rogues, vagabonds, and sturdy beggars."

The Stuart dynasty inherited these unsettled social conditions. Since it demonstrates the wide extent of the dangerous situation among the lower classes, the 1615 case of Ellen Pendleton, alias Floder, and her outlaw band (cited in Chapter I) serves as an excellent example. This is not an unusual incident; it reflects a social ferment quite prevalent at the time. The king's opponents, regardless of the forces causing them to act, certainly knew that they could count upon the disaffected masses for support in the Civil War. In this sense, therefore, the malaise of the common man figures as a cause or a cause behind the cause that ultimately dethroned Charles I. Tudor inability and callousness in dealing with poverty and vagrancy share much of the blame for his fall. Further investigation of this line of thinking, however, must await the results of additional research in the Stuart era prior to the Civil War.

ABBREVIATIONS

The abbreviations apply to the chronological lists given in this work. They also are used in footnotes where the author (cited in full) refers to his sources of information (cited in abbreviated form). Full citations are given in the bibliography.

APC   *Acts of the Privy Council.*

Becon   *Works of Thomas Becon.*

Bland   A. E. Bland et al. (eds.), *English Economic History, Select Documents.*

Burnet   Gilbert Burnet, *The History of the Reformation of the Church of England.*

CSP   *Calendar of State Papers.*

Cheyney   Edward P. Cheyney, *Social Changes in England in the Sixteenth Century: As Reflected in Contemporary Literature*, Part I: *Rural Changes.*

EJ   G. B. Harrison (ed.), *The Elizabethan Journals: Being a Record of Those Things Most Talked of During the Years 1591-1603.*

Heylyn   Peter Heylyn, *Ecclesia Restaurata; or, the History of the Reformation of the Church of England.*

Holinshed   Raphael Holinshed, *Chronicles of England, Scotland, and Ireland*, Vol. IV: *England.*

JJ   G. B. Harrison (ed.), *A Jacobean Journal: Being a Record of Those Things Most Talked of During the Years 1603-1606.*

JHC   *Journals of the House of Commons.*

JHL   *Journals of the House of Lords.*

Mackie   J. D. Mackie, *The Earliest Tudors, 1485-1558.*

NE   C. Roy Huddleston (ed.), *Naworth Estate and Household Accounts, 1648-1660.*

Rowse   Alfred Leslie Rowse, *The Elizabethan Age*, Vol. I: *The England of Elizabeth: The Structure of Society.*

RP   Robert Steele, *A Bibliography of Royal Proclamations of the Tudor and Stuart Sovereigns and of Others Published Under Authority, 1485-1714*, Vol. I: *England and Wales.*

SR   *The Statutes of the Realm.*

Stow   John Stow and E. Howes, *The Annales . . . of England.*

Thorns on the Tudor Rose

CHAPTER I

Why Were the Monasteries Dissolved?

A major cause of the Dissolution was Tudor regnal insecurity and fear of political and social upheaval. Aristocratic families often furnished monastic leaders, and monks had influence as alms-givers with vagrants who roamed England. Concerning monks, the bishop of Salisbury, Gilbert Burnett (1643-1715), says, "It was very visible that they were secretly disposing people to a revolt. So it was resolved to proceed against them all by degrees."[1] Within the religious community, monasteries offered the most resistance to changes made by Henry VIII. Monastic orders were more closely allied to the will of the papacy than the secular church, and after the Dissolution monks often figured in Rome's plots against the Tudors. The Pilgrimage of Grace and the Northern Rebellion show that monks opposed religious change and held the affection of common people. Because religious orders founded many parish churches, the danger was even greater. Approximately half the churches in Yorkshire belonged to monastic establishments.[2] Many secular clergymen, therefore, were monastically controlled. Henry ignored no dangerous situations, and with parliamentary sanction, he closed monasteries either directly or by pressure and "voluntary" surrender. He used monastic corruption as his excuse. Yet in 1544, after the English Dissolution, Hertford urged the king to destroy the threat from bishops and abbots in parts of Scotland.[3]

Because Tudors felt challenged by the Church and the aristocracy, they feared any popular discontent that might support these two factions. Ellen Pendleton, alias Floder, exemplifies such discontent. This female Robin Hood led her bands of rogues on raids throughout the shires of Norfolk, Kent, Lincoln, and Leicester. Because she flourished shortly after the Tudor dynasty (1615), her career was a climax to developments familiar to sixteenth-century England. It also reveals the legacy of social unrest that the Stuarts inherited from the Tudors. In this social drama one finds the elements of unrest and vagabondage among the poor masses. Reacting from apprehension and fear, the crown strictly applied the available laws designed to suppress, torture, and punish the unruly into submission.

Ellen and certain of her accomplices were arrested in the summer of 1615 and convicted of burning the town of Windham in Norfolk. Because of her pregnancy and her promise to reveal other names and crimes, Ellen received a temporary stay of execution. In its investigation of the matter, the privy council wrote several warning letters to the officials in shires where Ellen and her followers operated. A letter to Kent reveals the widespread nature of the danger. "It hath appeared that divers of her complices and associates are still wandring in severall partes of this kingdome, with intention to committ the like villany in other principall townes and cittyes which they have resolved to burne likewise, besides other treasonable practises, wherewith they are accused." The earl of Suffolk, Lord High Treasurer of England, received another letter. It, too, describes Ellen's crimes and those of her accomplices and warns that they "have conspired (if what she confesse be true), against his Majesty's sacred person, wee have thought fitting to acquaynt your lordship therwithall." The last letter went to the sheriff of Norfolk and reveals the probable fate of the protagonist of the investigation. Ellen had given false evidence to the king's council, and it moved to take vengeance. "We do therefore heereby signify unto yow that wee have not thought it fitt to continue her reprivall any longer, but that yow may proceede to the execucion of judgment given against her, notwithstanding any former direccions of ours."[4]

In the foregoing situation the first Stuart king, in Tudor style, avoided any attempt to get at the heart of prevalent discontent by pawning that obligation off to others at the local level. The towns and villages surrounding Windham were asked to give shelter to the fire victims who received rehabilitation by the royal grant of licenses to beg on the countryside. Ellen Pendleton's trial demonstrates that local discontent was widespread and that her vagabonds planned to burn other towns and even plotted against the king's life. They held several rendevous in which to hatch their plots, and the king's men chased from place to place in their attempts to apprehend the treasonable vagrants.

The misfortunes of Ellen Pendleton bring into focus the society and methods of the age, and one wonders how much torture she underwent as state officials tried to gain information. The rogues' gallery of the disaffected enumerated in the correspondence presents a microcosmic picture of much of lower-class society as it existed during Tudor and Stuart times. These rogues, vagabonds, and sturdy beggars formed a ragtag army, but an army capable of arousing anxiety and fear in the crown. Still, one must admire the audacity of Ellen Pendleton.

Ellen represented the chronic state of unrest among the lower class. The crown knew discontent could concentrate under leadership of either members of the aristocracy or the Church, and in the time of Henry VIII the monasteries could furnish the focal point. The king realized that the monastic establishment contained a major portion of papal power. He also knew that France and Spain, his foremost enemies, supported Rome's anti-English endeavors. Henry VIII could not take chances; therefore, out of fear of the mob and papal machinations, he consigned the monastries to extinction. This thesis will receive further attention in a later chapter. The Tudors had provided only palliative measures and had not penetrated the problem. Apparently Henry never concluded, as did Sir William Forrest during Edward VI's reign, that people at large supported the kingdom, not a few men of privilege. Therefore, the latter must not receive advancement at the expense of the former.[5]

Monastic wealth appears pertinent to dissolution, and it becomes inseparable from Tudor fear of the mob. The fact that monasteries held much of England's landed wealth increased Henry VIII's fear and caused him to act, for in the Tudor struggle for survival the possession of wealth remained vital. The king feared monastic power and the threatening linkage of that power with the pope and commonalty of the realm, and he wanted to eliminate the threat and thus gain the wealth. The major cause of dissolution, therefore, was neither fear of the mob nor desire for wealth, but a combination of both. Also, the same relationship existed between these two factors and the crown's fear of papal and other foreign interference in the realm, for in Henry's mind all these items formed part of one related threat to the Tudor throne.

The riches of the monasteries created a paradox for the crown. If Henry VIII anxiously dedicated his efforts to gaining monastic wealth, how could his agents proclaim the decay and poverty of the religious establishments? Perhaps this was true of the smaller houses, but Henry had larger fish in mind, and within four years he dissolved the entire monastic structure. The 1535 survey by royal commissioners of church wealth presents proof of royal awareness of monastic affluence. That survey (the *Valor Ecclesiasticus*) resulted from a statute whereby the first fruits and a new tax were consigned to the crown rather than the papacy. The survey enabled Henry to levy these impositions. David Knowles says that "the monastic income was underestimated by the commissioners of 1535" by about 20 percent or less. Wilbur K. Jordan in analyzing Yorkshire maintains that the monasteries absorbed much of the wealth that ordinarily went to the Church. He says about one-half of the 475 to 525 churches serving Yorkshire at the time belonged to monastic orders.[6]

The dissatisfaction and questioning in England provided another reason for the king's determination to check opposition. Thomas Starkey, royal chaplain, described the condition in his dialogue between Cardinal Pole and Thomas Lupset. Pole said England's disease thrived because "the temporalty grugyth agayn the spiritualty, the commyns agayne the nobullys, and subyectys agayn they rularys." They complain, bear envy and malice, and there is no health in this divided body. Pole presented an idea novel to the time when he stated that hereditary kings are seldom worthy; a country cannot prosper under a king who is not elected. Lupset, the traditionalist, warned Pole against treasonable words, for the king's position superseded all laws and questioning. Pole, preferring parliamentary rule, viewed Lupset's ideas as the source of England's disease.[7]

Monastic practices of dispensing alms and other charity served as one justification of the Dissolution. The ecclesiastical establishments supposedly increased beggary by their dispersal of "indiscriminate" and inadequate alms for the needs of the poor. Alexander Savine says, "The entries of monastic educational expenditure are very few in the Valor Ecclesiasticus." And, "there can be no doubt" that the number of people living upon monastic alms was fewer than the number of monks residing in religious houses. In terms of corrodians only, monks apparently dispensed little charity. Occasional alms given at monastic gates provided another form of charity. Wilbur K. Jordan reaches the equivocal conclusion that while "the charitable burden borne by the monasteries was, then relatively light . . . it cannot be dismissed as without importance."[8]

The monasteries and secular church of England had expanded to the point where, as Simon Fish said, they had acquired more than one-third to one-half of the realm. He refers to churchmen as "holy, and idle, beggars and vagabonds" who consume the substance of the king and the poor while they breed power for themselves, rebellion against the crown, and are stronger in parliament than the monarch himself. While the above estimates are questionable, historians acknowledge monastic control over much of England's landed wealth. Edward P. Cheyney concluded that monastic holdings amounted to at least one-fifteenth of English land.[9]

Despite such accusations, John Stow indicates popular support for monasteries. " 'It was' (sayeth mine author) 'a pitiful thing to hear the lamentation that the people in the country made for them: for there was great hospitality kept among them, and as it was thought more than ten thousand persons, masters and servants, had lost their livings by the putting down of those houses at that time.' " While this account is overdone, it reflects lower-class concern over destruction of the houses.

Many historians contend that monasteries contributed little to charitable needs. G. M. Trevelyan uses *scanty* in reference to monastic alms, and G. G. Coulton takes an equivocal stance by saying, "the problem of pauperism, though certainly hastened by the Dissolution. . . ." He then finishes the statement by a practical negation of what he has just said. W. E. Lunt maintains that the Dissolution happened less because of corruption than by a failure of monasteries to fill their former role in

medieval society. Only in the backward north country, he feels, did the
monasteries perform a vital function in the social life.[10]

As an excuse for dissolution, corruption provided the major charge
brought against the monasteries by the king's commissioners. The *Comperta Monastica* or visitation reports directed vile charges at the majority of religious inhabitants. A comparison of available documents
shows the falsity of a large portion of these accusations. The charges
against the houses form a repetitious pattern of superstitious practices
and sexual relations: sodomy, incest, "incontinence," masturbation. No
one knows how the commissioners discovered this in such a short time.
Many historians have disseminated this sad cry against the monasteries.
Geoffrey Baskerville speaks of the "slothful and ungodly life" of the inmates and says that their wealth "would be better employed" in the pursuance of various good deeds.[11] Perhaps it would have, if it had been so
used.

This chapter contains indictments against the houses and evidence
counteracting such indictments appears in Chapter II. First, an examination of visitation report charges of corruption: " 'Compendium
compertorum per Doctorem Layton et Doctorem Legh, in visitatione
regia in provincia Eboracensi ac episcopatu Coven. et Lichfelden.' "
This visitation contains a similar report for the diocese of Norwich. The
statistics of the two are here combined:

Number of houses in these two reports, 155.

Houses charged with superstitious practices, 60.
Houses with outstanding debts, 31.
Religious persons charged with sodomy, 109.
Religious persons accused of sodomy "per voluntariam pollucionem," 80.
Religious persons charged with incest, 4.
Religious persons charged with "incontinence," 178.
Religious persons accused of "incontinence per voluntariam pollucionem," 46.
Religious persons accused of "incontinence fatentur voluntar. polluciones," 11.
Religious persons charged with "peperit" (form of incontinence), 16.
Religious persons seeking release from the religious life, 68+ (one house: all
    except the prioress; another house: almost all; and in a third case: all except
    two).
Religious persons conspiring to murder the abbot in one house, 3.
Religious persons accused of theft, 2.[12]

Sexual crimes comprise the major charge, and the list contains 444 individual accusations. Since the king's commissioners looked for excuses for dissolving the houses, the alleged sexual activity of the religious "celebates" was probably overrated. In the case of the Grey Friars of London, "One Friar was so eager to show his loyalty that he laid information against one of his fellow brethren, misrepresenting a conversation of which he had only heard part. The accused managed to clear himself, but such spying must have made life unendurable, and gone far to justify the warden in declaring that 'all the house would willingly change their coats provided they have a living,' and that 'they all longed to change their coats.' "[13] The commissioners achieved success, for such an imposing list of eroticism cast a bad image of monastic life.

Even from the above list one can salvage items of monastic honor, for the following statistics of the 155 houses help ameliorate the situation. In this analysis indebtedness and the desire of certain members to obtain release from them are not considered as adverse factors to otherwise noncharged houses.

Houses listed and no charges made, 24. (One can assume that such houses either remained in good order or bribed the commissioners or had inside influence, for the commissioners certainly did not demonstrate backwardness in making accusations.)

Houses charged with superstitious practices only, 18.

Houses in which one religious person only was charged with misconduct, unless that person was the abbot or prior, 20.

Houses in which one religious person only was charged with misconduct, plus the charge of superstitious practices against the house, 5.[14]

A total of sixty-seven houses remained free of serious malfeasance. Such statistics, taken in conjunction with the probability that other accusations were greatly exaggerated, presents the idea that monasteries were more sinned against than sinning. This is something to remember when positive aspects of ecclesiastical houses are presented in the next chapter.

Given the efficiency of the king's dissolution-minded press gang, monastic establishments could not escape, for if the inmates refused to confess riotous living they were accused of "confederacy." Examples of this charge appear in the examinations of Bury St. Edmund's, Thetford, and Iklesworth. In the last instance it stated that, although one was "in-

continent" and " confesses voluntary pollutions . . . there also is suspi-
cion of confederation, for though 18 in number they have confessed
nothing."[15]

Contemporaries knew the king's intentions. Chapuys, the Spanish
ambassador, told Charles V that Cromwell was making a clean sweep of
monasteries. Concerning religious persons who could choose either to
leave or to remain in the houses, he said, "It is true they are not ex-
pressly told to go out, but it is clearly given them to understand that they
had better do it, for they are going to make a reformation of them so
severe and strange that in the end they will all go; which is the object the
King is aiming at, in order to have better occasion to seize the property
without causing the people to murmur."[16]

Certain commissioners made life severe for monastic inmates in
order to force capitulation and dissolution. Commissioner John Ap Rice
informed Cromwell that another commissioner, the ill-famed "Dr.
Legh," confined inmates to their houses, thus insuring that "as many of
these houses stand by husbandry they must fall to decay if the heads are
not allowed to go out." The commissioner acted more diplomatically
than his cohort, Dr. Legh, but John Ap Rice also served his king well as
he revealed in his addendum to a letter from Legh to Cromwell that
bears out what Chapuys said to the emperor: "Though it were well done
that all were out, yet to avoid calumny it were well they were dismissed
upon their own suit. They will all do this if they are compelled to ob-
serve these injunctions, and the people shall know it the better that it
cometh upon their own suit that they be not straight discharged while
we are here; for then the people will say that we came for no other cause
except to expel them."[17]

If the monks knew they were destined for expulsion, why did the majority of them desist from fighting the charges of corruption and accept
the dissolution of their houses? There are several aspects in the answer:
royal power exerted via the Reformation, lack of unity and leadership
among the houses, and the blitzkrieg fashion in which Henry moved
against them. The first item refers to plain bread-and-butter facts. Royal
commissioners informed inmates of religious houses that if they surrendered they would receive pensions for life; if they remained obstinate
they could expect a life of destitution. As the king anticipated, this went

to the heart of the matter. Most inmates succumbed to such reasoning when offered the promise of life pensions.[18] Man may not "live by bread alone," but he usually acts as if he does.

Contemporary reports leave open the question concerning promises of pensions. In 1536 the former prior of Folkstone wrote a begging letter, apparently to Cromwell. The prior complained of his poverty; he surrendered his house but had received nothing in return. A 1535 record of the voluntary surrender of Folkstone supports his statement. Here is another example of the nebulous nature of such awards: upon agreeing to the dissolution of the Grey Friars of London, Thomas Chapman, the warden, "was granted a life pension . . . and payments, but apparently not pensions, were made to twenty of the friars." The promise of pensions provided a handy device to encourage greater cooperation on the part of monastic inmates. Dr. London told the chancellor of the Augmentations that he had accepted the surrender of the "Charter house beside Coventry" and awarded pensions which he hoped would encourage others to make their surrenders.[19]

Although the Dissolution met little immediate opposition, resistance soon developed. Sir William Fayrffax told Cromwell that monastic houses were making friends and "wag" the poor to support them, and the monks of dissolved houses stay in the vicinity and "wag" the people to reestablish them. Apparently wagging paid off, for during the Northern Rebellion numbers of monks reentered their dissolved houses, and many in undissolved establishments resisted royal interference. The people supported them in spite of the published charges of corruption. "Yet that wrought not much on the people; for they said, why were not these abuses severly punished and reformed?" A good question, but Henry VIII offered no answer. He had other plans. According to Holinshed, the banishment of Cardinal Pole in 1538 brought those plans to full maturity. "After which, in the yeare following, the whole companie of professed votaries, moonks, nuns, and friers, were utterlie overthrowne."[20] Thus a great medieval institution ended.

The monasteries fell victim to fear and greed. Henry VIII held no concern for reform; his concern centered upon dynastic survival. The monasteries threatened Henry and he needed their wealth, this determined their fate. But why not reform? R. H. Snape reminds us that

monasticism had experienced declines and revivals before the Tudor
period. It is possible that this could have happened again. Snape says
that it was no longer possible because England was moving from Mid-
dle-Ages Catholicism to Reformation-era Protestantism. True, but one
must remember that this represented Protestantism that developed into
the Ecclesia Anglicana, a combination of both Catholicism and Protestantism. Perhaps the religious houses could have reformed and thus remained a valuable part of the established Church of England. Many contemporaries felt that monasteries deserved reformation and not dissolution. In the dialogue between Pole and Lupset the cardinal said, "I wold
not that thes relygyouse men wyth theyr monasterys schold utturly be
take away, but only some gud reformatyon to be had of them."[21] Many
of the poor commons agreed and felt the loss of their heritage; but no
one spoke for them, certainly neither Henry Tudor nor Cromwell. The
king held the power necessary to force monastic obedience out of its
papal mold, so that posed no insurmountable obstacle. Just as he had
forced reform upon the Church, he could have done likewise with the
religious houses. That was what he ostensibly set out to accomplish in
1535-36 with the Act of Dissolution for the smaller monasteries.

Once King Henry made his point about monkish corruption and thus
justified his intention to seize monastic wealth, he had to contend with
people who felt that true justification for the Dissolution resided in the
ultimate usage made of the newly acquired wealth. *Starkey's Life and
Letters* contains a proposal to Henry VIII that he should "dyspose thys
ryches, to the ayd succur & comfort of your most louyng & obedyent
subyectys." He further admitted that some persons would rather have
"a just reformatyon then thys vthur ruynose suppressyon." He informed the king of rumors that monastic lands would go to gentlemen
who had no need of them. He favored division of monastic manors and
the leasing of property to lesser men who needed land. Such yeoman
ideas also appear in the correspondence of Robert Southwell to Cromwell. "Divers of the poor men in these North parts wish to have the
farms of the suppressed monasteries in fee farm." Marillac, the French
ambassador, told Francis I that parliament, too, had ideas concerning
monastic property; members favored the conversion of certain abbeys to
bishoprics, schools, and hospitals for aid to the poor. Henry ignored the

advice. He spent the revenues to suit himself, in spite of the final words in the preamble of the 1535-36 Act of Dissolution to the effect that the wealth shall revert "unto the Kyngs Majestye & to his heires . . . to doo and use therwyth his and ther owen wylls to the pleasor of Almyghty God and to the honor & pfytte of thys Realme." It appears that two of the partners named in this statute were cheated of their shares; but they had dared to deal with Henry VIII and his heirs in the first place. Gilbert Burnet, bishop of Salisbury says: "And the fault was not in taking them [the religious houses] away, but in not applying a greater part of them to uses truly religious."[22]

With the foregoing qualifications, the monasteries were dissolved because King Henry VIII's power was such that he could work his will in parliament and bring about the necessary legislation. He could have used this same power to carry out monastic reform, thus eliminating his fears concerning monkish control of the masses and the monastic-papal affiliation. The lure of monastic property, however, tempted Henry beyond endurance—this, in combination with the above two fears, doomed the monasteries to extinction. The king knew that he had two alternatives for settling the problem, reform or dissolution, and he chose the one containing the additional factor of wealth.

During the years 1532 to 1540 England witnessed events that made Henry VIII head of the Church in fact as well as by statute. They were well planned and progressed by logical steps. In chronological order they are:

Repeal of the papal annates, 1532.
Act of Supremacy, 1534.
Bill awarding the annates to the crown, plus a 10 percent tax on spiritual benefices, 1535.
Valor Ecclesiasticus or results of surveys to determine the tax on spiritual benefices, 1535.
Act of Dissolution, 1535-36 (to close monasteries with revenue of 200 pounds and under per year).
Comperta Monastica or visitation reports for purpose of closing monasteries.
Act of Dissolution, 1539.
Last monasteries closed, 1540.

The crown triumphed over the Church, and king and parliament worked together with little friction. Even Ireland's parliament accepted the situation as indicated in the letter from "Brabazon to Crumwell." It names several acts and states that "the Common House is merveilous good for the Kinges causez" even though the proctors spiritual "sumwhat doo stick in diverz of thiez Actes." An ensuing statute removed any opposition that proctors might offer. In 1598 when a delegation went from the House of Commons to the House of Lords to discuss certain amendments to an act for erecting houses of correction, they received instructions that they could speak but that the amendments would remain.[23] Thus did Henry VIII and his daughter Elizabeth work their wills upon the parliamentary process. In short, Henry carried out a four-year program of controlled dissolution of the monasteries.

There is no point in going into the uncertain and complicated statistics relative either to the numbers of religious houses or the wealth involved. Authorities arrive at different sets of figures. A composite review of the statistics gives some visual indication of the magnitude of the monastic endeavor and the uncertainty of source materials. The total number of houses both large and small is usually established within a range of 469 to 825. The figure for the number of smaller houses, subject to dissolution under terms of the 1535-36 Act of Dissolution, is slightly over 200. Monastic establishments housed an estimated total of 7,000 to 9,500 religious inmates and maintained something over 20,000 laity who were direct dependents either as workers or corrodians. The estimates of the annual income of these establishments vary somewhere between 150,000 to 200,000 pounds. These figures appear in a population context of approximately 3.5 million people for the realm of England. They show that enough monastic wealth existed to put the gleam of anticipation in the eyes of King Henry VIII. This, plus his fear of the monastic-papal relationship with the mob were, in the final analysis, causes behind the dissolution of the monastic houses, and other factors remained auxiliary to them.

CHAPTER II

Did the Monasteries
Serve a Positive Role?

In examining the positive role of the monasteries, one should remember from the preceding chapter that even the grim report, *Comperta Monastica*, exonerates 67 of the 155 houses from serious irregularities. They were smaller monasteries that, according to the Act of Dissolution, formed the most unstable element in the monastic system.

The preamble of the 1535-36 Act of Dissolution of the smaller houses charged them with corruption. "Forasmoche as manifest synne, vicious carnall and abhomynable lyvyng, is dayly usyd & comytted amonges the lytell and smale Abbeys Pryoryes and other Relygyous Houses" to the end that they "spoyle destroye consume & utterly wast." The preamble accused inmates of wandering abroad as vagrants. Consequently all houses of less than 200 pounds annual income were designated for suppression and "the Relygyous psons therein comytted to greate & honable Monasteries of Relygyon in this Realme, where thei maye be compelled to lyve relygyously for Reformacon of ther lyves." For these are the "greate solempne Monasteryes of this Realme wherin, thanks be to God, Relygyon is right well kept & observed." Section nine of the Act ordered the heads of "suche Honable great Monasteryes" to accept those monks and nuns assigned to them from the dissolved houses.[1]

What has this act really said? The smaller houses stood guilty of malfeasance and the larger houses remained "greate & honable Monasteries of Relygyon" capable of receiving vagrant criminals from the lesser crime-ridden houses that they "maye be compelled to lyve relygyously for Reformacon of ther lyves." The larger houses represented the wheat and the smaller ones the tares. The Act of Dissolution seems to concede that the major portion of the monastic establishment, namely the larger houses, lived in a godly state of Christian well-being. If that was the case, have some historians accepted the *Comperta Monastica* or visitation reports of the smaller houses as representative of the whole monastic establishment without reading the Act of Dissolution? The king and parliament condemned themselves by their own Act of Dissolution which speaks seriously of the "greate and honable Monasteries of Relygyon." The government therefore had no justification for forcing the suppression and dissolution of those "great and honorable" institutions. Historians could well assume that, until they find contrary evidence stronger than the visitation reports of the king's commissioners, a majority of the larger houses performed a "great and honorable" function in the realm of England. In any case, the "great and honorable" clause in the Act of Dissolution (as an admission against interest) is one of the strongest pieces of evidence on behalf of the positive role of the larger religious houses.

The so-called second Act of Dissolution of 1539 was an act for regulating acceptance by the king of the "voluntary" grants of monasteries by their abbots and priors. As the preamble says, "of their owne free and voluntarie myndes good willes and assente, without constryante coaction or compulsion of any manner of pson or psons." This is legislative mumbo-jumbo, for the king's commissioners pressured monastic houses to surrender in order to satisfy the royal will. Hear Dr. Thomas Legh in his correspondence with Cromwell: "Whereas of late the King sent my lord of Winchester and Mr. Treasurer to see the order of Chertsey Abbey, and they reported all was well, you will know somewhat more by the 'comperts' which I send." Then he related that at Merton Abbey he wanted to dismiss ten canons but only dismissed two pending word from Cromwell. In a letter to Cromwell, the commissioner John Ap Rice brought an indictment against Dr. Legh for his manner of procedure as a commissioner. He used against Legh such terms as: "insolent and pompous . . . handles the fathers very roughly, many times for small causes. . . . He is . . . of intolerable elation. He is also excessive in taking." The tone of the letter of commissioner Richard Layton to Cromwell suggests that Dr. Layton belonged with Dr. Legh in the above indictment, for in reference to the prior of Lewes he says, "I laid to him concealment of treason, called him heinous traitor in the worst names I could devise, he all the time kneeling and making intercession unto me not to utter to you the premises for his undoing; whose words I smally regarded."[2] Nevertheless, the statute laid no charges against the "great and honorable" institutions so that parliament's words in the earlier Act of Dissolution still resound to their glory. They were dissolved without dishonor per the evidence left behind by the king in parliament.

An examination of a representative sample of the commissioners' reports resulting from the king's survey of the surrendered monasteries provides an apparently truer and more favorable assessment of the smaller monastic houses. The earlier commissioners having finished their work, these particular houses had capitulated to the king's pleasure, and there was no further point in dredging up criminal charges against them. Therefore, it is fair to assume that this source material merits more confidence than that provided by the original visitations recorded in the *Comperta Monastica*. In general, it supports the positive role of the monasteries.

Leicestershire:
Priory of Bradley: "of good conversation and living"—one desires capacity—house "in convenient repair"—they wish to continue—debt.
Monastery of Oulveston: all desire capacities—"religion not very duly kept for lack of numbers and because of age and insanity"—"clean house"—debt.
Priory of Kirby Bellers: "of good conversation"—"good hospitality"—two desire capacities—house in good repair—debt.
Priory of Ulvescroft: "refreshes many poor people and wayfaring people"—"prior, a wise discreet man"—"six are priests, good, virtuous, religious, and of good qualities"—wish to continue—house in good repair—debt.
Monastery of Garadon: "of good conversation, and God's service well maintained"—wish to continue—house old and in poor repair—debt.
Monastery of Gracedewe: nuns—"of good and virtuous conversation and living"—wish to continue—part of house fair and rest in good repair—debt.
Priory of Langley: nuns—"all are of good and virtuous living and conversation"—wish to continue—house in reasonable repair—debt.
Bredone cell: no news is good news, so, a clean slate.

Warwickshire:

Abbey of Pollesworth: nuns—"of a very religious sort"—wish to continue—"house in good repair"—debt.

Maxstokke: "2 of them suspected of incontinency, the others virtuous"—5 desire capacities if house dissolved—house "in good repair"—debt.

Erburie: "all of good conversation"—wish to continue—"the house in good repair"—debt.

Priory of Hynwood: nuns—"of good conversation"—"house ruinous and in much decay"—"discharged the nuns"—debt.

Carthusian priory nigh to Coventry: "in virtue and religion excellent"—wish to continue—"children brought up in virtue and learning found there of alms 12"—"house in very good repair"—debt.

Priory of Pynneley: nuns—"of good conversation"—"one desires a capacity"—"house in meetly good repair"—debt.

Stonely White Monks: "all of good conversation"—wish to continue—"the house being ruinous"—debt.

Priory of the Sepulchre by Warwick: "good conversation"—wish to continue—"house in meetly good repair"—debt.

Priory of Wroxall: nuns—"of good conversation"—wish to continue—house "in good repair"—debt, none.

Priory of Stodeley: "of good conversation"—"2 desire capacities"—house "in good repair"—debt.

Avecourte cell: no pertinent particulars.

Alcester cell: no pertinent particulars.

County of Rutland:

Priory of Broke: "The prior and no more . . . of good living by report"—house in decay—debt.

County of Huntingdon:

Huntingdon: "of good conversation"—wish to continue—"house well repaired"—debt.

Sawtre: no pertinent particulars—debt.

St. Ives: no pertinent particulars.

Hichinbroke: no pertinent particulars.

Stoneley: all desire capacities except one who wishes to continue—"house in decay"—debt.

County of Lancaster:

Cokersand: no pertinent particulars.

Cartmele: no pertinent particulars.

Conyshede: no pertinent particulars.

Burscough: no pertinent particulars.

Holland: no pertinent particulars.

South Wales:

Carmarthen Priory: This priory was under consideration for dissolution—"a

great number of people have their meat and drink in the said house."—
"hospitality is daily kept for poor and rich, which is a great relief to the country, being poor and bare."—"weekly alms is given to 80 persons, which if the
house were suppressed, they would want."—house "in good repair"—debt,
none mentioned.[3]

County of Sussex:

Tortington Priory: "incont. 1, desiring capacities 4, and the other desires to
go to other houses"—"the house wholly in ruin"—debt.

Boxgrave Priory: "incont. none, desiring capacities 8"—"house in good condition"— debt.

Hasting new priory: "incont. 4, desiring capacities 4"—"the house wholly in
ruin"— debt.

Mychelham Priory: "incont. none, all desiring capacities"—"house in good
condition"— debt.

"The Priory of S[hulbr]ede": "incont. none, desiring capacities 4"—"house
in good condition"— debt (record lost by mutilation).

Durford: "incont. nil, and all desiring capacities"—"the incompetent
estate"— debts (record lost by mutilation).

"[Priory of E] stbourne": nuns—no pertinent information.

Priory of Ruspar: nuns—"Nuns [two], desiring capacities and both continent"— debt (no information given).[4]

Various sources attest to positive features of several religious houses
(either dissolved or under consideration for dissolution):

Legh to Cromwell: Monastery of Holme— dissolved—nothing said against it.

Prior of Christchurch, Hants, to Henry VIII: against suppression—"Their
church is the parish church for the town of Christchurch"—a place of refuge
for miles around—feed the poor in surrounding country—a grammar school
for children— daily lecture in divinity.

Sir William Parre to Cromwell: "on behalf of the abbey and abbot of Pip-
well."—hard workers— daily aid to the poor. A previous entry gives, "very
small revenue, keeping continual hospitality, relieving the poor, maintaining
divine service in as virtuous and laudable a manner as any I know."[5]

Bishop of Rochester to Cromwell: "prior of the Black Friars at Cambridge, a
man of good learning and a preacher of God's true Gospel."

Evesham (Wales) abbot's petition: "that their monastery may be one of those
which the King proposes to alter into educational establishments."—buildings in good repair—noted for hospitality— daily aids many poor people.

Abbess of Godstow to Cromwell: no superstitious practices in this house.

Latimer to Cromwell: "Intercedes for the prior of Great Malvern."—keeps
hospitality—he feeds many daily in this poor county.

"[Dr. John London] to Cromwell": has accepted surrender of the abbess of
Delapray by Northampton—"a good aged woman"—house in good repair.[6]

Legh to Cromwell: commissioners at Chertsey Abbey reported all was well.

Richard Layton to Cromwell: prior of Boxgrave "a great husband, and keepeth great hospitality." At last, here is someone of whom Dr. Layton approved.

John Tregonwell to Cromwell concerning visitations made:

    Godstowe: nuns—"where I found all things well."

    Ensham:"all sorts of offences."—chaste abbot—house kept in good order—poor leader.

    Bruwerne: well learned abbot—house in good repair—good order.

    Wraxton: "The prior is a good husband, but rude and unlearned."

    Clathercott: "The house is old, foul, and filthy."

    Catesby: nuns—inmates "are free from suspicion."

    Canons Asbye: 160 pounds in debt—house decayed—"But the prior, though unlearned, is disposed well, and has a learned and religious sub-prior under him."

    Chacombe: prior well learned and is bringing his rude and unlearned canons to order.

    Burcestre: prior leads his house well and it is in good order except one runaway who is incontinent.

William Fordham, monk of Worcester, to Cromwell: received visitation—"I trust their books will show that I have lived religiously. . . . God be thanked, none went against us."

John Ap Rice to Cromwell:

    Lacock: nuns—"We found nothing at Lacock."—well ordered.

    Keyngton: three nuns—two incontinent.

    Edington: rector "a man of good name, but not so his brethren."

    Bradstock: prior adequate—two or three incontinent.

    Stanley: abbot incontinent before he became abbot, "and six or seven of the convent have confessed the same."

    Laycock: "no excesses."[7]

"[Prior of Henton] to his brother": "We have given no cause why we should be put down but have observed the service of God . . . hospitality, almsgiving and all other duties as well as any house in this realm."[8]

"Thomas Arundell to [Cromwell]": Monastery of Clyffe, Somersetshire—asks that house may stand—seventeen priests "of honest life who keep great hospitality."

The Duke of Norfolk to Henry VIII: houses of Bridlington and Jerves—"I think I should be at the suppressing, because the neighbouring country is populous and the houses greatly beloved by the people."[9]

Prioress of the Convent of Legborne to Cromwell: "We trust you will hear no complaints against us."

Prioress of Catesby to Cromwell: begs that house may continue—"I hope you have not forgotten the report the commissioners sent to me and my sisters."[10] It certainly must have been a favorable report.

Sir Richard Bulkeley to Cromwell: on behalf of the prior of Prestolme or Penmon, in diocese of Bangor—"shut up in his house by Dr. Elys Price and Will. Glyn., the King's commissioners. . . . He supports two canons, a priest, and 12 or 16 persons besides."

"Visitation of a Nunnery": The inhabitants want to know from Cromwell "whether Margaret . . . 12 years of age, being dumb and deaf, and Julian . . . 13 years, an idiot fool, shall depart or no."[11] Let us hope that the answer was "no," though they certainly had to depart ultimately.

Dr. London to the Chancellor of the Augmentations: "has taken surrender of the Charterhouse beside Coventry . . . the house is little in debt." —begs that they receive pensions.

Dr. John London to the Chancellor of the Augmentations: convent of Pollinsworth has surrendered and "have left it in such state that the king is put to no cost in despatching (sic) them." Therefore, pensions provided.[12]

"The Grey Friars": "The importance of the house may be gauged by the amount of plate in the church at the time of Dissolution."

"St. Henen's, Bishopsgate": "The satisfactory state of the house in the early sixteenth century is shown by the bishop of London's choice of one of the sisters to be prioress of Holy Cross at Castle Hedingham."[13]

Robert Southwell, Edward Carne and others to (Cromwell): "Have taken the surrender of Haylys, where the father and brethren were very honest and conformable, and the house out of debt."[14]

Favorable consideration for the monasteries appears in Sir Thomas More's *Utopia*. As R. W. Chambers explains, "*Utopia* indicates that, whilst he realized the faults of individual friars or monks, More believed their community houses to be on the right lines. In such institutions, as Burke put it later, there was 'a great *power* for the mechanism of politic benevolence, what our workmen call a *purchase*.' " They aided society and eliminated estate conversion to private holdings. " 'Reactionaries' like More and Vives [in reference to the monastically operated hospitals] could not see the logic of the argument that, because funds left for the aid of the sick were alleged to be badly administered, therefore they should be taken from the sick and given to the wealthy. The advice of [Simon] Fish and of Cromwell proved in the end more to Henry's mind."[15]

The dissolution of hospitals illustrates Henry VIII's greed and the fact that monasteries served a number of positive functions. Monks usually operated the hospitals, and many institutions suffered suppression in spite of pleas for their continued existence by such men as Sir Richard Gresham, mayor of London. Although not specifically mentioned in the 1535-36 Act of Dissolution, "Hospitalls" appeared in the 1539 "Acte for dissolucon of Abbeys." This illustrates an area in which monasticism provided poverty care. Both monasteries and hospitals certainly needed reform; but as to their absolute dissolution, the assumptions of Thomas

More, in the preceding paragraph, would apply. As Chambers remarks, the four great hospitals of London fell victim to the Dissolution and his majesty's Court of Augmentations only a short time after More's death. Chambers says of one of the hospitals, "It became the dwelling-house of Sir John Williams, Master of the Jewels, and the 'lodgings for the poor' became stables." Two of these hospitals were regranted: St. Bartholomew's by Henry on his deathbed and St. Thomas' by Edward VI. Of the latter hospital, the *Victoria History* . . . says that the convent accepted the changes in religion and "nothing was said against the brothers." Nevertheless, "Sir Richard Gresham's petition that the work done there in aid of the poor and sick might continue under the rule of the City Corporation was unheeded, the place being let to Thomas Mildmay." St. Thomas' hospital had established another such institution at Berkhampstead. Gresham's petition, however, finally succeeded in reference to St. Bartholomew's, as mentioned above.[16]

It is easy to understand why Henry was anxious to acquire the hospitals. Contemporary documents reveal that many of them held property in various parts of England:

St. Bartholomew's Hospital, London: dissolved and possessions listed in "cos. Midd., Herts, Essex, and the city of London, and elsewhere in England."

St. Leonard's Hospital, York: dissolved and possessions listed in "city of York, and in cos. York, Westmld., and Cumb., and elsewhere in England, Wales."

St. John the Baptist's Hospital, Exeter: dissolved and possessions listed in "Exeter and in cos. Devon, Soms., Cornw., and elsewhere in England, Wales."

St. John's Hospital, Bridgewater: dissolved and possessions listed in "Soms., Wilts, Glouc., Dors., Hants, Devon, and elsewhere in England, Wales."

The "Buckland or Minchin Buckland Priory": dissolved and possessions listed in "Soms., Wilts, Dors., Devon, Glouc., and elsewhere in Eng., Wales."

St. Thomas' Hospital, Southwark in London: dissolved and possessions listed in "cos. Surr., Suss., Kent, Midd., Essex, Camb., the city of London, and elsewhere in England."

St. Nicholas' Hospital, Portsmouth: dissolved and possessions listed in "cos. Hants and Wilts and elsewhere in England, Wales." No mention was made concerning pensions for the religious inmates.

St. James' Hospital, North Allerton: dissolved and possessions listed in "cos. York and Durham and elsewhere in England." No mention made of pensions for monks.

St. Wolstan's Hospital Worcester: dissolved and possessions listed in "cos. Worc., Warw., and Salop, or elsewhere in England, Wales." Nothing said about pensions.[17]

Many of these establishments apparently owned large amounts of land-ed and other wealth.

Several other London hospitals fell victim to the Tudor ax. Concern-ing the Hospital of St. Mary without Bishopsgate, the *Victoria County History* states that, regardless of one's position in reference to the religious operators, "there can be no doubt that good work was done in a hospital of 180 well-furnished beds." Again, Sir Richard Gresham begged the king, to no avail, to spare the house. A list of other—with the exception of St. Thomas', Southwark, listed above as having much property—London hospitals that were dissolved:

Hospital of St. Thomas, Southwark: "On 26 September, 1535, Richard Layton, the monastic visitor, wrote to Cromwell . . . that he was going to visit . . . 'the bawdy hospital of St. Thomas'." Annual income listed as 309 pounds 1s. 11d. "of which sum only 42 pounds 4s. was spent on the poor and infirm." Contained forty beds for the poor—dissolved January 14, 1540.

Hospital of St. Mary within Cripplegate: dissolved March, 1536. "There is no account of what happened to the blind and sick poor."

Hospital of St. James, Westminster: "for leprous women."

Hospital of the Savoy: dissolved in 1553 and refounded in 1556.

Hospital of St. Augustine Pappey: "The hospital came to an end with the sup-pression of the fraternities under Edward VI."

Hospital of St. Anthony: "The hospital was despoiled, not by the crown, but by a prebendary of Windsor named Johnson, who . . . turned them out."[18]

The following is a list of smaller London hospitals that the king allowed to continue: St. Mary of Bethlehem Hospital: a small asylum; "Hospital of St. Katharine by the Tower"; Whittington's Hospital; "Domus Conversorum": founded in 1232 as "a hospital for Jews who had been converted to Christianity." A small house.[19]

An act for the "suppression of the hospitals of St. John of Jerusalem in England and Ireland" apparently took care of this group of monastic hospitals en masse. In addition, three hospitals were dissolved in Yorkshire: Hospital of St. James near Northallerton, 1540; Rerecross Hospital, or the Spital on Stainmoor, 1545-46; St. Leonard's (first called St. Peter's) Hospital, York, 1540.[20] The abolition of these hospitals pro-duced tragic results and caused the poor to suffer.

Monastic schools require only brief treatment. They contributed little to the era's pedagogic development. Not until the reign of Elizabeth did the demand for educational facilities increase considerably. William

Cobbett thought that after school closure, no immediate effort was made to fill the vacuum thus created. Geoffrey Baskerville, quoting from A. F. Leach's *Educational Charters*, makes the point that the dissolution of the monasteries deprived about 1,500 poor boys of educational opportunity.[21]

A. L. Rowse comments upon the smallness of monastic educational facilities and thinks that the loss due to closure was insignificant. The dissolution of the large number of chantry and guild schools caused a heavier blow to education, "even if they were small and amateurish in themselves." Concerning the Elizabethan period Rowse says, "It is probably fair to say that there was a greater rate of school foundations in this than in any other period of our history."[22] However, a majority of the schools founded during the time of Elizabeth were also "small and amateurish." Besides, this spurt of educational development was related to the evolutionary process of the era's society and had no particular reference to either monastic establishment or disestablishment.

The final item for consideration in this chapter is alms-giving, the most controversial part of the monastic function. Much of the controversy concerns the fate of the poor after the Dissolution. From one viewpoint the Dissolution was a catastrophe because the monasteries contributed to the charity needs of the Middle Ages. Many historians, however, contend it was the welcome death of a decadent structure—a blessing in disguise since the Tudors, especially Queen Elizabeth, thereafter proceeded to a governmentally oriented program of semi-modern welfare legislation. And as proof of such progress, they maintain that vagabondage in England became insignificant as compared to that on the Continent.

Studies of the problem divide into three categories. Writers such as Francis A. Gasquet contend that the monasteries gave a maximum to charity. George G. Coulton and others believe that the religious houses gave an insignificant crust to the indigent population. A few writers take a middle position. Notable examples are David Knowles and Geoffrey Baskerville. Knowles says that Baskerville professes to stand aloof from the extremes but ignores many facts and uses innuendo and rhetorical arguments.[23] Knowles himself is scholarly in approach, but somewhat apologetic. Textbooks tend to follow either one or the other of the two extremes.

Even though the monasteries achieved much less than their potential, they contributed appreciably to the relief of the poor, served as places of hospitality for the traveler, and in some degree helped the cause of education. The dissolution and removal of this source of revenue was bound to have an effect upon the Church in its entirety and in its ability to carry out delegated charitable functions. In this respect, Keith Feiling considers the Dissolution a disaster to the Church's effectiveness in all areas.[24]

The Dissolution involved more than the institutional Church and people who shared the monastic life. It affected the lives of many who had some direct or indirect contact with the monasteries. The disruption of such a social corporation had many adverse effects upon the nation. These are not totally measurable in the statistics relating to charity or to corruption but they relate to ideals and traditions. This is not to say that monastic charity and corruption are not valid concerns of historical study, but they should not be isolated from other considerations to which they might contribute a deeper understanding. The source used by John Stow and the letter of the abbot of St. Mary's Abbey to Cromwell express emotionally the spirit of the ideals and traditions of the time.[25]

When evaluating the controversy over religious care of the poor, one should keep in mind that hospital care and various other types of poverty aid, including alms, were items of monastic charity. After allowing for the various types of such charity, the results are "disillusioning"— thus R. H. Snape summarizes the arguments of the detractors. He says, "The meagreness of the gifts of the monks during this time, the absence of any systematic distribution among the really needy, the haphazard way in which many of the gifts of the religious were obviously scattered, and the lack of living personal interest in the poor which lies at the root of all indiscriminate charity, cannot be ignored." Nevertheless the same problems continued in the post-Dissolution era. The lax inmates of religious houses did not furnish the only cause of pecuniary and social irresponsibility. The king and nobility abused their claim upon monastic hospitality. R. H. Snape provides an example from the

Chronicle of Evesham during the period 1467-77. " 'Magnates con-
volarunt adeo frequenter ad monasterium ut non sufficerent redditus.'
The house was burdened in consequence with a debt of 1000 marks."
Henry Brinklow refers to the "Antichrist of Rome," but admits that
monks kept hospitality, fed and gave alms to the poor so that "many
thowsandes were well relevyd of them, and myght have bene better, if
thei had not had so many great mennes horses to fede, and had not bene
overcharged with such idle gentylmen as were never out of the abbeys."[26] In view of the abuse of religious hospitality, the monarch had
little cause to deliver accusations against the monastic system via the
Act of Dissolution.

Jean Jusserand thought it was either the poor or the wealthy to whom
the religious houses extended hospitality, for the inns served the middle
class. Quoting E. M. Leonard's *History of English Poor Relief,*
Geoffrey Baskerville says that "much monastic charity was dispensed,
but only of the compulsory dole kind and the system 'did nearly as
much to increase beggars as to relieve them.' " After using this same
passage from Leonard's work, George M. Trevelyan concludes that the
problem of mendicancy was little, if any, worse after the Dissolution
and that "it was certainly less bad at the end of the reign of Elizabeth."[27]
The repression of a problem does not necessarily make it "less bad."

Other than previously mentioned items, there is further evidence on
charitable contributions of religious houses. Cardinal Gasquet was the
apologist for monasticism. A quotation from a late sixteenth-century
manuscript sums up the cardinal's position. The monasteries were
" 'oblations to the Lord' and 'the patrimony of the poor.' " It adds that
the monks " ' made such provision daily for the people that stood in
need thereof, as sick, sore, lame or otherwise impotent that none or very
few lacked relief in one place or another.' " The 1539 correspondence
between the abbot of St. Mary's Abbey, Ireland, and Cromwell contains
another defence of the monasteries. The abbot begged Cromwell to
spare his house because "We be but stewards and purveyors to other
men's uses, for the kings honour; keeping hospitality, and many poor
men, scholars, and orphans."[28]

The *Calendar of State Papers* for the reign of Henry VIII contains
other evidence supporting the monasteries. The Clergy of Bangor to

Cromwell: The king's visitors found "many" guilty of incontinence. Still, they desire "that we may maintain such poor hospitality as we have done hitherto." If they are not allowed to continue, then it will be a "great loss of the poor people who are by us relieved." Then there appeared the letter from the commissioners in Northamptonshire to "[Cromwell]" regarding Catesby nunnery. They found the house in "perfect" order, the prioress "a wise, discreet, and religious woman, with nine devout nuns . . . as good as we have ever seen." The house is so located that it provides "a great relief to the poor." The commissioners entered the admonition that if any house should remain none was more worthy than Catesby. "We have not found any such elsewhere." Another testimonial is found in "Aske's Examination." In reference to the Northern Rebellion, Aske testified that he and his fellow countrymen stood against the suppression of the monasteries, "because the abbeys in the North gave great alms to poor men and laudably served God . . . no hospitality now kept." Finally, Cardinal Pole informed the emperor Charles V that the English king, by seizing the monasteries, had thus taken from the people "almost their very support (*sua prope alimenta*) for such these monasteries were."[29]

Although antipapal, Brinklow supported the monasteries. He saw the rents raised by the receivers of abbey lands, and "It had bene more profytable, no dowte, for the common welth, that thei had remayned styll in their handys. For why? thei never inhansed their landys, nor toke so cruel fynes as doo our temporal tyrannys." Due to post-Dissolution rent increases, poor men could no longer live on the lands, and they left to join the vagrant band. In another passage, Roderick told parliament that even though the monastic system was under the "Antichrist of Rome," it administered to the needs of the poor to the relief of "many thowsandes."[30] This was admission against interest on behalf of the religious houses.

David Knowles says that many scholars, after reading Alexander Savine's study of the *Valor Ecclesiasticus,* have concluded that less than 3 percent of the monastic income went for charitable purposes. Because the king's commissioners were "often both inconsistent and grasping" and would not allow many charitable expenses on the official roll, Knowles thinks that the contributions were much greater. In addition, the monastic contributions in terms of schools, hospitals, almshouses, the daily dole, and "the uncovenanted largesse of the abbot and major officials" would boost the total to "certainly double and perhaps even treble the sums allowed by the commissioners." Thus, he adds, the total would be somewhere in the neighborhood of the traditional tenth. The real failure of the Church was not that it did not make sufficient charitable provisions for the poor, but that it was guilty of "a failure to provide scope" in the organizational sense.[31] This is true not only of the Church and the monastic system but of the Tudor effort after the Dissolution, for it, too, depended upon the Church at the parish level to administer charity.

The ideas of Frank Aydelotte are subdued but still on the positive side in reference to monastic charity. If the religious houses aided many of the poor, their indiscriminate system of alms probably added to vagrancy. When monastic aid ceased, the vacuum created remained unfilled. "The new clergy were notoriously uncharitable," and they lacked the necessary wealth. This added to the burden of the English curse of vagrancy.[32]

Many historians have failed to concede the positive features of monastic charity. The monasteries do not appear as paragons of virtue in this work, for they faced many problems without adequate structural and spiritual equipment to handle the task. Nevertheless, they used some of their wealth and energy on behalf of the poor while the king seized and wasted this wealth and dodged his own obligations by shifting the burden of poverty care from the monastic Church to the secular Church or parishes. The monasteries gave the poor something; the monarch gave them nothing. The Dissolution made little difference, for the Church continued to carry the burden of poor relief. The demand for monastic restoration by the people in the North during their rebellion indicates that the religious institutions had satisfied certain needs. In many areas the Dissolution produced shock and caused hardship among the poor, especially in northern England.

The pecuniary impact of the Dissolution was of secondary importance to the psychological and social impact of the sudden death of a structure deeply involved in political, economic, religious, social, and traditional life of the nation. This structure furnished the only available succor for many paupers who looked to it for some charity. The blow struck suddenly without planning for the consequences. The poor-law legislation of 1535-36 made the first provision for work, and it stipulated that the officials of cities, shires, and parishes should put idle persons to work.[33] Furthermore, officials and churchwardens were to collect noncompulsory alms for the impotent poor. This legislation came too near the time of the Dissolution to be immediately effective and to alleviate the impact resulting therefrom.

Considered in terms of its beneficial effect upon the poverty problems of England, one can say much on behalf of a continuance of the monastic system as an aid to the government's newly launched efforts. The two systems could have continued giving mutual support to each other as they did between 1536 and 1540, thus eliminating the damage done to the social, economic, and religious institutions by the violent death of monasticism. It would have given the monasteries a chance either to survive by reform or to continue a gradual decline to extinction.

CHAPTER III

What Were the Results
of the Dissolution?

Poverty provided a natural and holy state of life during the medieval period; this philosophy grew especially among the religious orders, but under the Tudor monarchy it became an abomination accused of creating social chaos and crime and therefore scorned. There always had been a criminal element among the vagabond class, but with the new Protestant attitude, more of them were apt to accept criminal living because society considered and treated them that way. The beggar assumed the role of "dirty beggar" when treated like one; that resulted from the Reformation and the dissolution of the monasteries. Concerning the Dissolution, Francis Gasquet wrote that "the condition of pauperism as distinguished from that of poverty may certainly be traced for its origin to that event." This happened because, socially speaking, the English Reformation caused "the rising of the rich against the poor."[1] This provides an interpretation that most historians would not accept, but Gasquet interpreted the situation correctly in that he realized a change of attitude concerning poverty had taken place during this era. It had lost its medieval halo of holiness. That being the case, it is obvious that the ministration of charity to the disreputable would have a lower priority than previously when the recipients walked a religiously respectable pathway in the footsteps of their Lord. In reference to the poverty measures of the era, Gray asserts that they "are lacking in depth and discrimination," and the amount of poverty

30

ministered to during the Tudor period was "less than that for which it was unable to provide."[2] Part of the failure to fulfill the needs of society resulted, therefore, from the new attitude or "Protestant ethic" relevant to poverty.

The secular Church also suffered as a victim of the Dissolution, for when the state took control of the religious houses the Church lost a major source of income. Besides this, the Church received the burden of administering the system of poor relief that formerly had been the monastic duty.

Henry VIII gave the false impression that post-Dissolution monastic lands and other wealth would apply to the establishment of new hospitals, colleges, and dioceses to the benefit of the poor. Instead, the confiscated wealth went to the king. Robert Crowley's poem, "Of Almes Houses," gives a contemporary example of what happened to the hospitals. It reflects a dialogue between a merchant returning from his travels abroad and a beggar concerning the closing of a local "spittlehouse." The man of wealth who had purchased and torn it down had replaced it with a dwelling. What happened to the inmates?

> Alas! syr (quod the pore man)
>   we are all turned oute,
> And lye and dye in corners.
>   here and there aboute.
> Men of greate riches
>   have bought our dwellinge place,
> And when we crave of them,
>   they turne awaye their face.[3]

A. L. Rowse comments on the conversion to secular usage of much of monastic architecture.[4] Crowley also points to what use the suppressed houses might have served.

> O Lorde (thought I then)
>   what occasion was here,
> To provide for learninge
>   And make povertye chere?[5]

In this transaction the king who appropriated the monastic possessions and the wealthy landowners who purchased the land from the king benefited, and the poor people of the realm lost. The new owners of the land often exacted more as landlords than had the monks before them, and under the changed ownership the tenants suffered more from eviction due to enclosure and sheep farming. Brinklow reminded the king of his duties in these respects by telling him that, inasmuch as he realized great wealth from the Dissolution, he owed it to his poor subjects to ease their burdens. How did the king respond to this social challenge? Hear the words of Thomas Becon in reference to the new owners of monastic lands. "And yet, where the cloisters kept hospitality, let out their farms at reasonable price, nourished schools, brought up youth in good letters, they did none of all these things." And in another place he says, "How slenderly are the poor members of Christ provided for now-a-days!"[6]

The Dissolution caused change in the towns and cities of England, especially London, for now they could acquire the buildings and land from the crown either by purchase or donation and thus have more facilities for development. E. J. Davis investigated the idea that this transformed London: "Thus were founded the five Royal Hospitals, and the City acquired for social purposes much property once ecclesiastical." A. L. Rowse states that the Dissolution projected one-sixth of the nation's agricultural land upon the land market. This had the effect of aiding the growth of major cities and towns because they could more easily satisfy their increasing demands for foodstuffs. That is, agricultural production increased because the new owners were individuals rather than institutions and would presumably have more interest in the land and its efficient production of crops. This also served, he felt, to give impetus to the gentry who acquired a considerable portion of the monastic lands.[7]

What did the Dissolution contribute immediately to the poverty problems of Tudor England? A definitive answer to this question is not possible, for the sources of information are incomplete and misleading, and all kinds of considerations enter into the analysis. Some of the abbots, priors, and monks received pensions or entered the body of parish clergy. Nuns obtained release from their vows in order to reenter the secular world, and most of them presumably returned to their families or married. As for the people who earned their livelihood as secular employees upon monastic properties, many of them were retained at their old jobs under the new masters who purchased the confiscated lands from the crown.

Some casualties resulted from the change, especially since enclosure affected monastic lands. The greatest problem resulted from the plight of beggars and impotent poor such as the corrodians who depended upon the monasteries for all or part of their subsistence. These people caused an impact as they joined the growing numbers of beggars and vagrants. Certain of these received aid from alms of the laity, the subsequent government legislation, and the parishes. For these reasons, nothing definite can be determined relative to the immediate impact of Dissolution versus pauperism. The most important point of the situation, however, is that neither the monasteries nor the Tudor poor laws dealt at all adequately with the increasing poverty and vagabondage of sixteenth-century England.

Beyond considerations of how much or how little monasteries contributed to the care of the poor, is the psychological impact of the Dissolution; people in the north, especially, identified with the monasteries, and this greatly aided the cause of rebellion as one result of the Dissolution. The monks at least gave something while Henry VIII took all and gave nothing. The psychological aspect is presented in Sir Thomas More's reply to Simon Fish's *A Supplication for the Beggars*. Gilbert Burnet concerning the reply: "So he answered this Supplication by another, in the name of the souls that were in purgatory, representing the miseries they were in, and the great relief they found by the masses the friars said for them, and brought in every man's ancestors calling earnestly upon him to befriend those poor friars now, when they had so many enemies."[8] In assessing the consequences of the Dissolution, one must remember that England's poor people had a traditional and profound faith in the effectiveness of monkish prayers on behalf of their problems both in this life and in the next. When the monasteries closed, the loss of prayers was just as unendurable as was that of alms which they might also have lost in the process.

Historians have analyzed the normal flow of the rise and fall of the fortunes of the monastic houses as indicating respectively either periods of well-being or of decadence. That is one of the reasons why the charges that Henry VIII brought against these establishments have often received too much credence in historical accounts of the Dissolution. In reality, King Henry used the handiest weapon at his disposal, the charge of decadence, and used it as an excuse to suppress the monasteries without putting anything in their place to fill the vacuum left in terms of alms aid or hospitals. He assumed a perfunctory attitude toward the poor and put the burden of their care upon the parishes and officials at the local level. Those monarchs who followed him on the throne did the same and thus provided an increment of social problems and unrest. Socially and economically the times were changing, but the Tudors failed to change with them.

One cannot say, therefore, that the poor laws of Queen Elizabeth rested upon any sweeping concern for the plight of paupers as the result of a grand awakening of the new Protestant ethic. On the contrary, Elizabeth, as her father before her, remained religiously conservative, but she saw the wisdom of making concessions on behalf of comprehension. The same divided allegiance emerged as she approached the problems of the common people. She did not set forth as a poverty program trail-blazer. On the contrary, she continued the policy of her father, for Henry and Elizabeth simply took the administration of poverty relief away from one religious system of operation (the monasteries) and forced it upon another religious body (the parishes). The latter had a record in the field of poverty care no better than that of its predecessor.

Such judgment of the Dissolution is warranted in view of the case of the appropriation of church benefices and the consequent need for a reminder that they still carried the customary alms obligations. Furthermore, in 1544 the anonymous writer of *A Supplication to . . . Henry VIII* informed the king that part of the extensive possessions of the Church should go toward the relief of the poor. In 1546 the anonymous writer of *A Supplication of the Poor Commons* stated that "the king gives and allows to be given to the priests the portion of the poor with the result that the poor are forced to beg, borrow and steal and remain in idleness."[9] These are the same charges that had been brought against the monasteries. Thus, one can note that the system of Henry and Elizabeth contained no radical departure from that of the monasteries in terms of actual distribution of alms and care of the needy. In both cases the actual implementation remained in church hands. Moreover, in reference to the employment provided, one can ask: was there a great deal of difference between working in monastic fields and working in a workhouse or houses of correction? Perhaps the monastic work would appeal to many as the preferable choice of the two.

Therefore, if, as many writers have contended, the system under Elizabeth was so necessary and adequate, why should not practically the same type of system have been just as adequate under continued monastic jurisdiction as was formerly the case? That is, were not the monasteries doing such a necessary welfare service that the Tudors saw fit to continue it? The answer to this question spells out the very essence of the problem. The Dissolution cut off the major source of alms without preparation for a better system to take its place.

The basic problem finds definition in terms of the conflict between poverty's need of a humanitarian and constructive approach and Tudor desires for a controlled and well-ordered indigent society. This they proposed to bring about by suppression contrary to human welfare. Therefore, from a humanitarian point of view, the monastic system of poor relief was preferable to that of the Tudors. The monk, at least, might say some harmless prayers for the poor beggar and give him a few alms. He certainly would not horsewhip him and return him with an empty stomach and bloody back to his home parish. Even Job might have been dubious of such pauper care.

In any case, some hopeful signs appeared at the time in reference to private donations and the fact that not everyone took the hard-line Tudor attitude. This divergence of opinion in reference to the pauper and beggar finds expression in a childish chant of the period:

> Hark! hark! the dogs do bark;
>   the beggars are coming to town.
> Some gave them white bread,
>   and some gave them brown,
> And some gave them a good horsewhip,
>   and sent them out of the town.[10]

CHAPTER IV

Was There a Secularization of Charity After the Dissolution?

With the monasteries closed, the major responsibility for England's poverty problems shifted from church to state. Secular control appeared novel. One school of historical interpretation proposed that secularization received guidance from the Protestant ethic which replaced the Roman Catholic ethic of holy poverty, and the paternal absolutism of the Church. The Protestant ethic, which considered poverty a crime or sin of laziness, put the sturdy beggar to work.

Poverty legislation developed at an increasing pace because of changing patterns in society and changing attitudes toward poverty. A statute of Edward III stipulated imprisonment for people who wandered at night or otherwise acted suspiciously. The introduction of another statute of Edward III accused the "valiant beggars" of idleness and crime and threatened imprisonment to anyone who gave them alms or other aid. A statute of Richard II stated that vagrants were "running in the country more abundantly than they were wont in times past." They must either give surety for their good behavior or go to prison to await trial. These are the earliest of many statutes intended to control the poor element of society. Richard II issued another law stating that, unless they had permits, poor wanderers must return to their places of birth if the people where they were would not have them.[1]

The government showed some concern for the poor. Widespread appropriation of parish church benefices in the late fourteenth century was followed by a statute requiring the recipients of benefices to set aside a "convenient sum" according to the value of the church property for support of poor parishioners of churches involved. A statute of Henry VII moderated the harshness of former legislation. Hitherto, vagrants served lengthy prison terms, for the statute mentioned "the long abiding of them therein, whereby by likelihood many of them should lose their lives."[2] Governmental concern for the poor antedated the Dissolution and the Protestant ethic of the Reformation. These only intensified the concern that led to the poor-law legislation of Queen Elizabeth.

A qualification is necessary when relating the "Protestant ethic" to English poor-law legislation. Ecclesia Anglicana was and is Catholic as well as Protestant. The guiding principle was not so much a religious ethic of any type as it was a pseudosecular ethic, grounded in the Tudor desire for control, to which the Church acted as handmaiden and religious department of state implementing the governmental poor laws. The problem from an ecclesiastical point of view related to the fact that neither the Roman Catholic Church nor the Tudor Church of England created a conscience tuned to the real problems of poverty.

Since Wilbur K. Jordan has dealt more fully than most historians with the subject matter of this chapter—and in the process sums up some of the outstanding historical conclusions—a careful analysis of his ideas now follows.

Jordan's system of argumentation depends upon statistics, and they offer inexact proofs in the Tudor period because the sources are incomplete, often inaccurate, and are widely scattered in numerous collections of materials. As a result, Jordan develops some questionable theories. Additionally, critical historians have pointed out so often this fact in reference to Jordan that it needs only brief consideration here. Since he presented a static statistical analysis without any reference to the rising curve of prices during the period with which he is dealing, the conclusions based upon such statistics are often faulty.

Jordan is the leading proponent of a Tudor secular ethic—based largely in the "new urban classes and . . . the . . . Protestant gentry." Although reluctant to give credit to the monastic system, he concedes something, particularly in the case of Yorkshire. This shire, he says, "had continued to bear honourably a considerable burden of alms." Moreover, the Dissolution here "had an immediate and most serious consequence, which we have not noticed in any other county examined." He adds, however, that this vacuum was filled within approximately twenty years by "private charity." Yorkshire furnishes a good example of how Jordan's statistical conclusions ignore other pertinent considerations. In his treatment of the shire he said, "the great revolution in aspirations in Yorkshire occurred during the Elizabethan era, when . . . the substantial total of £11,275 11s was left for various forms of poor relief. . . . In this same amazing interval only £1,543 9s was provided for the needs of the church."[3] Jordan failed to take into account that the money given for poor relief was, since the Church at the parish level collected and administered the relief, definitely ministering to a major need of that institution. Formerly much of this money had flowed into the Church in the form of donations to the monasteries for poor relief and other purposes, and now it still came into the Church, as an instrument of state, for the same purposes.

Another example of statistical theorizing that ignores other issues emerges in Jordan's conclusion that the monasteries received less and less secular support and, therefore, "had outlived their social usefulness and very possibly their spiritual usefulness as well." Yet he says on the following page in reference to the secular clergy that, as he had often observed, "the Reformation on balance brought no real financial relief for an already hard-pressed parochial clergy in England." One could apply this same formula that equates the lack of support with a lack of usefulness and say that they too "had outlived their social usefulness and very possibly their spiritual usefulness as well."[4]

In this formula the lack of secular support is equated with lack of growth, and this in turn is offered as proof that the monasteries had no useful future. Such thinking ignores the fact that the monasteries had experienced development and growth throughout the medieval period and possibly had reached the point of greatest feasible expansion by the Tudor era. By the very nature of things—geography, population, economics—there is an outside limit placed upon the expansion of any organization. This does not mean, however, that the organization cannot continue to play a vital role in society. Historians agree that the monasteries controlled a great deal of landed wealth before the Dissolution.

Jordan failed to consider that if the religious houses had attained such wealth and position, they did not need as much gift income as they had received during earlier periods of establishment and growth. After all, they received annual profits from their landed wealth. When Jordan finds the monasteries, in terms of gifts, "almost wholly repudiated by the burgher class" he is not proving repudiation by the lower class of society. The Pilgrimage of Grace and the Northern Rebellion during the period of the Dissolution show the contrary. In demonstrating repudiation by the burgher class, Jordan says that in London the crown and the clergy provided 80 percent of all gifts to the monasteries.[5] However, that 80 percent ultimately came from the people of England. The burgher class knew this and had a good reason for not contributing a second time. One can hardly call this a repudiation of the monasteries.

Jordan says that rural parish bequests during the period 1545-1555 shifted to the degree that the proportion of gifts for "the poor" rose dramatically while those for "religious purposes" were hard put to hold their own. After a brief period the latter went into a period of decline. Therefore, after the monastic dissolution Jordan finds a surge of secular-oriented concern for the poor that climaxed in the "first generation" of the seventeenth century. This produced an increase of contributions for their care that brought an amelioration such as England had never witnessed. By this, he says, "the basic institutions of the modern society were securely established." In similar language Jordan maintains that, "though remedial legislation was adopted, it was our conclusion that men of the age reposed their principal confidence in private charity, gathered by the instrumentality of the charitable trust into large and disciplined aggregates of wealth with which formidably effective social institutions could be founded and endowed, as they undertook to relieve widespread and degrading poverty and to secure its prevention by a vast enlargement of the ambit of social and economic opportunity."[6] This evokes a picture in the reader's mind that sixteenth-century source materials do not support. The passage misleads when it says, "Though remedial legislation was adopted . . . men of the age reposed their principal confidence in private charity." Distinctions of this type about the Tudor period are not possible, for long before and after that time there existed an essential integration of the religious-secular, public-private aspects of life. For example, during a time of famine a wealthy man might contribute (a private donation) more than his ordinary share to the poor rate (public or "remedial" legislation) because the laws of God require proper Christian stewardship (religious). To what classification—private, public, religious, or all three—would a historian attribute such a donation? If the will of the giver determines the intent of the gift, how is that will known? Under such varying pressures for giving as just described, the donor himself probably did not know.

Tudor welfare consisted of state legislation (secular) and parish implementation (religious). Much of this remained true even before the Reformation and Dissolution; therefore, charity was not greatly changed or "secularized" under the Tudors. The Church administered the English poverty program after the Dissolution as she had before. The same money from the same people went for the same purpose to the same place both before and after the disruption of the monastic system. The only change concerned the secular officials of the state who now issued the orders, but this had little effect on the amount of poverty care available for England. B. K. Gray says that "Catholic charity" associated itself with the "doctrine of poenitentia" whereby the donor expressed more concern over the effect of giving upon his own soul than with its benefit to the physical needs of the recipient. This approach to benevolence survived the Reformation but the fact is often ignored, "for the post-Reformation period when, although this motive was still operative, it was ceasing to be explicit."[7]

Another defect in Jordan's hypothesis is that, while the amount of private charitable donations look impressive as statistics, most of such gifts remained small: the establishment of schools of one master and a handful of pupils or hospitals and almshouses to care for five to fifteen inmates. Jordan, like A. L. Rowse, emphasizes the founding of schools during Elizabethan and later times. He then adds that education in monastic institutions was not available, with few exceptions, to boys from outside. But the boys on the inside had originally been boys on the outside. It is doubtful, the royal visitation reports to the contrary, if many of them were born inside the convent walls. This point bears repeating: granted that only a small number of students received instruction in a few monastic schools, this probably adequately filled the limited educational needs of the society of the period. Many privately founded establishments appear makeshift and poorly endowed, if at all, and often resulted either from the deathbed desire of a wealthy person who used this as a means of propitiation for his past sins or to perpetuate his memory or for genuine humanitarian purposes. In speaking of the almshouses in Norfolk, Jordan admits that "most of the establishments were small and modestly endowed." "Milbournes Almshouses" provides another example. Sir John Milbourn founded this institution in 1535 in London to care for thirteen poor men and, if married, their wives. Peter Laslett says concerning Tudor-Stuart almshouses: "Few seem to have contained more than a dozen or twenty inmates, but in 1660 something like 1,400 people may have been living in such institutions in London."[8]

In the above quotations from Jordan, he appears to equate endowments with private charity and speaks of endowments and the establishment of almshouses in the same context as if informing the reader that private donations by the Protestant middle class had produced these houses. The medieval system, he says, operated haphazardly in its charity. However, endowments supervised by trustees superseded this method. "This may be said to have begun the institutionalizing of poor relief, the ultimate form of which was the almshouse." While some of the almshouses resulted from private enterprise, the Elizabethan basis for looking forward to the building of such houses on a nationwide scale was a parliamentary act that provided for the levying of a parish rate for the establishment of these institutions. Frederick G. Marcham provides information on this when he talks about the duties of the overseers of the poor. These church officials aided in the control of vagabondage and accepted the obligation to "provide a workhouse for the able-bodied poor of the parish, to acquire raw materials on which the able-bodied poor could be put to work" and to administer other relief for the poor. In order to raise funds, the overseers assessed property and collected taxes. Turning to the sources, one finds in the *Acts of the Privy Council* a 1578 letter to the Bishop of Winchester saying "that where there is latelie finished within the Castle a House of Correction *erected at the charg of the whole countie* for the setting on worke of suche idle people as run from contrie to contry."[9] (Italics mine.) The letter then asked that the Church contribute to the cause. This was not private charity; it was public effort resulting from state legislation and enforcement. The historian can assume, therefore, that a majority of workhouses would be of the statutory type.

Although he seems impressed by Tudor social action, Jordan does say that "these monarchs were not moved by sentiments of piety or pity." He adds that they got at the heart of the problem due to their recognition that, allowed to go untreated, the disease of poverty would create such unrest that might well "flame across the whole realm." For that reason, Elizabeth, while passing many repressive laws, did not strictly apply them but kept them ready should the need arise.[10] This thesis is incorrect on two counts: the Tudors did not get at the core of England's poverty problem, and the numerous restrictive legislative measures received enforcement in many cases. Any lack of application of the letter of the law did not result from Tudor leniency, for these monarchs, especially Elizabeth, constantly prodded local officials for stricter application of the laws. The *Acts of the Privy Council,* and other sources, demonstrate this fact. Laxity or leniency existed at the local level where the magistrates either thought the laws were too strict for practical application or simply did not care and applied them indifferently.

Private secular donations for charitable and godly purposes offered nothing new either in England or on the Continent. The *Cartularies of Cluny* record thousands of such donations all over Europe. In Spain, for instance, one can learn about the Monasterio de San Salvador de Cornellana: "El Monasterio se enriquece con dones de los monarcas, de los nobles y con las limosnas de los devotos." In the case of the mother house of Cluny, it is well known that William, duke of Aquitaine, provided its charter of gift. There is the case of Leotbald and his wife who gave four churches and three vills with churches and serfs. "Eva" gave her part of two vills and a manor to go to Cluny at her death, and another "Eva" gave a manor, serfs, one-third of a meadow and of a field. And here is a rather homely gift that, compared with those preceding, serves to illustrate the wide range of giving. "Un des chevaliers du comte de Ponthieu . . . donne à Saint-Martin dix muids de sel et deux réserves de poisson."[11]

In England William de Warenne founded the Priory of St. Pancras, and a baron, Roger Bigot (Bigod) founded the Priory of Thetford in Norfolk. King Henry I granted the Priory of the Holy Trinity of Lenton plus numerous other gifts, and Henry II made a grant of the manor of Letcombe-Regis to the Cluniacs. This example is given due to its unique nature; and it involves a gift to the Hospital of St. Thomas, Southwark. "In 1299 Isaac the Jew conveyed a house to the hospital, and that his grant might hold good, instead of a seal, he subscribed his name in Hebrew characters according to the Jewish custom." In 1414 a statute of Henry V mentioned the founding of the multipurpose "hospitals" of the day. "Forasmuch as many Hospitals within the Realm of England, founded as well by the noble Kings of this realm, and Lords and Ladies both Spiritual and Temporal, as by [divers other Estates] . . . to sustain [impotent] Men and Women, Lazars, Men out of their Wits and poor Women with Child, and to nourish, relieve, and refresh other poor People."[12] In view of such evidence, and there are thousands of examples, it appears that the surge of secular charitable giving flourished as strongly in the medieval period as in Tudor England.

This brings up the question concerning the effectiveness of the so-called Protestant or secular ethic that dominated society in the years following the Dissolution. In London, St. Mary of Bethlehem Hospital escaped dissolution and continued its existence under the "new" system. "In 1632 commissioners were appointed to inquire into the state of the hospital, which was found to be very unsatisfactory." The master and the steward had used most of the money for themselves, and the poor inmates went without treatment and food. The Hospital of the Savoy in London was dissolved in 1553 and refounded in 1556. "This new foundation had been in existence only a few years when it was almost ruined by Thomas Thurland, the master." In the case of the London Hospital of St. Katharine by the Tower, the king spared it and appointed a layman as master in 1549. One master used the position "merely as an opportunity for plunder." Then in 1698 another master underwent investigation and removal due to complaints against him, and a new set of rules was devised.[13] Brinklow sums up the situation, although the description may be overdone. "But now that all the abbeys, with their londes, goodes, and impropered personages, be in temporal mennys handes, I do not heare tell that one halpeny worth of almes or any other profight cometh unto the peple of those parisshes where such personagys and vicarages be. Your pretence of putting down abbeys was to amend that was amysse in them." Things seemed better when the "Antichrist of Rome" ruled, for the monks at least kept hospitality and helped the poor. G. B. Harrison gives an illustration of similar character when he considers the poem by Thomas Churchyard: "In this poem, he lamenteth that great lack of charity in our days."[14] From these examples, the fact emerges that charity administration, in spite of the new ethic, still operated deficiently. The act of changing names from "Catholic" to "Protestant" did not work any miracles, for the people and their manner of operation remained much the same after as before the dissolution of the abbeys.

Besides these examples pertaining to hospitals and monasteries, how did the problems of charity and poor relief progress otherwise under the "new" system? An examination of the multiplicity of statutes of the realm, acts of the privy council, and royal proclamations relating to vagrancy and poor relief during the latter half of the sixteenth century provides valuable information concerning the nature of Tudor poverty care. A perusal of these documents shows reiteration and amplification of acts and proclamations following the original pronouncement. These measures did not work as anticipated, and additional proddings provided desperate attempts to shore up a deficient charity and vagrancy control structure.

In spite of the passage of so many poor laws, the effort remained bogged down in a plethora of petty details and household squabbles because of improper delegation of function. This applied especially to the privy council, for time after time under Elizabeth one finds her advisors dealing with soldiers' pensions on an individual basis. The council would recommend a soldier for a pension or almsroom, but the shire, parish, or institution concerned ignored the recommendation. Why?— see to it!—and so on. Individual items would often take up time in from one to four council sessions as responsibility shifted back and forth. The justices of the peace supposedly handled these matters, but in their office resided a major portion of the problem in the first place. They operated as part of the Tudor system of local administration carried out by local, amateur, unpaid, untrained civil servants. Such a structure produced corruption, noncooperation, and lack of interest and laziness. Most of the local officials, trying to hold down the charges upon their jurisdictions, would often send the recommended cases back to the privy council. In speaking of the plight of the poor destitute, J. H. Thomas observes that "few greater blunders could have been made than to give them the right to 'poor relief' by a statute that did not provide the necessary finance nor the administrative machinery to make it workable." As to vagrancy control, the local magistrates either often stood in sympathy with the vagrants or suffered intimidation by their numbers and threats and refused to take other than nominal action against them. In certain instances the magistrates avoided the whole problem. "For avoyding of greate Travaile and Chargs risinge thereby, manye [rogues] are suffered to passe and wincked at." These problems caused a constant plague to the monarch and council. The system of central control of local authorities under Elizabeth and the first two Stuarts, as described by A. V. Judges and others, existed more in form than in effectiveness.[15]

The biggest defect of the Tudor post-Dissolution charity effort, therefore, resulted from the dumping of responsibility upon the local authorities and institutions, especially the parish. These ecclesiastical units had to supervise the collection of poor rates, control vagrancy, maintain roads, and carry out other duties. The central government enacted the necessary legislation and then passed authority on to the parishes to "see to it." Parliament passed legislation for the establishment of houses of correction but made no provision, other than the overworked poor-rate levy, for raising necessary funds for their construction. Still, the privy council constantly belabored the point and demanded the establishment of these houses in all the shires. The Tudor government consistently followed a policy of getting necessary things done if the local subjects and institutions were willing to pay for them.

The government itself was unwilling to assume proper responsibility for formulating a comprehensive program, including the means of raising funds, for the amelioration of the poverty-vagrancy problem and the advancement of the realm as a whole. The crown with its perfunctory attitude, followed a policy of jealously guarding its revenues while leaving the nation to its own resources in terms of social welfare. The Isle of

Guernsey, for example, received an indignant call to task from the queen's attorney who questioned the island's representatives: "By what power do they grant the poor the penalties of the Court belonging to Her Majesty, and why fines are not enrolled in the Court rolls? Ans., The bailiff and jurats ordered a fine of 4d. every time anyone blasphemed God, to be employed towards relief of the poor. Rep., Under colour of paying the poor these fines, they also pay them the fines due to the Prince, thus bringing the revenues to nothing."[16]

R. H. Tawney remarks upon this heel-dragging tendency of the Tudor-Stuart monarchs. He says that they were reluctant to admit that the impotent poor and the sturdy unemployed had any claim upon the state except punishment for the latter. "Governments make desperate efforts for about one hundred years to evade their new obligations. . . . When merely repressive measures and voluntary effort are finally discredited, they levy a compulsory charge rather as a fine for contumacy than as a rate, and slide reluctantly into obligatory assessments only when all else has failed." Tawney thinks the crown finally decided upon this course out of the desire to prevent the upheavals in society resulting from economic conditions over which the crown had no control.[17] The source materials support Tawney.

Even the Tudor method of punishment for vagrants, as the Water Poet demonstrates, was not completely secularized. It provided the one area in which sixteenth-century monarchs made their most concentrated effort for efficiency, for, as Tawney said, they exerted themselves trying to prevent social disorder in the realm. The period abounds with statutes, privy council acts, and royal proclamations prescribing punishment for vagrants. In a royal proclamation of 1530 the justices of the peace received instructions to carry out the statutory punishment, "leaving aside vain pity." While the major portion of such severe justice went to the lower orders, the law dealt just as rigidly with anyone caught in actions that might precipitate state problems. In May, 1574, the queen issued instructions to the Council of the North to prevent enclosure and oppression of the poor, and if any of the wealthy transgressed the rules they should undergo severe punishment "for example's sake, yet so that the common people do not violently redress themselves, but wait the redress of law."[18] The words *for example's sake* form a recurring theme in Tudor proclamations and laws, especially in application to disorders among the commons. Royal nerves remained constantly on edge about such matters, and the "example" had become the Pavlov reaction to them. In 1630 John Taylor, the Water Poet, in his poem "Whip of Pride," summed up the situation quite well:

> In London and within a mile, I weene,
> There are Iayles or Prisons full
>   eighteene
> And sixty Whipping posts, and
>   Stocks and Cages
> Where sin with shame and
>   sorrow hath due wages.[19]

The words *sin* and *due Wages* support the proposition made at the beginning of the preceding paragraph concerning the nonsecularization of punishment. Like Tudor charity, punishment was carried out at the behest of the secular state, but supported religious orientation in terms of content of social thoughts and attitudes of the time. Even the state and its laws failed at secularization for here too existed an abundance of the religiosity of the period. The monarch and the state served as God's instruments for carrying out his will on earth. Such religiously centered thinking in the realm of the "secular" appears repeatedly in the sources of the period. In the following century, for example, the Puritan ethic carried this thinking a step farther by equating failure in life with God's displeasure and success as a sign of his blessing. Success in life may be a secular occupation, but as interpreted by the Puritans it carried a burden of rationalized religious content. It would take a long while before the secular ethic dominated English life.

For those who, nevertheless, discern a secular ethic with a charity-oriented content, the wealthy middle-class townsmen furnished potential for such benevolence. Here again the evidence points to the conclusion that bourgeois charity also remained religiously conditioned. In his praise of the town of Salisbury, John Taylor told the inhabitants that when they contributed to charity "(with religious piety, open hands, and relenting hearts) do acknowledge that your goods are but lent in trust unto you." Speaking of the supposed middle-class charitable urge to provide for the poor, Brinklow says that the citizens of London developed a selfish interest in increasing their wealth while allowing the innumerable poor to suffer and die "to the greate shame of the, oh London!" For, such provision for the poor "shalbe demaunded of you at the greate daye of the Lorde."[20] Such remarks qualify the bountiful benevolence of town-dweller charity.

The middle-class city population desired to make money, and charity failed to motivate them. In 1603 the privy council "intreated" the burgesses of the town of Westminster to provide 100 pounds for immediate relief of the poor. The townsmen received assurance that the money would be repaid by "the Lords." In this case, the great outpouring of citizen generosity had failed. As late as 1614 the county of Middlesex, in spite of much legislation on the subject, still did not have a house of correction. In that year the privy council pointed out the problems of vagrancy and roguery both in Middlesex and in and around London and suggested that the City should contribute to the building of such a house or houses. London provided 500 pounds but only as a belated gesture and after much prodding from monarch and council. If such a situation existed in London and the heart of the realm, one would certainly expect much worse conditions in backward and less wealthy areas. Even orphans had to seek privy council protection from the citizens of Bristol, for in 1589-90 the council wrote to that city demanding assurance that orphans not "be defrauded of what is rightfully theirs." John Taylor speaks of the "great number" of poor inhabitants in Nottingham who dwelt in "vaults, holes, or caves" cut into the soft sandstone of the hill.[21]

A stream of acts and royal proclamations forbade the building of housing for the poor in London. Hugh Latimer in his "Sermon of the Plough" takes Londoners seriously to task. In the past, he remarked, London was full of "pity and compassion" but in present times the poor and sick die in the streets and no one cares. B. K. Gray says that "the supply [of hospitals] was far from being equal to the demand, and if we consider the country as a whole was altogether inconsiderable."[22] In general, town fathers were more interested in repressive than benevolent measures:

> At Halifax, the law so sharp doth deal,
> That whoso more than I 3. Pence doth steal,
> They have a Iyn that wondrous quick and well,
> Sends thieves all headless unto Heav'n or Hell.[23]

English towns operated as semiautonomous units by the sixteenth century, and king, council, and parliament could do little to enforce urban obligations. "The important fact is that within the limits set forth in its charter the town authority was an independent unit with practically the power of a sovereign state." Because of lack of concern for enforcement of vagrancy statutes and for instituting adequate poverty care, problems multiplied under the sporadic but harsh repressive measures. Poverty and vagrancy did not undergo a decline during the Tudor era. As late as 1616 the privy council was still exhorting the City to take steps for control of the multitude of rogues, vagabonds, and sturdy beggars in and around London, Westminster, the borough of Southwark, and other nearby areas. City officials did little about the situation. The crown issued another proclamation demanding proper execution of the laws against vagabondage and requesting the appointment of provost marshals to exercise martial law within the shires of Middlesex, Kent, Surrey, Essex, Hertford, and Buckingham.[24]

The foregoing picture does not deny that townsmen contributed to welfare activity. Source references illustrate that towns as corporations and their inhabitants as individuals concerned themselves with public welfare. They paid the poor rate, built almshouses, houses of correction, hospitals, and engaged in other charitable deeds. Many towns, due to decay resulting from economic changes, found it difficult to relieve the poor. A statute passed in 1543-44 indicates this, "An Acte touchinge the repayringe and amendinge of cten decayed Houses & tents [tenements] as well in Englande as in Wales." The statute lists twenty-four towns. In 1598 the crown granted remission of 300 pounds due from the city of York because of the city's decay and the fact that they maintained six bridges, and provided for poor relief.[25]

Having examined the obvious deficiencies of Tudor welfare, it is appropriate to consider the meritorious activities of both town and crown. During times of famine and high prices they provided either free or reasonably priced grain for the poor. Attempts multiplied in reference to enforcement regulations for the buying and selling of foodstuffs in order to maintain fair prices. Such measures were not unique for they operated both before and after the Dissolution. They provided social insurance against food riots for towns and government.

Royal alms provided another form of charity relief. Edward VI's deathbed bequests gave Grey Friars' church, revenues for an orphanage, St. Bartholomew's for a hospital, and his palace of Bridewell for a house of correction. The will of Henry VII dispersed 2,000 pounds in alms, and the poor along the route of his funeral cortege received their portion. This would assure the king a solid departure into the next life. His will also provided alms to sixty rural parishes, to the poor prisoners in the "clynke," and many other items. The monarch regularly distributed alms during his lifetime and had a special official, the king's almoner, who took care of these matters.[26]

Private donations represented a well-established source of charitable aid to the monasteries. After the Dissolution such benevolences went into the replacing medium of welfare care, namely the Church-operated poor-law effort consisting of both the poor rate (made compulsory in 1563) and the otherwise unfunded, noncompulsory statutes for the building of hospitals, almshouses, and houses of correction. Private donors made innumerable contributions to welfare needs. Sir William Cordell's will donated lands and tenements for the maintenance of a "hospital or almshouse in Suffolk for certain poor people." Sir William's was a double contribution, for he had built the hospital. The Hospital of St. John was endowed by Simon, earl of Northampton, "who gave all his lands in Northampton to pray for the soul of his father." Sir John Hawkins received permission to build a hospital for the "relief of ten or more poor mariners" at Chatham, Kent. Lord Cobham's will provided for maintenance of the poor and the establishment of a college for the poor. G. M. Trevelyan says "the 'lady Bountiful' of the manor-house and her lord often did as much for the poor as had been done by the later monasteries."[27] Perhaps she and her lord were doing it from monastic example, for in the cases cited above a religious content prevailed as motivation behind the donations.

Another form of charity widely used before and during the Tudor era was the charity brief or license for private collection. Ecclesiastical authorities granted permission for these originally, but by Tudor times the crown issued the licenses. Public collections for individual and community needs served as social insurance and often provided aid in cases of loss by fire and other needs.[28] The briefs provided that individuals; officials of towns, church, or state; and proctors of institutions could travel in accordance with specified areas and lengths of time collecting or begging on behalf of towns suffering fire losses, individual fire losses and sickness, repair and building of churches, hospitals, and almshouses, ransom of prisoners held by foreign powers, maintenance of gaol prisoners and other emergency cases. A simpler form of this, the individual license or brief to beg, provided relief for the poor.

This form of charity created abuses. A proclamation against decay of churches cites those who delay repairs in the "hope of having the work done by a public collection."[29] Queen Elizabeth discontinued (39 Eliz.) the practice but in emergencies ignored her decision and allowed collections. Forty-eight examples of charity briefs issued during the Tudor period and the reign of James I were readily found in the sources used in this study.

This chapter has dealt largely with problems and weaknesses of Tudor poor-law and vagrancy control measures. Implicit in criticism is the suggestion of a better method of performance. Tudor England contained the potential for improvement of welfare implementation and vagrancy control. Tudor welfare failed to improve over pre-Dissolution poverty aid because it largely retained that same system, with repression added, which the Tudors themselves had criticized. Tudor monarchs never arrived at the discovery that government cannot effectively ameliorate welfare problems with palliative measures: alms, make-work programs, and repression. Rogues, vagabonds, and sturdy beggars needed a program of rehabilitation through work, as opposed to make-work, and it could exist only within a socially concerned political and economic system. The Tudor-age mind had the ability to formulate such a program, for certain contemporary thinkers saw answers to the social problem and tried to do something about it. They failed because they could not awaken sufficient concern to carry out their experiments, and vested interests opposed change.

The city of Lincoln attempted to provide employment and began an economic experiment as early as 1517 when the city council promised capital aid to any member of the clothing industry who would establish a business within the town. Lincoln, in 1551, attempted to entice the cloth industry to her environs but again failed, for "the scheme appears to have been opposed by the Weaver's Gild." Around the year 1571 Leicester attempted a similar and also unsuccessful program. Several other towns experimented with industrial enticement ventures as well as make-work (houses of correction) programs for the vagrant unemployed, and the Elizabethan government adopted this latter system of make-work. Peter Laslett remarks that workhouses furnished the "closest approximation" to a factory system at that time.[30] This is true if one is willing to equate factories with penal oriented institutions.

In one case at least the government stepped into the economic realm to act as regulator: "Form of a letter of Privy Seal for a loan. The Queen to ___. We wish for relief of the poor tinners and their families, 12,000 in number, and for the good of the kingdom in upholding the price of tin, to take the management of it into our own hands." Therefore, in order to carry out this government project, she requested a loan from Mr. ___ in order that the transaction might continue.[31] Working in the Cornwall tin mines was no picnic, but the miners probably fared much better than the vagabonds who worked as prisoners in Elizabethan houses of correction. Presumably the queen succeeded and the tin miners remained on the job and out of the workhouse prisons.

A tract of 1580 ("A Politic Plat . . .") provided a unique plan of economic salvation by an Elizabethan named Robert Hitchcock. As a scheme for the whole of England, this man's idea is dubious. However, it illustrates the fact that some Tudor minds imaginatively worked on their problems. And who knows, perhaps his plan would have benefited the fishing industry. The author proposed the creation of a fishing fleet composed of 400 vessels from coastal towns and manned by vagrants who would abandon their manner of living because of dignity acquired through useful work. The opening paragraph criticised weakness in public welfare provisions. "Yet, nevertheless, all these laws, so circumspectly made, could not, nor cannot banish that pestilent canker [vagabondage] out of this common weal by any degree; but that the same increaseth daily more and more: to the great hurt and impoverishing of this realm."[32] Regardless of the feasibility of his plan, Hitchcock realized the inadequacy of Tudor methods.

"Stanleyes Remedy," from the reign of James I, also condemned the charitable usages of the age. The poor, he stated, suffered whipping, branding, and hanging before anyone would provide them with work. "The Publike must joyne their shoulders to the work or else it will never be done." A keen observation that still applies. It appeared shameful, he said, that the poor received severe punishment because they were unable to find work. "I have heard the Rogues and Beggars curse the Magistrates unto their faces, for providing such a Law to whip and brand them, and not provide houses of labour for them." He informed the king that vagrancy had never more prevailed than at the present time.[33]

John Taylor offered a plan to Salisbury that, he assured them, would eliminate their vagrancy problem. "Now to turn from beer and ale to fair water, (your river I mean) which if it be cleansed, then with the profit of your Town-brew-house, and the commodity of the river, I think there will be scarce a beggar or loiterer to be found amongst you."[34] Oversimplified perhaps, but containing much truth.

The watermen of the Thames appealed to London's mayor concerning abuses by the masters of their company.[35] It is not known what action the mayor took in this situation, but England certainly suffered from a lack of governmental action on behalf of the nation's economic problems.

Finally, in Starkey's *Dialogue* Pole explained to Lupset that the felon should receive employment on public works rather than having to face death on the gallows, for "dethe ys over-strayte punnyschement for al such theft pryvely commytted."[36] Many Englishmen decided that it is more productive of a sound society to provide men with employment and self-respect than to expose them to the punishment and humiliation of hanging, the alms dole, and the make-work of houses of correction.

The Tudors sat on an insecure throne and, like the monasteries, were victims of social change. They reacted to maintain the old system. In the struggle to survive, however, the Tudors gave an impetus to secularization, and this finally offset their more conservative measures and eventually overcame them altogether. Such effect was not felt in any appreciable amount until long after the Tudor dynasty's era. The struggle of the monasteries and that of the House of Tudor were parallel phenomena in that both were elements of the old order washing away in the current of change leading to the modern age.

The Tudors never went beyond the medieval system of Church alms and alms based upon private contributions.[37] Any secularization of charity was accidental and not the result either of an adequate system of governmental planning or a burgeoning display of the Protestant or secular ethic. Instead, the Church—operating under loose secular jurisdiction and by means of the parish rather than the monasteries as formerly—was still carrying forward, with little or no advancement of pace due to state prodding, the pre-Dissolution, ecclesiastically oriented system of poor relief. Practically speaking, there was little secularization of charity in Tudor England.

CHAPTER V

Was Tudor Insecurity and Fear
of the Mob Reflected in Poor-Law
and Vagrancy Legislation
Plus Other Measures?

Henry VII's amelioration of legal severity against vagrancy soon ended. The legislation of Henry VIII and Elizabeth activated suppression, control of mobility, and severe punishment or torture, even for children under age fourteen. The legislation of Henry VIII finally distinguished between the punishable sturdy beggar and the aid-worthy impotent poor who either received alms or a license to beg. Another poor-law measure of Henry stipulated that the sturdy beggar, after his whipping, be sent back to his place of birth and put to work.[1] Provision for work remained under the home parish's discretion.

The same parliamentary session (1535-36) that provided for the dissolution of the smaller monasteries also passed a poor-law bill.[2] It expressed concern over the increase of vagrancy and crime. This, and the vagrancy legislation prior to Henry VIII's reign, refutes the theory that the Dissolution caused an explosion in the indigent population and a resultant avalanche of poor-law legislation.

With an abundance of legislation and apparent concern by the government, why did vagrancy and poverty remain a problem in England? The answer lies in the Tudor approach or attitude toward the situation. From a Christian or an ethical standpoint, neither they nor their officials showed much concern for the poor. Their concern sprang from apprehension and fear of the possibility of uncontrollable dissatisfaction among the lower classes. Henry VII won his throne on

Bosworth Field, and this left him minus a legal claim to it. The Tudors feared the possibility that anti-Tudor factions among the nobility would exploit unrest among the commonalty. Therefore, because they only wanted to apply stringent repression to vagrancy and palliative measures to poverty, the Tudors failed to get at the heart of these social problems, and they constantly flared up anew at any opportune moment.

Enough rebellions erupted to warrent royal fear. The sources give a long list of them. They ranged from major rebellions to local riots and disturbances. The Tudors suppressed them harshly. In 1497 Cornwall rose, and Thomas More says the rebellion was "suppressed with great slaughter of the poor people engaged in it." London rioted against foreigners in 1517; Coventry attempted insurrection in 1524; and Kent planned an uprising in 1528. The backward northern shires caused much trouble. Rioting and rebellion broke out in Northumberland in 1518 and again in 1528. In January, 1528 the earl of Northumberland informed Henry VIII of the surrender of the Lisles and other outlaws. Stow's *Annales* describe the major uprisings: 1536-37, the northern Pilgrimage of Grace; 1549, widespread revolt in many shires including Kett's Rebellion; 1554, Wyatt's Rebellion in Kent; 1569, Northumberland and Westmorland in rebellion; 1607, rebellions in Northamptonshire, Warwickshire, and Leicestershire.[3]

During the 1590s, England faced depression, famine, and revolt. Additional poor-law legislation passed in 1597 and 1601. In 1594 the queen issued the Proclamation for Staying Unlawful Assemblies. The wording indicates the prevalent chaos and fear.[4] Suppression of public disorder was the major reason for Tudor concern with poverty, for legislation and other measures point to that conclusion.

After the foregoing introduction and brief outline of major events, it is time to consider the specific issues at stake. Since the major concern of this chapter is to demonstrate the effect that rebellions, riots, and other forms of violence had upon Tudor legislation and actions, a full chronological listing of these disturbances will make clear the impact of such events upon Tudor governmental policies. Taken mostly from sources, this information presents the prevalence of social discontent. Paradoxically, the repressive measures used by the Tudor monarchs only caused further unrest. The sequence of disturbances presented in Appendix I, herein, extends from 1536 (Pilgrimage of Grace) to 1603 (death of Elizabeth). To illustrate that social unrest continued after the reign of Elizabeth, a few incidents are given after 1603, but that list is not complete. For convenience of comparison, the listing is broken into decades.[5] Having diminished briefly during the 1560s, mounting social unrest reached its peak during the 1590s, as recorded by this and the following chronologies. The disturbances resulting from enclosure, famine and grain shortages, religious discontent, vagrancy, discharged soldiers, mutinous troops and seamen, elections, unemployment, and an inequitable system of punishment produced a lawlessness and discontent that threatened the monarchy's existence. Combinations of these elements of dissatisfaction had produced dangerous situations in the past, such as the Pilgrimage of Grace, and the crown's anxiety stemmed from a desire to prevent them from again happening and perhaps succeeding.

The above information helps to dispel the myth that the Elizabethan period produced a Protestant ethic that destroyed a decadent Roman Catholic world and produced a middle-class Protestant world dedicated to efficiency and the secular ethic. Instead, the "new" ethic maintained, with minor changes, the same inefficiency of that earlier era, and Tudor repression made the situation much worse. The Stuart era saw the climax to such conditions when the unrest among the lower classes greatly strengthened the antiroyalist party in the events leading to and during the Civil War. During this period the common people grumbled that "the gentry 'have been our masters a long time and now we may chance to master them, and now they [the lower classes] know their strength it shall goe hard but they will use it.' "[6] Or, listen to the words of a poem of the commons:

> Since then the anti-christian crew
>   Be prest and over-throwne,
> Wee'l teach the nobles how to crouch,
>   And keepe the gentry downe;
> Good manners hath an ill report,
>   And turnes to pride we see;
> Wee'l therefore cry all manners downe,
>   And hey then up go we.[7]

The lower classes had known their strength for a long time and had used it on many occasions; during the Civil War period, however, they used it to much greater effect than heretofore, for the Roundheads needed their support.

Tudor-generated social discontent continued to plague the first two Stuart kings as illustrated by a 1631 privy council directive to the justices of Rutlandshire. The letter expressed concern over the report that a shoemaker was stirring up trouble among the poor due to the lack of grain and employment. The letter ordered the justices to apprehend the ringleaders and to gather up all arms in a safe place. Then followed the standard advice concerning the application of palliatives rather than measures for extirpating the real causes behind the discontent: "and likewise (which is indeed most considerable and the best means to prevent all disorders in this kind) that you deal effectually in causing the market to be well supplied with corn and the poor to be served at reasonable prices and set on work by those of the richer sort, and by raising of stock to relieve and set them on work according to the laws."[8] Due to an overdependence on coercive measures, this typical Tudor procedure allowed the situation to get out of hand and then applied too little too late in terms of remedial action.

Gladys Scott Thomson deals with the Tudor mania for control. She points out that the dynasty remained continuously anxious lest the spreading of local disturbances end in loss of the throne. The Tudors felt compelled to keep every shire, hundred, and parish under strict surveillance. A.V. Judges says that the cause of charity took second place to action against the malcontents.[9]

Historians sometimes ignore the obvious fact that major affairs of state are intimately related to local problems. These writers are so involved with "higher" problems of state that they forget the people in their homes and communities. This lack of local analysis impedes understanding of Tudor history where local events exerted a more than ordinary impact upon contemporary developments. Much earlier than the Tudor period there existed examples of vigorous public opposition to the monarch. According to Jusserand, the murder of Archbishop Thomas Becket produced opposition to the king, for the people demonstrated their approval of Becket by visiting his grave in unceasing numbers and thus created a saint by popular acclamation.[10]

From early times, leaders sprang from the rebellious lower classes. The vagrant priest, John Ball, provided leadership of this type, and Wat Tyler emerged from the same background even though his ancestry is disputed. The priest's role as preacher carried great influence in medieval and Tudor society. He kept close touch with the people, held sway over them and often sprang from their uncouth milieu. In 1517 Londoners, inflamed by a preacher and others, rioted against foreigners dwelling in their city. Forty leaders of the Evil May Day riot suffered hanging and quartering by will of the king. Contemporary correspondence tells the barbarity of such punishment. "Nothing is to be seen at the city gate but gibbets and quarters." Four hundred of the rioters received pardon, after appearing before the king for the death sentence, and they jumped with joy and praised the magnanimity of their ruler.[11] King Henry was able to take his vengeance, provide deterrent examples, and still resolve the situation by propagandizing the extent of his benevolence in the extension of pardon to his unruly subjects.

Many more examples demonstrate that the common people did not always depend upon upper-class leadership in their revolts but often provided the leaders for their own plots. Sedition prevailed in Kent in 1528, and contemporary documents introduce several of the rebels of the third estate: Robert Banks, cutler; John Bigg, clothmaker; Thomas Hyklyn, fiddler; Wrigg, fuller; Hoge Owin, "a birler of clothes"; Robert Warre, clothmaker; John Armistrong, laborer; John Ungely, husbandman; Mr. Oliver, shoemaker; and Peter Tailour, a smith.[12]

One of the greatest popular disturbances was the "Pilgrimage of Grace" of 1536-37. It began in Lincolnshire, spread to Yorkshire, and most of the remainder of northern England soon joined. The people rose in rebellion and "took certain Lords and gentlemen . . . causing them to be sworn to them upon certain articles." Again, popular leaders were present such as the shoemaker, Melton, although the leader in Yorkshire, Robert Aske, was a gentleman and lawyer. And as one correspondent of the time expressed it, "all this insurrection rises of persons of no reputation; 'it is the dangerest insurrection that hath been seen.' " Another writer thought there was a common confederation of the northern people that would require astute treatment and that the people should have wages.[13]

Why did northern England explode into widespread rebellion? This part of the realm suffered from poverty, backwardness, and a feudalistic society. It had never fully accepted control by the monarchy, and the people often gave greater allegiance to members of the local nobility than to the king. Also, the Scottish border was the scene of raids, revolts, and outlawry in general. Local disturbances remained standard in northern England. Lord Dacre, in answer to Henry's inquiry about the cause of certain riots in Northumberland, had told the king as much in 1518.[14]

During the Pilgrimage of Grace, the demands of the people presented both to the king and to society at large expressed dissatisfaction in the areas of politics, economics, and religion. They asked for a return of the earlier customs and tenant rights, reasonable rents, the old form of religion, the restoration of monasticism, the removal of Thomas Cromwell and other such corrupt advisors of the king, the pulling down of enclosures, and the strict enforcement of the statutes against them, repeal of the Act of Uses, removal of certain taxes, and removal of extortionate fines. In addition, the rumor mongers further disquieted the people by reports that the king intended to collect all the gold of the realm, to take all unmarked cattle, to loot the parish churches, and to levy a series of "fines" or taxes on weddings, baptisms, burials, and the eating of wheat bread, goose, and capon. Such tales of the king's intentions persisted and he anxiously denied them—perhaps to too great a degree for his denials to sound genuine. This set a precedent for Tudor strictness toward rumors, especially during the reign of Elizabeth. While monastic dissolution was the most often cited cause of the Pilgrimage of Grace, it supplied only the spark that finally ignited a combination of social ills. Norfolk, writing to Cromwell in 1537, summed up the issue concerning the poor commons, "and what with the spoiling of them now and the gressing of them so marvellously sore in time past and with increasing of lords' rents by inclosings, and for lack of the persons of such as shall suffer, this border is sore weked and specially Westmoreland; the more pity they should so deserve, and also that they have been so sore handled in times past, which, as I and all other here think, was the only cause of this rebellion."[15] The participants in this revolt did not consider themselves rebels against their king but pilgrims on the holy cause of a Pilgrimage of Grace "for the love that you do bear to God's faith . . . preservation of the king's person . . . purifying of the nobility."[16]

The king refused to give thanks for the "preservation" of his person, and he expressed his displeasure in an answer to the petitioners of Lincolnshire:

How presumptuous then are ye, the rude commons of one shire, and that one of the most brute and beastly of the whole realm and of least experience, to find fault with your prince for the electing of his counsellors and prelates? Thus you take upon yourself to rule your prince. As to the suppression of the religious houses we would have you know it is granted to us by Parliament and not set forth by the mere will of any counsellor. . . . We pray God give you grace to do your duties and rather deliver to our lieutenant 100 persons than by your obstinacy endanger yourselves, your wives, children, lands, goods, and chattels, besides the indignation of God.[17]

To say nothing of the indignation of Henry VIII which could strike more severely than that of God.

The king sought revenge. In corresponding with the duke of Norfolk in 1537, he demanded severe punishment for certain rebels as an "example" for the rest. Every community that took part in the rebellion provided victims "as well by the hanging of them up on trees as by quartering of them and the setting of their heads and quarters in every town . . . which we require you to do, without pity or respect, according to our former letters." Further proof that the indignation of Henry VIII rather than that of God caused most fear among the people is provided by a letter written by the lord chancellor. Referring to further executions, he informed Cromwell that, "as the gates of London are full of quarters not yet consumed, has ordered the heads of these prisoners to be set up at London Bridge and at every gate, and the bodies to be buried." Apparently the wild birds of carrion were not as busy as the human birds of prey, for the king must have his examples in order that he might again feel secure upon his throne of fear. If any again rebel, he told the Duke of Suffolk in 1536, you shall advance rapidly to "destroy, burn, and kill man, woman, and child the terrible example of all others." He should spare those gentlemen capable of future service to the king.[18] Therefore, as the commons well knew, Tudor social life displayed a goodly amount of benefit of gentry.

The king emerged victorious over his people, but the northern revolt warned him that the situation could generate further problems. The people acted from desperation, and their king, rather than taking steps to solve their problems, treated rebellion with further repression. Nevertheless, the warning to the crown remained explicit, and the king knew that there was a point beyond which he dared not go. An undated manifesto spelled this out for the ruler. It was directed from "The Diggers of Warwickshire to All Other Diggers." The "diggers" complained of the poverty of the times, the robbing of the poor by wealthy landlords, and other grievances. They asserted loyalty to the king but warned the opposition: "But if you happen to shew your force and might against us, wee for our partes neither respect life nor lyvinge; for better it were in such case wee manfully dye, then hereafter to be pined to death for want." The anonymous author of *A Supplication of the Poor Commons* spoke in similar fashion.[19] These outbursts warned the king against using repression beyond a certain point unless he was prepared to defeat, hang, and quarter his common subjects.

Henry Brinklow suggested a solution to the problem. If the king provided a just system of government for all peoples of his realm, he would have nothing to fear.[20] Robert Crowley provided another voice of moderation. In his poem, "Of Commotionars," he observed that when the sword fails it is time to make use of "discrete counsell" in order to undermine the power of rebellion. Then he continues,

> When the hertes of the people
> be wonne to their prince,
> Than can no Commotioners
> do hurte in hys province.[21]

The king realized the truth of such argumentation and proceeded to put into operation a minimum of such governmental philosophy in the vain hope that it would prevent further rebellion. His instructions given in 1537 to the earl of Sussex demonstrates this mode of operation. To prevent impoverishment of the commons, the king ordered him to control enclosures and extortionate fines in order that gentlemen and "the poor men may live in harmony."[22] This meant that the gentleman wanted to live free from disturbance while the poorer classes lived slightly above the line of deprivation and rebellion. The Tudors and Stuarts discovered that this was an impossible balance to maintain. The crown established the Council of the North in 1537 to apply control and palliative measures to this dangerous area.

In 1549 widespread rebellion again erupted, and the government passed "An Acte for the punyshment of Unlawful Assemblyes and rysinge of the Kings Subjects." In the same year a royal proclamation threatened disturbers of the king's peace with death by martial law.[23] Kett's Rebellion in Norfolk produced the most famous disturbance. Here again the people had spawned a leader, for he started as a tanner and became a landowner who opposed enclosure.

The causes of the 1549 troubles were much the same as those enumerated earlier in reference to the Pilgrimage of Grace and remained the major items of discontent throughout the Tudor and early Stuart monarchies. The following quotation sums up the varied nature of the discontent.

The causes and pretences of thes upprores an Risynges are diveres and uncerteine, and so full of varietye almost in Every Campe, as they call them, that it is hard to write what it is; as ye knowe is lyke to be of people without head and Rulle, And that wold have that they wotte not what, some Criethe 'plucke downe inclusures and parkes'; some for their Comones; otheres pretende the Relygeone; A number wold Rulle an other whille and directe things as the gentlemene have done; And indeed, all hath Convayed a wonderfull hate agaynste gentlemen, and takethe them all as their Ennemyes.[24]

This letter displays a sense of bewilderment as deep as that of the participants in rebellion. All classes felt the pressures developing within a changing society. The government fearfully retreated behind a façade of repressive legislation and refused to deal with the problems realistically.

The spirit of discontent, as witnessed by Wyatt's Rebellion, remained active during the 1550s. Compared with the chaos of Edward VI's reign and the uncertainty of the religious state of the realm under Mary, the 1560s were much calmer. Still, discontent and revolt did not disappear, especially in 1569. The troubles of that year again arose in the north. Sir Ralph Sadler told Sir William Cecil that,

There are not 10 gentlemen in all this country that favour her [the queen's] proceedings in the cause of religion. The common people are ignorant, superstitious, and altogether blinded with the old popish doctrine, and therefore so favour the cause which the rebels make the colour of their rebellion, that, though their persons be here with us, their hearts are with them. . . . For if the father be on this side, the son is on the other; and one brother with us and the other with the rebels.[25]

In January, 1570, the queen reproved the earl of Sussex for the lack of executions by martial law "of the meaner sort of rebels in the North." She ordered him to do his duty "for the terror of others." Servants of state could not long ignore the Tudor penchant for "example" and "terror." Elizabeth learned her father's lessons and executed them herself. Suppression of the rebellion brought the usual toll of lives. The victims came from rebels "that had no freehold nor copyhold, nor substance of lands." The earl of Sussex reported to William Cecil that he guessed that the number of commons scheduled for execution would be six to seven hundred. By killing some and fining the remainder he boasted that he would "thereby raise a commodity to Her Majesty; and I trust she will not mislike that." He added that he had no intention of bringing martial law against those of wealth, "as I knew the law in that case."[26] The poorer sort knew where they stood in the affections of the crown.

From the 1570s to the end of Elizabeth's reign, popular dissatisfaction rapidly increased, especially during the last decade of the century. For the most part, large-scale rebellion remained under control. Nevertheless, the common people's disenchantment burst forth in a plethora of small-scale acts of violence that made up in numbers and social turbulence what they lacked in terms of the brute threat of former rebellions. Adding to this social discontent, famine prevailed during the latter part of the sixteenth century. Grain or food riots, mutinies of troops, lawlessness, disorders, vagrancy, local riots of various sorts, unlawful assemblies, religious riots, enclosure riots, affrays, conspiracies, and plots against the queen's life filled this period of Elizabeth's reign.

In 1589 hundreds of the vagrant, disbanded soldiers who had just returned from Sir Francis Drake's expedition to Portugal threatened the peace of London. Troops were called out to protect the City by the application of martial law. In Gloucestershire the mob looted a malt-laden ship. The participants maintained that they did this because of starvation by famine that forced them "to feed their children with cats, dogs, and roots of nettles."[27]

In order to minimize turbulence, the government provided palliatives for relief of the poor. These consisted of the provision of either free or reasonably priced grain supplies during times of famine or they might consist of the provisions of the poor-law system itself. The privy council in 1595 told the mayor of Norwich not to tolerate the plots and disturbances within his city but at the same time reminded him of his obligation to satisfy the needs of the poor which he had heretofore ignored. The council informed him that the condition of unrest was his responsibility and that he should prevent it by reforming his former laxity as chief magistrate. The standard governmental order in such situations, besides the palliative measures cited, demanded control of the disorder by martial law via the commission of the provost marshal as the increasingly used curb. Even with grain riots, the government still operated on the basis of "example" and "terror." A grain riot broke out in Kent in 1596, whereupon the privy council ordered the justices to bring the culprits to trial and punishment as an "example" for others.[28] By supplying grain for the markets and administering punishment to the hungry looters, the government of Elizabeth managed to stay slightly ahead of its fear of the angry mob.

England witnessed many colorful and dangerous events during the reign of Elizabeth. A bizarre trespass in London in 1591 was called "A Conspiracy for Pretended Reformation." It happened through the efforts of "three fanatical preachers . . . [who] began to proclaim . . . that Christ was come again from Heaven." A crowd gathered, and one of the three presented himself as Christ's vicar on earth and king of Europe. They denounced the queen and other officials and were arrested. Small wonder, then, that in 1595 there appeared: "The Queenes Maiesties Proclamation for staying of all unlawfull assemblies in and about the Citie of London, and for Orders to punish the same." This document provided for usage of the provost marshal to control lawlessness and vagrancy by military force. If lawbreakers remained unwilling to conform, the provost marshal would execute them "upon the gallows by order of martial law."[29]

The Stuart dynasty inherited this social situation, and the same conditions of unrest continued under the new reign. In 1607 a renewed concern over enclosures caused rebellions throughout Northamptonshire, Warwickshire, and Leicestershire. Under these circumstances the "Levellers were busily digging" but were also busily arming themselves. When defeated, the participants of rebellion received Tudor-type punishment.[30]

An integral part of the larger picture of treason, rebellion, and revolt, and therefore just as much a concern for the crown, was the problem of rumors, false reports, and sedition. Robert Crowley's poem, "Of Inventers of Straunge Newes," expresses contemporary concern over this issue.

> Such men cause the people,
>   that els woulde be styll,
> To murmour and grudge,
>   whych thyng is very ill.
> Yea, sometyme they cause
>   the people to ryse,
> And assemble them selfe
>   in most wycked wyse.[31]

In an era of limited communications how did rumors and reports undergo such wide dissemination? To begin with, England formed a geographically compact realm thus making it relatively easy for people to travel from one area to another. Jusserand provides an answer concerning the identity and method of the scandalmongers, for he states that the ideas arose orally and the itinerant rogues, vagabonds, sturdy beggars, and Gypsies transmitted them throughout the realm. By this means, there existed a linkage of information and ideas among the various shires, and source materials bear out his explanation.[32]

The spreading of tales, rumors, and demands during the Pilgrimage of Grace provides an example of how efficiently the system operated. Wandering ministrels, included among vagrants, often spread revolutionary ideas in the form of songs. "It was a popular song which furnished John Ball the text for his famous speech at Blackheath in the revolt of 1381: "When Adam delved and Eve span, Who was then the gentleman?"[33]

The printed word in the form of handbills, posters, pamphlets, tracts, and books furnished another medium for the dissemination of seditious information. Vagabonds often distributed these during their wanderings. The Water Poet, John Taylor, writing during the reign of Charles I, explained how Henry Walker the ironmonger published works against church and state and employed about 500 vagabonds from London and neighboring shires, "and they were all suddenly . . . transformed into wandering booksellers." The printed cry of this man against his ruler was that of the ancient Israelites when they desired rebellion against their king, namely, "To Your Tents O Israel; as if the King were a tyrant."[34]

The Reformation and religious discontent as causes of fear and trouble for the government are too well known to deserve special treatment here other than that given in connection with the dissolution of the monasteries. Religious discontent operated in esoteric ways. Persons who were trying to cause trouble for the king apparently encouraged the "Maid" or "Nun of Kent" in her prophesyings and messages from God. In 1554, according to Holinshed, a young woman in London pretended to speak under the influence of heavenly spirits. Certain persons at the sessions interpreted the messages as sedition against the queen and her religion.[35] Heaven-sent sedition was too powerful to be ignored.

As an example of the involvement by the common people in the various antiroyal machinations of the time, Holinshed presents an interesting character sketch of William Parrie, "one of the yoonger sonnes of a poore man." The father was an alehouse keeper. Young Parrie entered into a plot with some Jesuits who planned to kill the queen.[36]

In terms of sedition, with or without rumors, one can find literally hundreds of cases from the sources. No local disturbance was too petty to merit the attention of king, privy council, and state officials. Many incidents bordered on the ludicrous and Rabelaisian as demonstrated by the following scene. In 1537 William Lord Sandys wrote to Cromwell concerning an examination of Perot de Latur, a tailor of Guisnes, for "tedious and unsitting words." Perot and another man began fighting at a drinking party and were "pulling each other by the hairs of the head when Morgan and others parted them and charged Perot to keep the peace in the King's name, when he answered 'A turde for the King.' " In another humorous incident, the parson of Whatcote was sent to the Warwick gaol for "railing words." These words resulted from his having read to his congregation the king's injunctions concerning religion. The language of the parson, rather than "railing," echoed the frustration of many a clergyman who finds that he has taught the word of God, read innumerable announcements to his congregation, and preached long and hard to little or no avail. Listen to his lament: "This must needs be conned, for by God's bones I have read this unto you a hundred thousand times, and yet ye be never the better. . . . Here is an hundred words in these injunctions where two would serve. . . . There was never a man in Westminster Hall thet would for 20 nobles read so much."[37] Part of the accusation stated that he had read certain of the king's and bishop's injunctions only once. Apparently his majesty's servants had no sense of humor whatever.

The king punished many of his unfortunate subjects with various forms of esoteric torture and maiming in order to bend them to his will. Judge Manwood gave his opinion to Sir Walter Mildmay relative to a man who had suffered the pillory and had his ears chopped off but who still continued to slander the queen. The only remaining alternatives, he felt, were either life imprisonment or removal of the man's tongue. Perhaps the method later used for silencing Charles I was more efficient and humane even though the blade cut a bit deeper. Thomas Norton's letter to Walsingham, in which he bemoaned his bitter fate at being named in an uncomplimentary fashion in a recently published seditious book, presents another torture case. The book's author called him " 'Mr. Norton the Rackmaster,' who vaunted to have pulled one Briant 'one good foot longer than ever God made him.' " Poor Norton justified himself on the basis that he simply had followed orders. Technically, he was correct, for during the previous year the lieutenant of the Tower had told Norton and another man to exact a confession from Briant, a Jesuit, on the condition that if he would not talk voluntarily then they should " 'put him unto the torture, and by the paine and terrour of the same wring from him the knowledge of suche things as shall appertayne.' "[38]

The eyes and ears of the monarch were ever alert. On the Isle of Guernsey in 1597 a man was accused of speaking against the queen, but, for some reason, the justices of the peace appeared reluctant to bring him to trial. The privy council thereupon ordered the transfer of his case to the council's court on the charge of sedition. In the same year the privy council accused an Oxfordshire man of a similar crime and ordered his arrest and appearance before the council.[39]

The three chronological lists in Appendix II demonstrate the magnitude of Tudor concern over rumors, false reports, and sedition and show what a large portion of governmental effort these problems required. The first presents the statutes relevant to these items; the second gives the royal proclamations; and the third shows a listing of the persons and areas charged with rumors and/or sedition during the period under examination. For purposes of comparison, a few examples are given outside the limits of the sixteenth century.[40] These accounts of various social disturbances illustrate the weakness of Tudor society. Repression drove major disturbances underground, but their destructive force still surfaced as a plague of smaller acts of violence and lawlessness. The Tudors did not solve the problems but only borrowed time.

Vagrancy loomed as another nightmare—closely allied with the concern over rebellions, rumors, false reports, and sedition—that the crown must face. Samuel Rowlands gives an account of vagrancy that, while perhaps not always historically accurate, reflects plausible conditions for the author and his readers. Certain precedents warned the Tudors concerning the danger resident in the numerous bands of rogues, vagabonds, and sturdy beggars who roamed England. For example, Rowlands recounts that the gang of vagabonds led by Hugh Roberts, lately returned soldier from France, aided Jack Cade's Rebellion. Roberts died a vagrant fighting against Henry VI. The knavish throng elected his successor, Jenkin Cowdiddle, who met death while leading his group of some three hundred men. Spysing, successor to Cowdiddle, joined forces with the pirate Thomas Nevell and his following. They marched against King Edward IV with "seventeene thousand men" and suffered defeat but Spysing escaped only to die on the gallows later. After this, a leader of the vagabond army, Lawrence Crosbiter, joined the cause of Perkin Warbeck in his attempt to seize the crown from Henry VII. Rolands tells of a meeting between the Gypsies and the regular vagabonds, now led by Cocke Lorrell, at "Divels-arse-a-peake." There they worked out their canting language.[41] This account is

highly stylized and dramatized, for vagabonds never organized themselves so thoroughly, but it illustrates the impact that the vagrant life
made upon the contemporary English mind in fact and fiction. The
Tudors never sat easily on the throne while the marching feet of hungry
bands of vagrants echoed throughout the realm.

Frank Aydelotte reports that vagabonds gravely threatened the
monarch. They were ever "ready to join in any rebellion. . . . It was
this danger which was responsible for the rapid development of the
English poor law between 1530 and 1600." It was a poor law designed
more for repression and control of the lower classes than for aid thereto.
B. K. Gray testifies to the crown's concern over vagrancy and the attempt to suppress it by strict police measures.[42]

The Tudors arbitrarily designed methods for policing vagrancy. "For
there is not one yeare commonlie, wherein three or four hundred of
them are not devoured and eaten up by the gallowes." The same writer
of 1587 gives what appears an exaggerated number when he states that
Henry VIII "did hang up threescore and twelve thousand of them in his
time." This, he says, intimidated the remainder, but they rapidly increased after Henry's death. Despite rigorous measures, vagabonds continued to multiply, and the officials blamed this on weak laws poorly
enforced. The Tudor mind failed to understand that it would require
more than repression in order to effectively control the situation. Strype
blamed the 1596 crime increase by vagrants in Somersetshire on the laxity of local officials. Yet in the same paragraph, he reports that in two
assizes of that year "in all 40 were executed, 35 burnt in the hand, 37
whipped and 112 were acquitted."[43] This hardly proved magisterial
slackness. Obviously he favored the hangman's noose for all of them.
"The only good 'un is a dead 'un" has been a popular theory of social
control throughout history—this was especially true in Tudor England.

Who were vagabonds? Some of them acquired that status by birth,
while others entered a life of vagrancy owing to adverse circumstances.
Among the latter appeared dispossessed yeomen: victims of enclosure,
high rents, inflation, and famine years. Some had fallen from higher
social status for various reasons: dissolute living, poor management, and
accidents of fate. Gypsies roamed the land as an esoteric gathering of
communal vagrants. Disbanded soldiers and men posing as such formed

one of the most bothersome and dangerous vagrant societies, especially during the latter part of the sixteenth century. Queen Elizabeth, as will be fully discussed in Chapter VIII, continuously attempted by means of parliament and privy council to cope with this dangerous problem. Concerning these vagrants, a contemporary writer says, "but of these wandering idle people there are 300 or 400 in a shire, and grown so strong that the constable dare not apprehend them." A. V. Judges says that most of the dangerous vagrants arrived at that calling by way of service as soldiers, sailors, or retainers. He quotes Somerset justice Hext who wrote to the privy council in 1596 describing local fear and intimidation created by vagrants. He warned in closing: "I may justly say that the able men that are abroad seeking the spoil and confusion of the land are able, if they were reduced to good subjection, to give the greatest enemy her Majesty hath a strong battle; and as they are now they are so much strength unto the enemy."[44] The "strength unto the enemy" phrase had power to arouse the monarch.

The government adeptly devised new regulatory methods. The parliament that passed the Dissolution also forbade the asking and giving of alms, for, as the government recognized, the gathering of beggars into groups for benevolences from individual benefactors posed a dangerous situation in which such mobs might support rebellious causes. Despite these regulations the problem of vagrancy continued unabated. In 1603 the privy council still complained "that rogues growe againe to increase and bee incorrigible and dangerouse, not onely to his Majesty's loving subjects abroad, but also to his Majestie and . . . his Court." Blame fell upon the justices of the peace because of their lack of effort, and the absence of places designated for the sentence of transportation. The council forthwith took care of this item by so designating Newfoundland, "the East or West Indies," France, Germany, Spain, and the Netherlands.[45] One wonders what the sovereign nations on the list thought of this decision of His Majesty's privy council.

The chronological list pertaining to vagrancy (Appendix III) reinforces both the previously presented chronologies and this chapter's earlier statement about the epidemic nature of the Tudor social disease. These several items present in microcosm, as collectively foreshadowed by many small eruptions, an explosive force that served as a major support to the antiroyalist forces that finally ended the life of a Stuart monarch. Tudor repressive measures and the people's dissatisfaction with them emerge in this table. Because the Tudors aided and abetted begging and vagrancy by issuing licenses to beg, the granting of such charity briefs rates inclusion in the listing. This chronology cites: statutes of the realm, royal proclamations, the problem in general, and cases at law. For purposes of perspective, examples from before and after the Tudor era are included, although the list is not complete.[46]

Allied with and in most cases a part of the general problem of vagrancy, the category of arms and the peace often appeared with vagrancy statutes and royal proclamations as a cause and effect unit responsible for much lawlessness throughout the realm. The king issued a proclamation in 1487 against the unnecessary carrying of weapons, causing disturbances, and for suppression of vagrants. Because of disturbances in churches and churchyards, a proclamation of 1556-57 limited the usage of certain weapons. In 1559 a proclamation placed a restriction—one of many such orders and statutes on guns both before and after this date—on the use of handguns and "dagges" (pistols) due to the usage of these weapons in criminal acts throughout the realm. The continued use of weapons and other disorders produced a regulatory proclamation in 1594. "Lawlessness near London" was the subject of a 1598 measure which dealt with the problem of vagrants, many of them armed with petronels and pistols. Then in 1600 a royal proclamation dealt with the linkage between the problem of the high rate of criminal actions and the common practice of carrying firearms.[47]

Statutes and proclamations had attempted to control the use of unauthorized weapons since medieval times. Under the Tudor monarchs, especially with the advent of firearms, such usage was related to the many disorders of the realm that served to make the crown fearful for the loss of either life or throne. Certain proclamations forbade the carrying and shooting of weapons within proximity to the monarch. Appendix IV provides a chronological listing of the statutes and proclamations from 1487 to 1616 relating to arms and the peace—in conjunction with the former three appendixes on revolts, rumors and sedition, and vagrancy—as further evidence concerning the extremely unsettled nature of the period under consideration and of the inadequacy of Tudor attempts to cope with it.[48]

Enclosure and the related economic problems of rack-renting, engrossing, and regrating furnished other causes of dissatisfaction among the common people. Interest in the enclosure movement has produced many historical works describing it both as a widespread disruptive phenomenon of the time and as an economic irritant virtually unnoticed by the majority of England's common people. One can agree that, although sporadic and spotty in application, the enclosure movement affected the society of the era in magnitude that exceeded its relative extent. Race relations in the United States afford a modern example of how a problem of limited proportions can have a profound effect on the whole social fabric. The American Negro is in a minority and the explosive areas are, relatively speaking, limited in extent; but the psychological, social, political, and economic ramifications of the situation have infested the whole nation. The same thing applied to land enclosure in England. Land furnished the status and economic symbols of the time; the aristocracy and gentry controlled most of it to the disadvantage of the resentful common people. Therefore, enclosure, beyond the fact that it caused acute problems in certain areas at certain times, produced a social cause célèbre from a psychological point of view. It furnished the focal point to which contemporaries related most of the socioeconomic problems of the Tudor reign. Furthermore, it afforded a theme whereby the social malaise of the period was bitterly discussed, written about, acted upon in parliament, and acted out in everyday life.

The following contemporary examples will serve to expose the sensitivity of the social nerve as reflected in enclosure and related problems. They will not only demonstrate the volatile nature of society at the common level, but will also depict the Tudor reaction to the threat.

First, to set the tenor of the age and to demonstrate the relationship of many of England's social ills to enclosure, the historian can turn to Sir Thomas More's *Utopia*. In a conversation with "the Cardinal," the protagonist explained the chief cause of thievery in England.

"Your sheep," I replied, "that used to be so gentle and eat so little. Now they are becoming so greedy and so fierce that they devour the men themselves, so to speak. They lay waste and pillage fields, homes, and towns. . . . Whole families, poor but numerous (since farming requires many hands), are forced to move out. . . . What is left for them to do but steal and so be hanged, doubtless justly, or to go about begging? And if they beg, they are thrown into prison as idle vagabonds. They would willingly work, but can find no one who will hire them. . . ."

"This enclosure has likewise raised the price of grain in many places."

. . . .

"Curb the engrossing of land by the rich. . . ."

"If you do not find a remedy for these evils, it is idle to boast of your severity in punishing theft."[49]

More set the stage for the controversy that continued to rage around the subject of enclosure.

Two contemporary writers expressed the attitude of governmental policy. Robert Crowley, during the reign of King Edward, criticized the gentry for their oppression of the poor, but after figuratively saying "naughty, naughty" to them, he proceeded to castigate the poor for daring to rise in revolt because their oppression really came from God as punishment for their sins. Therefore, they must "be obedient, and suffer patiently." It is a neat trick of mental gymnastics to denounce an action in the first instance and in the second to seek justification by attributing it to the providence of God. This would seem to justify the gentry, for they were only doing the dirty, but necessary, work of God. Crowley finally conceded the wrongness of the wealthy, for if the commons were to "commit their cause to God, you may be sure He will fight for them." This committal must be by prayer and long-suffering and not by means of revolt, for they dare not take up sword against God's anointed.[50]

As the editor of Crowley's tracts informs the reader, this was a time when men examined their fears and their Christian consciences and spoke their opinions in secular life and in churches. In the latter case, "The Prayer for Landlords" from the liturgy of King Edward provides the flavor of the situation.

We heartily pray Thee that they (who possess the grounds, pastures, and dwelling-places of the earth) may not rack and stretch out the rents of their houses and lands, nor yet take unreasonable fines and incomes after the manner of covetous worldlings, but so let them out to others that the inhabitants thereof may both be able to pay the rents and also honestly to live, to nourish their families, and to relieve the poor. . . . Give them grace also that they may be content with that that is sufficient, and not join house to house nor couple land to land to the impoverishment of other, but so behave themselves in letting out their tenements, lands, and pastures, that after this life they may be received into everlasting dwelling-places.[51]

In one of Crowley's tracts, "An informacion and Peticion agaynst the opressours of the pore Commons of this Realme," the author directed an appeal to parliament on behalf of the common people who suffered under the extreme pecuniary exactions of their landlords. He pointed out that the upper class of society had an ethical obligation to care for its less fortunate brethren. In his "Epigrammes" the author continued his attack on the aristocracy as he took issue with the "Forestallers," the "Leasemongers," the "Marchauntes," and the "Rente Raysers."[52] He repeated the message in "Pleasure and Payne," and told the rich man that God would punish him for his sins of enclosure and high rents against the poor commons, for he has a God-given obligation to:

> Let the pore man have and enioye
>   The house he had by copyholde,
> For hym, his wyfe, and Iacke hys boye,
>   To kepe them from hunger and colde;
> And thoughe the lease thereof be solde,
>   Bye it agayne though it be dere,
> For nowe we go on oure laste yere.[53]

"The Way to Wealth, wherein is plainly taught a most present Remedy for Sedicion" gave Crowley his opportunity to establish a cause and effect relationship between the evils he denounced and the infection of the realm with sedition, especially during Edward's reign.[54] Although Crowley complained of his age's evils, the historian cannot label him a reformer. He asked men to examine their Christian consciences and to continue the old policies in their God-given purity rather than in the form to which they had degenerated under the wealthy aristocracy. This furnished the theme of his message in "The Voyce of the Last Trumpet," for, as he says in reference to the yeomen,

> If thy landelorde do reise thy rent,
> Se thou paye it wyth quietnes;
> And praye to God omnipotent,
> To take from hym his cruelnes.

. . . .

> For God, who ruleth ech mans herte,
> Shal turne thy landlords hert, I saye,
> And shall all his whole lyfe convert,
> So thet he shall by thy greate staye.

If the yeoman decided upon a quicker and more earthly form of justice he was certain to lose everything.[55] Thus spoke Crowley and God.

The second author, Thomas Becon, wrote in the early 1550s. He too lamented the deplorable condition of the poor but agreed with Crowley that they deserved such suffering because of their sins. He denounced their rebellions, and pointed out the obligation that the wealthy had toward easing their sufferings. By their actions of enclosure they caused the downfall of common people and created suffering in the realm. "And the cause of all this wretchedness and beggary in the common-weal are the greedy gentlemen, which are sheepmongers and graziers. While they study for their own private commodity, the commonweal is like to decay." He ended his tirade of "O unnatural disposition! . . . O cumbrous confusion! . . . O preposterous order!" by telling the poor that "if oppression be done to the poor of rich worldlings, shall they avenge themselves? God forbid!"[56] Men of this caliber (Becon served as chaplain to archbishop Cranmer) knew that they could not go too far in denouncing the evils of the day. These men tried to pour oil on the waters of discontent. They, like their ruler, could only agree with the palliative measures then in vogue and had nothing concrete to offer by way of basic alleviation of society's problems. Their ejaculations of con-sternation expressed royal fear of the mob and the unsettled times. They expressed their reluctance to witness to any real social change by the sermonizing approach reflected throughout Becon's and Crowley's writings.

Under governmental policy, the aristocracy took all and the commons received, by the grace of God, as much or as little as their overlords wished to give. This served as an excellent socioreligious philosophy for the aristocrat as long as he could convince the common man that it was the world's God-given mode of operation. Thus the aristocrat had the advantage, even when wrong, of being the arbiter of God's justice, and the common man had to suffer in silent subjection before the dual wills of God and the aristocracy. Small wonder that many Englishmen ultimately turned their backs upon the image of God presented to them by *Ecclesia Anglicana* and accepted in its place the more attractive image presented to them by the radical reformers.

Another contemporary writer, Sir William Forrest, reinforced Becon's and Crowley's message of warning to the men of wealth. He stated that the individual should not operate against the advantage of the public by enclosing of lands, by trade, and by hoarding grain.[57]

During the reign of King Henry VIII, Thomas Starkey, Chaplain to the king, wrote his *Dialogue* between Cardinal Pole and Thomas Lupset, a lecturer at Oxford. The protagonists discussed the pros and cons of enclosure and related problems, and Pole concluded that the rent-raising desire of the landlords plus other faults of their class had produced a national sickness. "Thus it may be seen that in the head is a great disease, and the state is as a man in a frenzy." He then proposed a solution for many of the realm's problems "yf the statute of inclosure were put in executyon" in order to return enclosed lands to the plow. Philip Stubbes, in the 1580s, added his voice to those who blamed the wealthy aristocracy for enclosing, rack-renting, engrossing, and thus destroying the health of the realm by abusing the lower classes and driving them to extreme poverty.[58]

Hugh Latimer, in his "Last Sermon Preached before King Edward the Sixth," expressed the basic fear of all these men when he said, in reference to the suffering caused to the poor commons by enclosure, "Therefore, for God's love, restore their sufficient unto them, and search no more what is the cause of rebellion. But see and 'beware of covetousness;' for covetousness is the cause of rebellion." In spite of such warnings the situation did not change. In a play written about 1625 Philip Massinger was still concerned with the same problems and personifies them in the character of Sir Giles Overreach, a cruel extortioner and social climber. The play portrays this man as he plotted to seize land that belonged to others, and when confronted with the accusations of those whom he had cheated and robbed, he replied, "I only think what 'tis to have my daughter right honourable; and 'tis a powerful charm makes me insensible of remorse, or pity, or the least sting of conscience."[59]

As the above examples testify, the controversy of fear raged not only in the secular life of England but in the prayer life and sermons for the king as well. Both he and his ministers faced the fact that many problems plagued the realm. The numerous statutes, royal proclamations, acts of the privy council, and legal decisions relating to enclosure present proof of this. For example, the instructions to the duke of Norfolk in reference to the Northern Rebellion state that, "one ground of the late rebellion was that certain lords and gentlemen have enclosed commons and taken intolerably excessive fines." The letter of Dr. John London to Cromwell and of Roger Wigston to Cromwell give additional examples, and there is an abundance of these, of the king's and his ministers' concern over the continued enclosure of land.[60]

Parliamentary statutes provide additional information on the problem. An "Acte concernyng pulling downe of townes" dates from 1514-15, and it outlines the evils resulting from the destruction of towns due to the use of tillage land for grazing. In the same vein are the statutes titled: "An acte concernyng Ferms & Shepe" (1533-34), and "An Acte concernyng decay of Houses and inclosures" (1535-36). Elizabeth's reign produced, among others, "An Acte againste the decayinge of Townes & Howses of Husbandrye," and "An Acte for the maintenance of Husbandrie & Tillage." The latter outlines the benefits of tillage for keeping people occupied, fed, and out of mischief. The threat of an unruly people maintains a basic though unstated theme running throughout the foregoing examples, and the chronological list in Appendix V serves to complete the picture of the extensive nature of the enclosure problem and of the crown's attempt to deal with it. This list overlaps the Stuart reign to the year 1618 in order to show that the problem continued after the death of the last Tudor monarch. Also, see the chronological listing of "revolts, rebellions, riots" presented in former appendixes for such major enclosure disturbances listed there but not here.[61]

Men of Tudor England exaggerated the role played by the enclosure movement in producing the evils of the age; nevertheless, enclosure of lands created acute problems in certain areas, and furnished a focal issue to which Englishmen related the social ills of Tudor society. The psychological impact of the enclosure movement had a greater effect on English society than it merited from its innate importance. A phenomenon is important for an era when the contemporary actors believe and act out that importance. Given that qualification, the enclosure movement, in view of the kind of evidence just presented, had a profound effect upon Tudor society, especially in terms of the crown's concern for the maintenance of peace and order in the realm.

Although only a remnant from the medieval period, the problem of livery and maintenance remained another of the social plagues affecting the Tudors. Sir Thomas More wrote: "These noblemen carry around with them a great train of idle fellows. . . . As soon as their lord dies or they themselves fall ill, they are straightway turned out of doors. . . . Those who are turned off soon take to starving, unless they take to stealing." Then he says, "The custom of keeping too many retainers is widespread here."[62] Many of these people, leading a shadowy existence between the men of substance and the poor, eventually joined the hordes of vagrants who kept the government on the alert.

The several statutes of laborers under the Tudor dynasty were designed not only to control the wage level of the worker but also to force idle persons to work and thus serve as a means of vagrancy control. The following chapter develops this subject more fully.

Henry VII, having just won the crown for his family and wanting to restore public order out of the chaos resulting from civil warfare, attempted to placate the common people by ameliorating the former severe legislation against vagrants and beggars. Henry VIII, however, felt secure enough to continue a policy of strict control over the masses rather than continue what he considered the dangerous precedent of reducing the severity of the legal process. For this reason, poor-law legislation throughout Henry's and Elizabeth's reigns developed into a legal maze designed for suppression and control of the common masses. The punishment for securing control covered a wide gamut: whipping, the stocks, pillory, imprisonment, death sentence, deportation, registration, sending wanderers back to home parishes, apprenticeship of children, ear-boring, ear-cutting, branding, overseers of the poor, houses of correction, and workhouses. These measures partook more of a repressive philosophy than of an enlightened Protestant ethic that, as some teach, operated in a manner superior to the decadent and medieval Roman Catholic ethic that had damned the monasteries to destruction.

Conservatism, reinforced by fear of the mob, caused the Tudor monarchs to ignore the positive steps that they might have taken toward a solution to the social problems. Contemporaries saw certain alternatives and pointed them out to the government. They called upon Tudor officials and institutions to initiate positive programs of welfare action and to stop depending upon the dangerous policy of enforcing social control by means of punishment and intimidation. As certain of these concerned individuals stated, a king who rules justly and wisely has little to fear. The example of direct governmental control in the case of the destitute Cornwall tin miners shows that the crown had the capacity to act positively in such matters.[63] However, the fact that this provides an exception rather than the rule demonstrates the fatal weakness of the Tudor monarchs.

CHAPTER VI

What Laws and Other Measures Were Used by the Tudors in Combating Poverty and Vagrancy?

T he Tudors felt obligated to consider the welfare of the commons because the realm's peace depended upon their contentment. "The Maiestrates Lesson" by Robert Crowley reflects this attitude. The magistrate's duty was to administer justice and see to the enforcement of statutes, for neglect would cause decay of the realm and oppression of the poor. Attorney General Coke's list of articles for the observance of constables at the beginning of the assizes provides similar instructions, especially article number ten: "How vagabonds are taken up and punished, and impotent poor provided for."[1] After the Dissolution the state tried to establish some form of equitable poor relief, but it still placed the burden upon local parishes, and they often reacted by shirking this responsibility. Historians have made too much distinction between monastic and parochial alms—it was all part of the Church's effort, and the Church continued to handle it after the Dissolution.

Ecclesiastical alms operated capriciously and without a centralizing discipline. This Elizabeth attempted to give but failed because she still depended on local rate levies and local administration of the program. "A long series of statutes, beginning in the reign of Henry VIII, assigned increasingly complex and important duties to the parish as a secular unit of administration, while the Elizabethan poor laws were to fix the status of the parish as a unit of secular government." In the following passage from Philip Massinger, one sees the important role played by local officials, especially that magistrate of many functions, the justice of the peace. Here is Tapwell, an alehouse keeper, speaking to Wellborn, a prodigal: "Your dead father, my quondam master, was a man of worship, old Sir John Wellborn, Justice of peace, and *quorum,* and stood fair to be *Custos rotulorum;* bore the whole sway of the shire; kept a great house; relieved the poor, and so forth." Upon being accused by Wellborn of making his money from whores, and other questionable sources, Tapwell replied that he was better off than Wellborn, for by his business acumen he had acquired money and the position of "Parish Scavenger" and had hopes of eventually becoming overseer of the poor. "Which if I do, on your petition Wellborn, I may allow you thirteen pence a quarter, and you shall thank my worship."[2] Upon amateurs of this caliber the Tudor poor-law effort depended.

The queen expressed her obligation toward the people in the instructions of 1574 to the Council of the North requesting that members prevent unlawful enclosure and oppression of the poor. Wealthy persons transgressing these rules should suffer prosecution to the full extent of the law "for example's sake, yet so that the common people do not violently redress themselves, but wait the redress of law." This last line reveals the true concern of the queen; it derives not from a humanitarian motive but from fear that the people might "violently redress themselves." Robert Crowley expressed contemporary philosophy when he said that beggars should trust in God and He would feed them.[3]

The queen's concern relative to the situation of 12,000 Cornwall tin mining families was explained earlier.[4] This is one of the few times when the government took constructive action in reference to a socioeconomic problem. Mostly the crown passed statutes and issued proclamations designed to place responsibility on local institutions and peoples.

Statutory evidence of vagrancy problems emerged as early as the reign of Richard II. In 1388 a law appeared providing punishment of stocks and gaol for wandering beggars. People unable to work remained where they were at the time of the statute's proclamation, and if the residents would not have them they returned to their places of birth. Beggars with permits were excepted. Presumably, the ones who returned continued to live by begging. George G. Coulton remarks that this arrangement "has some right to be called our first real Poor Law, providing for all cases." That may be true in one sense, but it certainly was a negative "Poor Law." Allowing a pun, it introduced a rather poor law for a poor law. Henry VII moderated provisions of Richard's penalties whereby long imprisonment caused the death of some vagabonds. In spite of this, Thomas Starkey has Cardinal Pole say that men suffered hanging for petty thievery.[5] So much for Tudor leniency.

The 1517 orders in the journal of the *London Common Council* reveal that the privy council prodded the Londonites toward controlling their vagrants. The impotent poor had to register and receive tin badges for legal begging. Others suffered punishment and return to places of origin. Legal beggars aided authorities in expelling unlicensed ones. Ill persons went to hospitals where proctors received licenses to beg for the institutions.[6]

A royal proclamation in 1530 ordered magistrates to whip ("leaving aside vain pity") all persons caught as illegal vagrants. Because of the problems they created, they received certificates of whipping and then returned to places of origin or birth. A reiteration of the above regulations appeared as a statute in the 1530-31 session of parliament. It made a distinction between beggars who could not work and should continue begging and sturdy beggars who should receive punishment. An additional statute of 1530-31 dealt with another facet of the problem, that is, the bands of Gypsies who roamed the English countryside engaging in vagrancy and crime. This act ordered them to vacate the realm within sixteen days of the statute's proclamation on pain of imprisonment and forfeiture of their goods. A royal proclamation in 1535-36 dealt with the problem of clerks and pretended clerks who went about preaching seditious sermons and granting pardons and indulgences for money. They often leagued with thieves and were to receive the same treatment as sturdy vagrants.[7]

These poor-law provisions received a new element in the 1535-36 parliamentary session. It reiterated the Statute 22 Hen. VIII. C. 12. which provided for punishment but made no provision for employment of sturdy beggars. This present act remedied this by stipulating that officers of cities, shires, and parishes should provide work for sturdy vagrants, but made no provision for the source of employment. In addition, it ordered church wardens and other officials to gather alms for both employment of sturdy vagrants and maintenance of those unable to work. Alms were donated on a voluntary basis. This act provided as punishment for unlawful begging the usual whipping plus the loss of part of the right ear for second offenders, and third offenders could receive death as felons.[8] Thus, for the first time, the law provided positive features for control of vagrancy and begging.

In spite of these provisions for keeping peace, the government issued a circular letter of exhortation in 1541 to the justices of the peace demanding that they look to their duties relative to suppression of Roman Catholics, seditions, rumors relating to the king, vagrancy, and administration of justice in general. The Tudors discovered that it was one thing to pass strict laws to control the realm but another when it came to enforcing them. Henry VIII found it necessary in 1541-42 to issue a statute in which he took the justices of the peace to task for not properly executing laws against vagrancy. The statute lays down certain rules and regulations for better observance of their duties. Still, the problem was far from a solution, for the king could not even keep his own court free of vagrants. A proclamation of 1543 declared that statutes against vagrancy should apply to vagrants who infested the royal court.[9] Apparently this attempt to clear the court of undesirable characters was unsuccessful, for this problem recurs time and again throughout the century by the evidence of proclamations, statutes, and acts of the privy council.

The first year of Edward VI's reign marked the apex in severity of treatment for vagrants. That year's statute, while retaining earlier provisions, subjected them to branding and slavery in neck irons. Here one sees Tudor mentality formulating its law of paradox: if harsh measures produce undesirable results then use even harsher measures in order to produce the changes desired. They never tried to understand the causes of social upheaval but stuck to their formula that all things would right themselves in the end by means of severe punishment as "an example for others." They did not realize that this approach only worsened an already impossible situation. Latimer voiced his concern when he preached before Edward VI relative to the injustices of the time and then continued that "another poor woman was hanged for stealing a few rags off a hedge that were not worth a crown."[10]

Apparently the severe Statute of 1 Edw. VI. C. 3. caused more problems than it solved, for parliament in 1549-1550 repealed it and 22 Hen. VIII. C. 12. was revived in its place. This act further provided for the forcing of poor children over age five into servitude without parental permission. The act even admitted in reference to the laws that "thextremitie of some whereof have byn occation that they have not ben putt in ure." The statute passed in 1555 added little to these provisions with the exception that it stipulated that each parish should elect two men to serve as collectors for relief of the poor. Voluntary collections remained with the instruction that a person refusing to contribute to the poor fund should receive exhortation to reconsider. Firstly, he was approached by priest and church wardens who "gently exhort" him, and if this failed the bishop provided additional persuasion.[11] This was more in the nature of a voluntary-compulsive system than one based upon mere voluntarism.

Early in the reign of Elizabeth the former poor-law and vagrancy statutes (22 Hen. VIII. C. 12. and 3 & 4 Edw. VI. C. 16.) received confirmation, with certain amendments. The parishes still elected collectors of alms to gather and distribute alms to the poor. The contributions were made compulsory, for those refusing faced imprisonment. When the poor became too numerous for parish relief, they received licenses and badges to beg.

The privy search provided another deterrent to vagrancy. By this system, shires, cities, and towns received privy council letters ordering them to conduct general searches for apprehending vagrants. "The searches ordered in 1571 affected eighteen counties at the least, and took place on agreed days at monthly intervals throughout the whole area concerned. The ones ordered during the years 1569-1572 were the most elaborately organized on record."[12] Unsettled conditions prevailed, therefore, the fewer vagrants left to participate in rebellious activities the better for the crown.

Apparently finding the existing laws unsatisfactory, parliament, in 1572, repealed 22 Hen. VIII. C. 12.; 3 & 4 Edw. VI. C. 16.; and 5 Eliz. C. 3. and replaced them with "An Acte for the Punishment of Vacabondes, and for Releif of the Poore & Impotent." The preamble pictures a land infested with beggars and vagrants who caused disturbances and crimes. The new law was largely a repetition of laws just repealed, but provided harsher punishment for vagrancy than heretofore, with the exception of the severe statute of Edward VI. Elizabeth's statute again serves to reveal the Tudor tendency of vacillation and irresolution. They might relent for the moment, but fear of the mob drove them in the direction of severity for "example." This statute provided imprisonment for unlawful beggars over age fourteen, whipping and ear-branding for beggars convicted of vagabondage, unless someone would take them to service. If they ran away from serving, the above punishment went into effect. Second offense beggars became felons unless they could find masters, and third offenders became felons subject to death. Begging children under age fourteen received the whip and stocks. In addition, justices of the peace received orders to register persons unable to work and see that they received maintenance in their districts of birth or residence. Also, the justices assessed the poor rate quota per parish inhabitant and yearly appointed collectors and overseers of the poor to receive and distribute alms. This statute also furnished the Tudor listing of persons who represent rogues, vagabonds, and sturdy beggars: wanderers, minstrels, gamers, fortunetellers, bear-warders, players, jugglers, peddlers, tinkers, petty chapmen, begging scholars, and gaolees (unless any of these were licensed).[13]

Since the above statute made no provision for work for the poor, this oversight received an amending statute in 1575-76. A new feature appeared among the poor-law provisions, i.e., make-work, for this act called for building and maintenance of houses of correction throughout the realm. These were to receive stocks of materials for employment of beggars. "Houses of Correction shall be provided in each county for punishing and employing Rogues and unsettled poor, etc." This act further provided for punishment of parents of bastard children. Small wonder that social conditions worsened in Tudor England, for the whole state system remained geared to punishment and little else. Even the system of make-work offered punishment; the statute described houses of correction as places of "punishing and employing" and the former was always in the ascendancy. These two acts furnished the heart of the Elizabethan poor-law structure. According to Aydelotte, "the famous poor law of 1597 was nothing but a modification of these two statutes."[14] This applies to the additional poor law of 1601.

In spite of these statutory regulations for controlling the actions of society's riffraff, the crown instituted even more severe measures for control. This happened when provost marshals received martial law power for dealing with and hanging vagrants without court trial. Harrison states in his publication of 1587, "The punishment that is ordained for this kind of people is very sharp, and yet it cannot restrain them from their gadding; wherefore the end must needs be martial law." As a result, he further says, several hundred of these poor wretches gave up their lives on the gallows. Such severity resulted from the fact that the crown made little distinction between seditious persons on the one hand and rogues, vagabonds, and sturdy beggars on the other. In the eyes of the Tudor government, they all stood together as part of a common mob and threat to the throne. A royal proclamation of 1594 reveals this threat. It indicates the court's infection with vagrants, especially former Irish rebels against the state. One such Irishman confessed plotting to kill the queen. The Tudors saw sedition and treason lurking amidst every vagabond group, and they desired to control them at any cost. Dynastic fear of this threat appears in a royal proclamation of 1595 for London and environs. It stipulated that no one, except officials and known persons, could venture abroad "after sunset or nine o'clock at night," and no assembled groups could meet except in places of worship, law courts, and guild halls. Persons caught writing or posting seditious bills would suffer execution. Twenty pounds reward was offered for information on persons engaged in these activities.[15] This provided the structure for dictatorship except that Tudor law enforcement was too hotch-potch and amateurish to provide such regulation in the fullest sense. Nevertheless, the intent persisted and all that prevented Tudor monarchs, especially Elizabeth, from carrying it out fully was the wherewithal.

Nothing rested safely from Tudor control, and this included the playhouses of London and vicinity. In 1597 the privy council sent letters to the area officials directing an immediate closure of plays and destruction of houses. The council condemned the players as an unruly lot and the buildings used by them as disorderly and seditious places. For instance, a play in a "Bancke Side" theatre was charged with "contanynge very seditious and sclanderous matter." The players, when apprehended, went to prison.[16]

Capital punishment served as a favorite means of social control during the Tudor monarchy, for not only did the crown and provost marshals mete out the death penalty, but the county quarter sessions acted just as severely. The Devonshire sessions and assizes sentenced a total of seventy-four persons to death by hanging in the year 1598 alone. Thirty-nine received sentence by quarter sessions and thirty-five by the assizes. "Indeed foreigners commented on the cheapness with which life was held in Elizabethan England."[17] This reveals the real heart of the Elizabethan poor-law and vagabond control program. The noose of the hangman always formed a shadow in the background serving as an "example for others." Small effort went into solving the socioeconomic problems of society, and the hangman worked busily when all else failed.

Until now, this chapter has dealt primarily with statutes, privy council acts, royal proclamations, and the laws of the land in general as they related to the control and combatting of vagrancy, vagabondage, and poverty. As previously pointed out, this control sometimes acted constructively, but more often it degenerated into a system of harsh punishment and control. Presently, this study will consider the "other measures" (other than those of a more or less legal nature) that went into the Tudor attempt to deal with the lower-class problems of the time. This will mainly have to do with the various types of charity available to the poor people of that period.

As in earlier times, philanthropy played on active role during the Tudor era. This approach to the problem of poverty did little to alleviate the matter. Charity based upon philanthropy haphazardly and inadequately served the needs of the people. It only provided the Tudors with an excuse for their perfunctory attitude toward poverty. For this reason, the Tudor poor-law system was never organized on a comprehensive and constructive basis of governmental concern and management. True, much legislation on the matter existed, but after legislative enactment, the government washed its hands of the whole situation and left the implementation of these laws almost entirely up to the philanthropic

whimsy of the local peoples, institutions, and customs. The dis-
organized, amateurish, and unwilling local institutions shirked these
burdensome duties and allowed a bad situation to further degenerate.
Even after Elizabeth made the poor-rate levy compulsory, the individual
communities reluctantly assumed responsibility for their charges and,
whenever possible, refused to provide for their maintenance. Time after
time the privy council devoted its concerns to attempting to force communities to shoulder their duties.

Individual alms or philanthropy in one form, or another had to provide for some maintenance of poor relief. This was customary and a
built-in feature of the era, for, since all things came from God and all
persons served as stewards of his possessions, what better stewardship
could one render than to give his (God's) worldly possessions to the
cause of charity and suffering humanity? Beginning at the top of society,
one finds the crown dispensing alms by means of the king's almoner.
He collected the royal alms and dispensed them to poor individuals,
groups, and institutions. For instance, an entry from the *Acts of the
Privy Council* reveals that certain money from the town of Maidstone
belonging to the queen was designated for usage by her almoner, the
Bishop of Bristol, "to be imployed to the increase of her Majesty's
almes." Also paid in augmentation of royal alms accounts were the
possessions of "felons *de se,* and deodands" as well as the goods of
suicides. Funerals afforded one of the favorite occasions for dispensing
alms, as cited earlier in the case of Henry VII. On one occasion at least,
two men made provision for dispersal of alms before their execution.[18]

The owners of great estates came next in social importance as alms-
givers. In this respect, the record of Naworth estate, although dating
from the middle of the seventeenth century, serves as a good example of
this type of charitable activity.[19] This listing has the advantage of being
typical of the scope and variety of private alms-giving of Tudor times
and also illustrates the fact that the Tudor monarchs had brought about
little change in poverty care despite the much praised Elizabethan poor-
law system.

The 1597 will of Lord Cobham, Lord Warden of the Five Ports and
Lord Chamberlain of the Household, affords another example of this
type of charity concern. For, he says, "My jewels, ornaments, and plate

are to be sold, to pay debts, funeral expenses, and maintain the poor at Cobham." He also left real estate and funds for the building and maintenance of a college for poor people at Cobham. On the other hand, the bequest might be simple and to the point as in the case of Thomas Trepe of Warburton in 1560. "I bequeath as much for refreshments to the poor at my funeral as my executor thinks fit."[20]

In the Tudor world, no chance was ever missed for almsgiving, not even at the parliamentary sessions. On January 2, 1563, the House of Commons alms collection amounted to nineteen pounds ten shillings. Lateness and nonattendance at sessions brought fines and this money went to the alms box. Not taking a back seat to Commons, the House of Lords also made its own collection on behalf of the poor. The church poor box provided the example for such collections, and the parliamentarians adhered to that traditional form of charity. These forms of almsgiving proved noteworthy and admirable, but they provided a spotty form of charity. Needy persons often suffered from destitution and hopelessness. For as A. V. Judges says concerning prisoners, "no public funds were available for the care and nourishment of prisoners; failing charity the poor starved.[21]

As stated earlier, the customary royal letter patent or charity brief served when ordinary forms of alms failed to satisfy charity's demands. These briefs or evasions of official responsibility placed the problem before the alms-giving potential of the general public and provided an admission of lack of concern and defeat on the government's part. Regardless of the names used, these permits for public collections were simply licenses to beg, for they served as customary relief and were not reserved for unusual calamities alone. The government recognized the problems pertaining to officially sanctioned begging activities and finally forbade them by statute (39 Eliz., 1597-1598) but continued to permit their use. In 1601 the town of Fordham (Cambridgeshire) suffered loss by fire, and the dwellers suffered impoverishment. They petitioned for a collection license under the great seal in spite of the prohibition of these by the preceding parliament. The queen granted a collection in Cambridgeshire and five other counties for one year. The towns of Walton and Bastingstoke also received permits for collections during the same year and for the same reasons.[22]

The following example taken from the 1598 privy council proceedings illustrates the use of licenses to beg as a last resort and admission of governmental perfunctoriness and failure. In Devonshire, fire ruined the town of Tiverton and the magistrates resorted to a collection throughout the realm as the only possible relief:

Which course of making collection having bin of late so restrained by the lawes of the realme upon very just causes as that there can be no license or warrent for it but such as proceedeth immediatly from her Majestie, wee do therefore commend the said humble suite of the inhabitantes for such collection to be presented by you unto her Majesty. . . . The case is extraordinary and the number of those whome it concerneth very great, their estate very pittifull, and therefore somme speedy course needfull for their relief.[23]

Furthermore, in the same shire, the town of Cullompton suffered heavily from fire in 1602. The justices levied a collection and saw to the quartering of the poor refugees in surrounding parishes. The shire of Cornwall in 1595 received a collection due to the recent invasion by the enemy. "Now it appeareth that this money was neither well ordered nor distributed, for the license to gather was sold by the parties that undertook the collection, and the villages most spoiled like to be defrauded of it." There is record in 1592 of a letter to the earl of Lincoln and others relative to the poor prisoners in Lincoln Castle who suffered from the lack of relief to them by "collection of the common releefe appointed to them by the statute within the shire." The report says that many of them had already starved. The wording of the following request is amusing and different. In 1514 the Church of St. Mary Axe, London, received a license for the gathering of alms for repairs to the building. "They state that their church was built in remembrance of St. Ursula, daughter of a King of England, one of the 11,000 virgins 'that tenderly shed their blood for our Christian faith and belief'; and that 'the said poor church is edified and honored by keeping of a holy relic, an axe, one of the three that the 11,000 virgins were beheaded withal.' The church is so poor that the parson has departed and left." Rome had generously granted 380,000 years and 100 days indulgence to those pilgrims who visited this church during certain holy seasons.[24]

As the evidence bears witness, collections such as those listed above were subject to abuse and caused disgrace for the Tudor government. They furnish typical cases of the government's attitude of "let Jack do it" when the poor needed relief. The sources record many such collections.

A major feature of Elizabethan poor laws was provision of work for able-bodied beggars and vagrants in the newly created houses of correction. In spite of pretenses to the contrary, these workhouses served as glorified prisons, for they operated like prisons and the inmates spent their time in prisoner fashion. Upon first entrance of male or female vagabonds into one of the houses they received twelve whiplashes upon bare flesh and children received six. Then the new prisoner "shall have putt uppon hym, her, or them, some clogge, cheine, collers of iron, ringle, or manacle." Unruly prisoners received harsher treatment, heavier shackles, less food, and harder work.[25]

The house of correction or workhouse idea seemed a good one if handled properly. However, the operation of these houses as prisons did not produce a successful program. As with so many other social endeavors, the Tudor government bungled the attempt at creating an adequate system of houses of correction to provide work for vagrants. Here, again, the government passed legislation ordering the building of these institutions and then sat back and expected both construction and operation of the houses to come from the good will of individuals and communities. In 1579 the privy council ordered the dean of Winchester to make a collection for supplies to stock the new house of correction. His efforts did not secure enough materials for the operation of the house. A follow-up letter from the privy council directed the establishment of a committee for a collection from all those able to pay. The failure of Middlesex and the City, the "place where his Majesty doth so ordinarily reside," to provide a single house of correction has been mentioned.[26]

The almshouse provided an interesting feature of Tudor poor-relief care. Wilbur K. Jordan says that for a long period (1480-1660) "household" relief by alms, food, clothing, and shelter was the prime concern of English society. Then during the latter part of this period poor people received an increasing amount of assistance by means of almshouses, "where the impotent and derelick might be separated from society as incurably charitable charges." The idea sounds good but the reality of the situation was far from ideal. The institutions were usually small and ill-equipped to care for their charges, for as Peter Laslett says, "Few seem to have contained more than a dozen or twenty inmates." The problem of maintaining these houses is revealed in a letter of 1595 from the privy council to the officials of Bristol where an almshouse existed for the benefit of disabled and aged sailors. The upkeep of this house came from a tax on the port's tonnage and a levy on the sailors' wages. The letter complained that some of the ships failed to pay the tax, and, rather than doing anything about it themselves as agents of the government, the members of the privy council passed the obligation to the city of Bristol.[27] The ideas supporting almshouse origins appear sincere, but like other areas of Tudor voluntary aid this too was poorly organized, amateurish, small in scope, and inadequate to the vastness of social care needed.

Of additional importance to the Tudors in keeping the masses of the people satisfied, especially during times of dearth and famine, was the food supply of the realm. This applied particularly to grain, the staff of the poor man's life. Poor harvests and the plague struck Cambridge in 1556. The privy council showed concern, but the city and university authorities organized and carried out the relief measures. They stamped out grain profiteering, made cheap grain available on the market, and imposed a compulsory poor rate on the wealthier segment of the population. Grain shortages and consequent profiteering by traders remained as recurring themes of the sixteenth century. On this subject, E. M. Hampson states that the main concern of the privy council under the Tudors was the control of vagrancy and "the securing of adequate food supplies at reasonable prices." Appendixes VII and VIII show the extent of this concern in its many ramifications and that the Tudors placed the obligation upon local, outmoded institutions and customs.[28]

A great number of statutes, acts of the privy council, royal proclamations, and other measures pertain to regulating the food supply: control of speculators, provision of supplies of cheap grain for the poor, prohibition of export of important food items, imports of such items from abroad, and directions to the justices, mayors, and other officials to look after food supply problems. Trevelyan observes that under the Tudors "the provision for the poor was better than anything there had been in an older England."[29] While it is probably true that Tudor monarchs fretted more over the situation, to judge from legislation, proclamations, and regulations, there is room to doubt the assertion that Tudor care for the poor "was better than anything there had been in an older England." One simply looks at the earlier royal proclamations to understand that a vital concern for the realm's food supply did not have its origin with the Tudor monarchs. During the period 1231-1482, there appeared sixty-six royal proclamations on the subject.

Although the maintenance of an adequate food supply in England remained a problem of varying intensity throughout the sixteenth century, the latter part of the century was especially troublesome in this respect. "The last quarter of the century was a period of general unrest throughout Europe, and in England this was intensified by a succession of bad harvests. During the worst years the Queen's Privy Council attempted to alleviate the hardships of the people and to prevent subsequent disturbances by closely regulating the price and supply of corn." Under such circumstances, town officials purchased grain and supplied it to the markets for the poor at less than regular market prices, and still they often made considerable profit.[30]

The chronology of statutes, acts of the privy council, and royal proclamations presented in Appendix VIII demonstrates the omnipresent nature of the food supply problem during the Tudor period and also indicates steps taken to deal with it. As this list demonstrates, England sustained many food problems. Major contributors to the crisis were those men of business, the food or grain speculators. They dared to venture into the environs of the royal court, and one can read about the 1540 dealings of the privy council with the four "tapsters that vagrantly followed the Court and caused the price of victuals to be enhanced, ordered to be set on the pillory." During the 1540s Thomas Becon produced a vituperative outburst against grain speculators. "What shall I speak of certain rich & greedy cormorants, those locusts and caterpillars of the commonweal . . . bring they forth their grain and sell it, unto the utter impoverishment and extreme undoing of the poor commonalty? O cruel murderers and unmerciful blood-soupers!"[31]

The speculators received contempt on all sides, and official pronouncements waxed in language as strong as that used by Becon. Elizabeth's proclamation of 1586 partly blamed the current shortage of food on the poor season, but added that she placed the blame "most of all . . . through the covetousness and uncharitable greedines of such as be great cornemasters and ingrosers of corne, using all the subtill meanes they can, to worke their owne present unconscionable gaine against the rules of charitie, which hir maiestie of hir princelie care and love towards hir people, utterlie condemneth, and earnestlie desireth to remedie, for the reléefe of the poorer sort." The queen ordered the supplying of the markets with food at reasonable prices for the relief of the needy poor. She closed with the admonition that those who failed to conform to her instructions would appear before the privy council "there to be further delt with by severe punishment for the better example of all others."[32] Again, note the usage of the famous Tudor phrase, "for the example of others." Those were the magic words that, in spite of their royal luster, never seemed to quite live up to their enchanting promise, for there were always those subjects upon whom the example had other than the desired effect.

One of the best illustrations of Elizabethan poverty-care plans working at cross-purposes is furnished by Herefordshire in 1586 where the money collected for building a house of correction was used to buy grain, due to scarcity, that it "maie be uttered to the poore people at reasonable prices." This furnishes an example of the "hand-to-mouth" method of care provided for the needy poor of Elizabethan England. This in the late 1580s: "If the world last awhile after this rate, wheat and rye will be no grain for poor men to feed on; and some caterpillars [grain speculators] there are that can say so much already." G. B. Harrison, using Stow's Annales and the Acts of the Privy Council, follows this up with further reports of food scarcity and rising prices in the latter half of the 1590s.[33] The Tudor dynasty stood unprepared to handle the economic and social instability of the age. The only response the privy council knew how to make was the policy of producing fulminating acts and proclamations blaming others and telling them to rectify the situation; this action fell upon justices, sheriffs, mayors, bishops, priests, and other local officials.

Meantime, the Elizabethan government continued coping with the situation with petty regulatory schemes. For instance, the 1596 letter of the privy council to the Lord Mayor of London directed him to see that

"all excess of fare might be avoided in public and private
diet . . . strict order shall be taken that no persons have meat dressed
in their houses at night on Wednesdays, Fridays or fast days; any that
offend therein shall be committed to prison." The same letter took exception to the many gentlemen leaving their estates in order to avoid
hospitality to the poor; the preachers should exhort them to shoulder
their responsibilities. In a royal proclamation of 1596, this gentleman's
obligation appeared in the form of "a prohibition to men of hospitalitie
from remooving from their habitation in the time of dearth."[34]

The government produced no better solution to the problems than the
medieval ideal of private alms; an ideal that Elizabeth and her advisers
should have realized was a thing of the past and inadequate in the present situation. Warning signs flew to tell the astute observer of the
bankruptcy of the old manner of handling such matters. The people
showed disaffection and anger, and the old alms-oriented structure of
society had left them hungry—so hungry in fact that in 1598 in the county of Lincoln "there is great discontent of the people; insomuch that they
were ready to break into great disorder."[35] What happened? One of the
leaders went to prison in order that he might appear before the queen's
privy council. The council, presumably, made him an "example for
others." Fine, but the "others" finally caught on to the system, and in
the next century they provided a force willing to help the Civil War
leaders make a Stuart king also an example for others. These conditions
of social unrest, though not the ideologic cause of civil war, furnished
the rebellious leaders with a paramount means of success. Therefore,
that which guarantees the success of such an undertaking is one of its
major causes, for without the means ideology remains worthless.

Now is the time for consideration of that most important workhorse
of medieval and Tudor charity care, namely, the hospital or "spital-
house." We think of a hospital as an institution with the specific function of caring for and curing the sick. During the sixteenth century those
were only two of a multiplicity of functions which the hospital served.
A. V. Judges provides a note of definition to Robert Copeland's "The
Highway to the Spital-House." It says that, "the 'Spital-House' was the
poor-farm of the era for the down and out." Copeland's poem presents
the types of applicants seeking shelter and aid in a Tudor English

hospital. A royal proclamation in 1560 gives additional information about the varied functions of such institutions. The proclamation deals with the four hospitals in and near London, "where are kept 200 scholars with daily meat and drink, the other hospital is for lame and impotent people. . . . The Hospitals are not sufficiently endowed to provide for the grammar schools in the said hospitals, the scolars of Oryall College at Oxford and the reparation of their Churches and Mansion Churches."[36]

This now poses the problem of the building and maintenance of these institutions in the first place. They had their origin in the medieval system of individual philanthropy and almsgiving. Kings, nobles, gentlemen, wealthy merchants, Church officials, and institutions established hospitals. In this way, men of importance could perpetuate their names and also salve their consciences for lifetimes spent as unworthy stewards of God's possessions. Sir John Hawkins received a license in 1594 to build a hospital in the town of Chatham in Kent. What to name the institution posed a real problem, so they named it Sir John Hawkin's Hospital, and it cared for "ten or more poor mariners and shipwrights."[37]

At the deathbed of Edward VI the preacher of the hour, Bishop Ridley, delivered sermons on the charitable obligations of the stewards of God's goods of this earth. The king, whose father had recently dissolved and plundered the four great hospitals of London, finally either suffered a twinge of conscience or had a desire to perpetuate his good name, and "did found erecte and establyshe three Hospitalles in and near the Cytye of London, called the Hospitalles of King Edwarde the Syxte, or Christe, Bridewell, and Sainte Thomas the Apostle. . . . And whereas our late Soveraigne Lord King Henrye the Eyght . . . did found an Hospitall . . . called Lytle Sainte Bartholomeus near London."[38] Two of these hospitals, St. Thomas' and St. Bartholomew's, were late victims to the Dissolution. Even the old dissolver himself, Henry VIII, had had second thoughts about at least one of his sacrifices. Bridewell served as one of the royal palaces, and it was converted into a workhouse or house of correction for idle vagrants and became a model for other houses of this type.

The maintenance of these establishments usually posed a difficulty.

A few received endowment to some degree, but most of them had to depend on the benevolence of others for the greater part of their expenditures. Queen Elizabeth gave permission in 1560 for a collection in Wales for the four hospitals of the London area. For endeavors of this type proctors carried out the collection campaign. As a sign that the situation neither improved under the Tudors nor for a long time thereafter, the information is given about the following charity brief of the late date 1684. It was issued for a collection on behalf of the Chelsea Hospital, a home "for 400 disabled soldiers on which much money has been spent. More is urgently needed. The bishops are to be called on to contribute and to collect in their dioceses liberally."[39]

In addition to pecuniary problems, the hospitals suffered the dangers of poor quality and dishonest administration. Most of them were not as lucky as Christ's Hospital of Sherbourne in 1585 when it petitioned the crown to increase its number of inmates from sixteen to thirty, "the revenues being able to maintain so many." The situation was more often of the following type as presented in a statute of 1414. "Forasmuch as many Hospitals within the Realm of England . . . be now for the most Part decayed, and the Goods and Profits of the same, by divers Persons, as well Spiritual as Temporal, withdrawn and spent in other Use, whereby many Men and Women have died in great Misery." This illustration points up the fact that institutional maintenance of this form had become inadequate long before the Tudor dynasty; yet that dynasty continued to rely on such outmoded means to care for the social problems of the era. The same conditions and complaints still prevailed in 1533 as indicated by an act of parliament to the effect: "That the hospitals and almshouses founded by the King's ancestors and other charitable persons, the profits of which are usurped by persons calling themselves masters, wardens, etc. (who call them free chapels), who take great fines for the admission of almsmen, send out pardoners to beg, and commit other abuses, by act of this present Parliament, certify into Chancery . . . their foundations."[40]

The Reformation and dissolution of the monasteries and many of the hospitals did not serve to improve matters any, for in 1572 Thomas Lever complained to Burghley about the "evils attendant on the present management of leases of impropriate benefices and hospitals. Proposed remedies for the same." There had been complaints against hospitals before the Dissolution, and St. Thomas' Southwark in 1536 furnishes a case to the point. Parishioners accused the monks who operated the house of harboring nonmeritorious characters of wealth and refusing relief to the needy poor. The master had closed the "free" school—for the maintenance of which four pounds per year was furnished—and he was also accused of disposing of hospital property to his own advantage. After the Dissolution, however, the same complaints prevailed at those houses that had managed to survive the greed of King Henry. The Hospital of St. Mary Magdalene, Ripon, was one of the latter, but in 1567 one hears this complaint against the master and two chaplains: "The howseis go to ruyne and decaie, and ther is no provision for releiffe of the poore." This 1568 letter of "James Bishop of Durham to Sec. Wm. Cecil" gives additional information on the post-Dissolution situation. He reported to Cecil on the "hospital that Mr. Lever had here" concerning its entanglements with leases, pensions, and fees to the extent "that he can neither keep it, nor the poor be relieved, except you stand his good master. . . . All these leases were made by the masters to their kinsfolk, and to impoverish the poor." Then he proceeded to say that "there was another such hospital here not long ago, where the poor is clean turned out by the like misusing of it."[41]

The Charterhouse Hospital, Hull, also survived the Dissolution, but in 1571 the mayor and aldermen complained that during the thirteen years of Thomas Turner's mastership of the house he had admitted persons with money and had shut out the needy and let to lease hospital property and lands.[42] The foregoing evidence indicates that Puritan dreams of a post-Reformation society of benevolent brotherhood, free of the evils of Roman Catholicism, existed as the product of the religious fanaticism of the age. They failed to take into consideration the greed of the era for which that of Henry VIII had set the example for others.

The medieval period produced statutes of laborers. Edward III's 1349 statute regulated labor conditions resulting from the plague-death shortage of working men and demands for higher wages. In fact, some commoners preferred begging to working. This statute forced able-bodied men and women either to work or go to prison. It stipulated a set wage scale with fines for the payers and gaol for the receivers of illegal higher pay. The Tudors accepted this system of semislave labor as a measure to combat poverty, at least to the extent of maintaining the worker at a bare subsistence level, and above all as a measure ready-made for control of the vagrant masses. An act of Henry VIII's reign established a wage scale for different types of work, but the document provides no indication that the formulators of this law desired to protect or aid the worker. Rather, its apparent design was to keep him in his place at the lowest scale of pay.[43]

The 1562-63 Elizabethan Statute of Labourers, as those before it, acted as a social control measure: enforcement, setting of a wage scale, and punishment were all delegated to the justices of the peace. The act placed certain obligations upon the employer but set forth a stricter set of rules and regulations for the worker: man, woman, and child. All the unemployed between ages twelve and sixty had to accept work, and workers could not leave their place of employment without permission from the local officials. Persons refusing to abide by the rules faced imprisonment, and this equally applied to anyone under twenty-one years of age who refused to become an apprentice.[44]

This set of rules for the laboring man, in conjunction with the various legislation for controlling vagrancy, formed the heart of the Tudor attempt to formulate a system of absolute control over lower-class physical mobility. Again, it provided an outmoded and outdated system, but in the process of trying to make it work, the Tudor government created a vast amount of hardship and social discontent. In the final analysis, it failed, for the lower-class population remained highly mobile as the continued increase of vagrancy bears witness. The sixteenth-century English monarchs never arrived at the truth that the restriction of a people's physical mobility will not produce social tranquility but, rather, will create the opposite condition as the history of Tudor England attests. A major problem resulted from the fact that there were more job seekers than jobs available, and those without employment often wandered to other areas searching for a living wage. The laws made this an illegal act. Many of the unemployed adjusted to this state of life, and a job was least in their desires. The government tried to solve the dilemma by means of prison-oriented houses of correction and failed, for this method robbed people of their freedom and dignity as human beings.

They were whipped like animals, reduced to a subhuman mode of exis- tence, and followed an animal-like form of daily life as a result. Tudor methods produced rather than reduced, as intended, an ever-growing population of rogues, vagabonds, and sturdy beggars.

The vast number of veterans returned from foreign wars, plus an ar- ray of beggars pretending this status, made a major contribution to the increasing number of vagrants in sixteenth-century England. They wan- dered about and committed crimes and disturbances throughout the realm. The many cases of vagrancy, rioting, mutiny, and desertion by troops emphasizes the critical nature of this problem. The situation first became serious in the late 1580s and reached a crisis stage in the 1590s. This resulted from England's levy of soldiers for the struggle with Spain as well as her involvement in warfare in both France and Ireland. The English practice of "pressing" or forcing vagrants to serve as troops in wars overseas made the situation worse. This became such an infamous part of the recruitment procedure that the Venetian secretary in England mentioned it in a dispatch to the Doge and Senate. The Venetian described it thus, "the Queen's ships are being manned, but not without using the violence of the press-gang in seizing men in the streets of Lon- don to send them on board, whether they like it or no."[45] These men, vagrants already, were forced into service and trained in the killing, looting, and pillaging of warfare—the finest type of vagabondage, vagrancy, and crime—and then returned home and set free in order to put this advanced training into operation among the citizens of the realm. With the Tudors providing such an excellent training school, the historian can expect to find that the results of the effort greatly in- creased during this period.

The government soon became aware of the danger involved and pro- ceeded—by statutes, royal proclamations, and acts in privy council—to deal with the situation by providing aid to the poor and disabled veterans and punishment to the able-bodied vagrant veterans and those who pretended such status in order to further their begging. The proclamation of 1591 so well defines the problem and also spells out the Tudor system of treatment in such lucid terms that the whole text follows.

Proclamation that there is a wandering abroad of a multitude of people, the

most part pretending that they have served in the wars, though that many have
not served at all, or have run away, and therefore ought to be punished instead
of relieved; but as others have served and fallen into sickness, and are
therefore licensed to depart to their countries, and deserve relief, officers of
justice where these resort are to use discretion between the unlawful vagrants
and the soldiers lawfully dismissed; all such vagrants as have not been brought
to sickness or lameness in the service, and cannot show sufficient passports,
are to be apprehended and punished as vagabonds, and if they shall allege that
they have been in Her Majesty's pay, and cannot show a passport from the
Lord General or some officer, they are to be committed to prison, and indicted
as runaways.

Those that have served as soldiers, and can show their passports, ought to be
relieved by some charitable means; and to conduct them to their country,
should have public letters from the justices of the peace to ministers spiritual
and temporal, for reasonable aid and relief for their passage, and be particularly relieved during sickness, by the parish or hundred from whence they
were levied, and placed with their former masters. But if they be found wandering abroad out of the ordinary ways mentioned in their passports, they are
to be punished as vagabonds. The Treasurer of War is to make payment, in every port where any shall arrive with lawful passports, of sums to conduct them
to the places from which they were levied, and all officers of ports are to be
allowed by the said treasurer any money paid by them to such soldiers. For
repressing the great number of mighty and able vagrants, wandering abroad
under pretence of begging as soldiers, although known to commit open rob-
beries by the way, the lieutenants of every county (having sufficient warrant by
their commission to execute martial law upon such offenders) are to appoint
some special persons to travel within the counties as provost marshals, and
direct the justices of the peace to assist them for apprehension of all offenders,
and to commit them to prison, to be punished by the laws of the realm.[46]

The crown expressed its concern over the situation in several ways. It
took great pains to determine who among the discharged soldiers
merited relief and who deserved punishment instead as counterfeits
and vagabonds. In 1593 the privy council appointed a commission to examine the claims of soldiers who affirmed that they were disabled as a
result of service to her majesty. "An Acte for Relief of Souldiours" was
passed in 1592-93. It stated that soldiers who suffered disability while
fighting in defense of the realm deserved relief upon their return home.
This act further ordered the rating of every parish within the nation for
the maintenance of these men. The rate, however, was very low: neither
over six pence nor under one penny weekly. That rate certainly would
not take care of very many soldiers, even after it was raised to ten pence
and two pence respectively by the statute of 1601.[47]

Preserving a careful distinction between those who deserved aid and those who did not, a statute in 1597-98 received the title "An Acte against lewde and wandering persons pretending themselves to be Soldiers or Marryners." Such persons, the act pointed out, gathered in bands on the highways where they terrorized the people and broke the laws as thieves, robbers, and murderers. To express it in the language of the time, they brought about "the disturbance of the Peace and Tranquilitye of this Realme." They either had to settle down in their places of origin and work or suffer felony charges without benefit of clergy and with the punishment pertaining thereto.[48]

A great deal of additional activity resulted relative to the disbanded soldiers: 1591-92, the officials of London and vicinity received instructions to check all soldiers in order to weed out the sheep from the goats; 1593, directions to the realm's sheriffs and justices told them to meet and plan how to implement the recent statute; 1593, the privy council sent letters to the sheriffs and justices relative to the enforcement of this statute; 1593, orders went to the Lords Lieutenant advising them to care for disabled soldiers pending the implementation of the recent statute; 1593, the House of Lords voted to levy a charitable contribution for maimed soldiers upon all lords temporal and spiritual.[49]

In view of the above official fanfare, it appears that disabled veterans received adequate relief. This, however, supplies another example of the Tudor propaganda machine founded upon a framework of statutes, proclamations, and privy council decisions but beyond this mostly depending for its practical operation upon alms of the people locally. As already mentioned, the statutory levy upon parishes operated in terms of pennies per week rather than pounds. From whence was promised care for war-maimed soldiers to come? The Lords offered something, but, since they rated themselves, they failed to dig very deeply into the noble purse. The balance and major portion of aid that soldiers received came from thrifty, penny-pinching people of the realm, but how was this collected and made available to the soldiers' needs? The chronology relating to the relief of the poor provides the answer.[50] That list, during the period after 1588 gives a multiplicity of cases concerning the plight of disabled soldiers seeking relief from their situations. In these "petty" records the historian gets beyond the propagandistic promises of those great records of parliament called the *Statutes of the Realm* and begins to approach the pedestrian truth behind the glittering façade of the Tudor poor-law system as set forth in these magnificent statutes. The difference between the promises and the truth is as great as that between the written constitution of a nation and the unwritten constitution of actuality at the level where the people live.

What relief did needy soldiers find? Often nothing, except the granting of the Tudor document of perfunctoriness, the license to beg. However, in view of the evidence furnished by the source materials, needy soldiers did not receive nearly as many charity briefs as did the civilian poor where their usage proved widespread. Apparently, the privy council remained fairly sensitive to the subject of begging soldiers. This may have been due to the possibility that banded together in a begging brotherhood, the soldiers posed a greater threat in terms of revolt than did the civilian beggars. In any case, here is another example of Tudor concern over allowing soldiers to beg. In 1593 the privy council wrote to London and Westminster pointing out that Lords and Commons were providing for the maintenance of about 100 poor and disabled soldiers in this urban area, and the officials received orders not to allow the soldiers to beg upon pain of losing their allowance and suffering punishment.[51]

The chronological list relating to the relief of the poor reveals another Tudor tradition making it difficult for needy veterans to extract their promised aid, namely the partially voluntary, partially extortionary method of individual almsgiving. *Individual* means not only individual persons but also local communities (towns, parishes), and institutions (churches, hospitals, almshouses). The government made its approach in the form of an invitation to the potential benefactor to live up to his or its Christian obligation as a steward of God's goods to give voluntary support to the needy poor—in this case soldiers. If the "voluntary" contribution did not materialize, then the privy council applied pressure in the form of righteous fulminations and threats. The above chronology contains many cases of the Tudor tactic of "passing-the-buck." It operated in this fashion: the needy soldier or civilian applied for his relief as promised by law and was sent to a local community or institution for perhaps either a pension or an almsroom. The organization, usually eager to escape the burden of aid, either procrastinated or sent the applicant away empty-handed to take his case back to the privy council. The council would remonstrate with the offender, and the relief seeker might or might not receive the specified institutional aid on the second try. This procedure often took months or years, and in the meantime the protagonist usually acquired his living by begging.

Here are some examples of the type of situation just cited. In the first case the privy council in 1591 took London to task for not adequately providing for disabled soldiers in her midst. The council heaped shame upon the City and pointed out that less well-endowed towns and villages fulfilled their obligations in this respect while in "that cittie where much land hath been given to those charitable uses no provision is had for the reliefe of such men." The council thereupon shifted to a tone of exhortation in asking that the poor men in question might have relief from hunger and begging, and then shifting tone again, there emerged the voice of threat, "or otherwise you will provoke her Majestie to have inquisition made howe those landes are imployed and to what spetiall uses, that thereby they maie be converted according to th' intention of the givers, etc."[52]

The council's threat apparently did not intimidate London, for in the following year that body again wrote to the City requesting that it turn over to the council money collected by the London butchers for soldier relief but which the City still held. The letter appears diplomatic but nervous in tone, as it might well be, for in the following year (1593) the council again wrote to the mayor of London demanding to know why the money had not been forwarded to the council as requested by the letter of the previous year. The tone was no longer diplomatically nervous but waxed emphatic: "Send it at once or we will send the soldiers to you with tickets for aid." In addition, London received instructions to collect more such alms as those recently collected by the House of Lords and the Convocation of the Clergy.[53]

Other English communities shared the guilt of not living up to the government-interpreted obligation to needy veterans. Durham Cathedral received a letter in 1591 in which the privy council took that institution to task for not giving aid to three soldiers as formerly requested. A second letter in the same year rebuked the cathedral for still not having aided the three men. The same type situation in 1591 also developed in reference to Canterbury Cathedral, except that it involved one man only. Kent, Monmouthshire, Hartfordshire, Berkshire, Leicestershire, Merionethshire, Warwickshire, Wiltshire, Salopshire, Berkshire, West Riding of Yorkshire, Dorset, Surrey, the dean of Rochester, and many others were reprimanded to a more or less degree by the privy council as an examination of the chronology relating to the relief of the poor reveals.[54]

Some other major areas receiving challenges from the privy council are worth mentioning. It accused Lancastershire in 1595 of making an unusually low parish levy for aid to the soldiers. Warwickshire in the same year suffered rebuke for not returning the certificate of collections made and received orders to send either the certificate or the treasurers to the council at once. Staffordshire returned a soldier to the council in 1595-96 with the remark that they had more soldiers than they could care for at that time. The council told them to care for the rejected soldier and said that they should prorate what they did have so that each would receive a little. Lincolnshire in 1596-97 had the infamous distinction of having rejected a blind sailor in a jurisdictional dispute with the town of Lincoln. The council demanded that they resolve the dispute and care for the man in question. Because of another jurisdictional dispute, this time between Hertford and Middlesex, the privy council stated that it had written several times to Hertford on behalf of a soldier who was still without aid.[55]

Last, but not least in terms of problems, one must consider that thorn in Tudor flesh, Ireland. In a letter of 1596 to the Lord Deputy of Ireland, the privy council took exception to the Lord Deputy's having sent a soldier to England for relief. The English promptly returned him to the point of departure with the admonition to Ireland to care for her own. Another letter went to the Lord Deputy in that year in reference to Ireland's having sent a second soldier to England. The privy council returned him to Ireland with the same advice as previously. Again, same year, same situation, and same request—the Irish paid little heed to the wishes of Her Majesty's privy council.[56]

Life for the disabled soldier may not have worsened under the Stuart monarchs, but it certainly did not improve if three royal proclamations issued in 1643 furnish a fair sample. They called for collections for wounded soldiers on certain Sundays in all colleges and churches.[57] The Tudor system of voluntary alms as the means of taking care of poverty needs still carried much weight.

An earlier statement said that the Tudors balked at initiating new measures into their poverty care. There were present at the time, as previously indicated, men with ideas concerning change and reform. The government ignored these ideas unless the method of trial and error gradually incorporated them into the processes of the age. The Tudors reluctantly followed even the most gradual of changes and failed as initiators. As A. L. Rowse points out, towns first devised most Tudor-credited projects, for there desperate need created new methods of dealing with social problems. For, as he says, "we have seen that London evolved something of a system as early as Edward's reign."[58] He is speaking of the five great London hospitals with their somewhat specialized systems of care: St. Bartholomew's for the sick; St. Thomas' for the sick, aged, and infirm; Christ's Hospital for children; Bedlam for the insane; and Bridewell as a workhouse or house of correction. Bridewell served as a model for other houses of correction. Rowse gives Ipswich as another example of institutional trailblazing at the time for having established by 1569 a combination hospital and house of correction. Also, the town organized a poverty-care program by levying a poor rate and licensing the beggars. The town of Norwich developed along the same lines, and both towns encouraged Dutch weavers to settle in their midst in order to open up a new source of employment for the inhabitants. Here is an interesting comment in relation to these towns: "It is worth noticing how many of the children were sent to school: popular education is no recent innovation."[59]

As early as 1537 John Prakyns expressed his ideas to Cromwell concerning care for the needy poor. He proposed the establishment of an almshouse in every shire "for impotent priests and others, and a free grammar school for poor men's children."[60] Robert Crowley expressed some definite ideas in the 1550s concerning poverty care. Needy beggars should receive alms but others should work, and if they refused to work let them starve. He continued:

> This realme hath thre commoditie
> woule, tynne, and leade,
> which being wrought within the realme,
> eche man might get his bread.[61]

The period witnessed a shortage of small coins, and this brought suggestions that the coinage of greater amounts of them would increase alms contributions to the poor. Sir Richard Martin, master and worker of the Mint, offered to reform the coinage of Ireland and to mint small copper money for England, "to relieve the poor from loss by the lead tokens delivered by alehouse keepers and others, and increase charity by enabling people to give coins of small value."[62]

England suffered no dearth of fresh ideas about the social problems of the age, but the Tudor monarchs did not support and encourage new theories and systems, even after they were developed.

CHAPTER VII

How Acute Were the Problems of Poverty and Vagrancy?

T he case of the "Unnatural Father": the story of John Rowse, a London fishmonger, who gave up his trade and acquired a landholding with an income of fifty pounds per year. This he lost to debt and men who cheated him of the rest. He then killed his two children. "Presently the Constable was sent for . . . who . . . demanded of him why and how he could commit so unnatural a fact, as to murder his Children? To whom he answered, that he did it, because he was not able to keep them, and that he was loth they should go about the Town begging."[1] This case serves as a two-fold example: it gives one of the causes for poverty, that is, poor management and also shows the grimness of the future faced by persons reduced to low estate. It demonstrates, moreover, the attitude of contemporaries, both the father of the children and the author of the account, to the horrors of the unmitigated poverty of the period. This happened in 1621 when Elizabethan poor laws supposedly worked their miracles in alleviating such conditions.

Or, revert to the middle of the preceding century for Latimer's sermon to King Edward VI about the causes and evils of poverty. "But to extort and take away the right of the poor, is against the honour of the king." He directed his words to landlords who caused poverty by enclosure and engrossing of land and tenements and by charging the people high rents for the same. He plainly told the king wherein his "honour" resided, that is, in his duty to protect poor people of his realm

109

against machinations of landed aristocracy. Merchants, too, received their share of blame for grinding down the poor with higher prices. The situation had reached such a stage "that poor men, which live of their labour, cannot with the sweat of their face have a living, all kind of vict-uals is so dear." He repeats that this detracted from the king's honor. "My father was a yeoman," and he proceeded to explain that his father rented enough land for three or four pounds per year upon which to support six men, a hundred sheep, and thirty cattle. He also served the king in battle with horse and equipment, sent young Latimer to school, married off two daughters with five pounds dowery each, and kept hospitality and gave alms to the poor. Presently, Latimer added, the same land rented for sixteen pounds, and the poor man who rents it "is not able to do any thing for his prince, for himself, nor for his children, or give a cup of drink to the poor."[2]

In the words of a modern historian writing about Elizabethan Eng-land, "The poor . . . became poorer, while the rich became much richer. Vagrancy and vagabondage increased greatly; poor relief became a question of the first importance for government."[3]

The messages of these three men suggest the development of a social upheaval in Tudor England that challenged the ability of the monarchs to deal with it. As Latimer said, it involved the honor of the king. How well did the royal honor withstand these pressures? Elizabethan historian A. L. Rowse gives the previously suggested answer. "There was a change going on in the balance of social forces which underlay the outward structure of the Elizabethan polity. It led to many tensions, which were just contained without bursting their integuments so long as the external danger of the war with Spain continued and the Queen reigned. With her death and the coming of peace, they were free to break out into the open in the form of constitutional conflict: they led ultimately to the Civil War."[4]

Rowse might have added that not only did Elizabeth just barely keep the social pressure below the bursting point, but that she and her dynastic predecessors held great responsibility for bringing the social situation to the bursting point in the first place. Latimer had told Ed-ward VI that the honor of the king was at stake, but instead of retrieving and maintaining that honor, the Tudor monarchs further besmirched it with the insincerity of their approach to poverty and vagrancy problems of sixteenth-century England. Captured by their fear and frustration, they continued to use an unmerciful system of control over the hapless poor when the needs of the age cried out for mercy and justice throughout the realm. As Rowse stated, Tudor minimal control died with Elizabeth, and the honor of a Stuart king ended soon thereafter upon a chopping block of dishonor. This serves as a measure of the acuteness of the problems, including poverty and vagrancy, during the Tudor era.

Poverty existed as a widespread and dangerous phenomenon of sixteenth- and seventeenth-century England. Further witness to this and the fact that the Tudor government did little to alleviate the situation is furnished by the 1641-42 petition to the House of Commons of "many thousand poore people, in and about the Citie of London." In the same year, another petition went to the Commons "of 15000 poore labouring men, known by the name of Porters, and the lowest Members of the Citie of London."[5]

What caused poverty on such a scale? No simple answer will suffice, for the socioeconomic forces during this period underwent a complex series of changes. Therefore, the answer must incorporate the many facets of these changes in order to arrive at a composite cause of poverty. In the case of the 1641-42 petitions to parliament just mentioned, the petitioners blamed their situation, rightly or wrongly, upon "the Bishops and Popish Lords who have hindered relief to the Irish Protestants, and occasioned the stoppage of trade."[6] In the case of "The Unnatural Father" the cause resulted from poor management by the father. The answer, as found in Latimer's first sermon to the king, relates to the general theme of the rich getting richer and the poor getting poorer, and the rapid increase in prices during the sixteenth century composed a major element in the process. Enclosure, engrossing, and the consequent levying of higher and higher rents on farmland furnish other items in the answer. Also, tenement owners in cities and towns gouged poor renters, and merchants increased prices of food and other essentials. Certain contemporary writers spoke strongly on the subject. Simon Fish placed the blame for England's problems on sheep farming and the enclosure movement. The increasing demand of the wool market for raw material drove yeomen off the land to a life of vagrancy.[7]

John Bayker in his letter to Henry VIII, mentioned an increase in the vagrant population in spite of the laws for control of the situation. Higher rents, he felt, forced tenants to leave their holdings and lead lives of vagabondage "to the depleation of villages and towns & the decay of the realme." Forrest's *Pleasaunt Poesie of Princelie Practise* adds another voice to contemporaries eager to place the blame for England's social evils. The rich-versus-poor theme is prominent in his message as presented in these lines: "As *Thowsandis* to lacke and *Twentie* to abownde, oh, howe it geavethe a myserable sownde!" How, he asks, in view of the rising prices and rents, can a poor man support himself and family on two pence or less per day?[8]

In addition to the increase of poverty caused by socioeconomic forces just mentioned, one must take into consideration forces of circumstance that added to the heavy burden of misery. In this sense, the recently mentioned 1641-42 petitions of the poor to parliament developed due to peculiar historical conditions of the 1640s. During this decade crop failure, famine, and plague ruled the land. In another such period: "The question reached a culminating crisis in the years 1594-1597: all years of bad harvests, great scarcity and distress." This was the worst of several famine eras that greatly added to the problem of poverty. A change of location for plays presents an example of the creation of economic deprivation as a result of the vagaries of community life. London players had held their plays on the "Bankside" thus causing considerable pecuniary increment to Thames "watermen" who ferried playgoers across the river. Then the players moved their stages to London and Middlesex thus depriving many watermen of their customary employment. In January, 1613, these men placed their grievance before the king.[9]

In the foregoing examples of social disaster, what could the government have done to either prevent or avoid the consequences of such events? Granted that a monarch cannot prevent drought years, famines, and plagues, and stop the process of historical change, he does know from experience that such things have happened in the past and will continue to plague the future. Therefore, if he is a wise ruler and has the interests of his poorer subjects at heart, he will take steps to prevent the harsher results of such eventualities. He can build granaries in which to store grain in years of plenty, and he can listen to the problems of his subjects and use the forces of governmental planning to alleviate their needs. It is in this area of humanitarian concern that the Tudors were most deficient, and social unrest increased when people realized it. The government told the poor that they had to work or starve. Many of them wanted to work but either could not find jobs or discovered that those available paid substandard wages, so they starved while the people responsible for administration of the realm ignored the situation except to apply repressive control measures. Much of the repercussion over monastic closure was psychological. The people realized that religious houses suffered dissolution because of greed and that members of the landed aristocracy who had bought the monastic lands were required by parliamentary act to provide traditional alms for the poor but usually managed to evade the obligation. In his consideration of English philanthropy, Gray says that "it is in this increasing cost and decreasing means of living that the causes of destitution and vagabondage are to be found."[10] This situation worsened, he contends, because dissolution of monasteries destroyed the traditional system of poor relief.

Just as the sixteenth-century population suffered problems of poverty, it also faced the closely related situation of a high incidence of vaga-bondage. Even playwrights such as Shakespeare peopled their plays with rogues, vagabonds, sturdy beggars, and Gypsies. Other writers dealt with the subject. In his "Epistle to the Reader" preceding his *A Caveat* . . . , Thomas Harman explains why he wrote the work. He did it, he says, in order that people might benefit from a true under-standing of the infamous life and deeds of vagrant bands. This knowledge, perhaps, could lead to England's reformation. Though often pictured as thieves and cutthroats, a body of popular legend of the Robin Hood type grew up around the vagabond class. Parson Haben tells the story of seven thieves who robbed a parson and then forced him to preach them a sermon in praise of thieves and thievery.[11]

John Awdeley in his work on vagabonds, as does Thomas Harman in his *Caveat*, sets forth the whole order or "fraternity" of rogues, vaga-bonds, and beggars, and he tells how they operated according to their different titles of specialization. Richard Head does the same thing in a largely biographical book. He ran away from home and joined a band of Gypsies. He tells of his participation in their life of drinking, loving, stealing, and begging. He left them and went to London where he joined the society of rogues, vagabonds, and beggars and learned the fine art of thievery. Samuel Rowlands' work colorfully pictures the fraternity of vagrants. He has them meeting in great convocations: "Meane time the Rogues of the North, had before met at the Divels arse apeake, hearing of this unexpected newes with rage inflamed, trot on their lustie tentoes, with bagge and baggage toward the Southerne Regiment."[12] They raged because the "Bel-man" of London had exposed and denounced their manner of living. Upon meeting with the "Southerne Regiment" they held a court relative to Belman at which he gave his defense to their charges.

The government, as explained earlier, expressed concern over control of these people but failed to provide remedies. As late as 1598 the privy council still debated the fact that in London tenement owners continued building and converting dwelling houses in order to charge high rents to vagrants. As on many previous occasions, the council ordered this activity stopped. This furnishes another of the government's steps in defense of a negative approach to problem solving. It would destroy the only source of housing that the poor had without giving any suggestions as to what should fill the vacuum thus created. Granted that tenement landlords provided poor quality housing and high rent, but at least it was something in which to live. The only solution that the Tudor government offered was "hit the road Jack and don't come back." Considering that the rose was a Tudor symbol, one can say that vagabond thorns grew thick upon the stem of this English blossom. It was especially true near the heart of the flower, for in 1596 the privy council still belabored Middlesex and London to control their rogues, vagabonds, and sturdy beggars because of the laxity of the shire and City in this respect.[13]

In his *Dialogue* between Cardinal Pole and Thomas Lupset, Thomas Starkey puts these words in the mouth of Pole concerning the vastness of the vagrant population. "For thys ys sure, that in no cuntrey of Chrystundome, for the nombur of pepul, you schal fynd so many beggarys as be here in Englond, and mo now then have byn before tyme; wych arguth playn grete poverty.''[14] All during the sixteenth century bands of vagrants plagued and terrorized the realm. John Taylor recounts that when his party landed their small boat at the town of Cromer, while making "A Very Merry-Wherry-Ferry Voyage" from London to York, the people reacted in terror:

> . . . Some women, and some children there
> That saw us land, were all possessed with fear:
> And much amaz'd, ran crying up and down,
> That enemies were come to take the town.
> Some said that we were Pirates, some said Thieves,
> And what the women says, the men believes,
> With that four Constables did quickly call,
> Your Aid! to arms your men of Cromer all![15]

Harman in his *Caveat* is equally explicit in depicting the fear of Englishmen for vagrant bands. He says that when beggars approached a yeoman's farmhouse for alms they traveled three or four in a group. "Where for feare more than good wyll, they often have reliefe." Moreover, sometimes as many as forty rogues, complete with their "doxies" or female companions, would bed down at night in the farmer's barn. He could not object to this, "or els they threaten him to burne him, and all that he hath."[16]

Aydelotte sums up the Tudor-era problem of vagrancy by saying that during the sixteenth century the population of that segment of society was greater, in proportion to the total population, than that at any other time in English history.[17]

Although the subjects of poverty and vagrancy are so closely related that it is practically impossible to distinguish between their causes, the factors contributing to the latter need some consideration. One must remember that most of the formerly mentioned causes of poverty equally well apply as causes of vagrancy and vice versa.

Vagabonds and beggars thrived in England throughout most of the medieval period. Historically, however, the habit developed of associating the rise of this way of life with the fourteenth-century onslaught of the Black Death. A. V. Judges, quoting the Webbs, thinks that the century following the plague produced a disruption of traditional social and economic patterns, and this in turn was responsible for the bands of wandering poor.[18] There is some truth in this theory, but it is too simple an answer to carry the whole burden of historical cause and effect. The Hundred Years' War furnished another of the more obvious causes of vagrancy.

Jusserand adds an item to the causal background of the wandering life by stating that the sentence of outlawry usually provided its starting point and a life of crime its economic necessity. A person acquired the sentence of outlawry easily, for it only required the committal of a petty crime and "to come within sight of the gallows, no great guilt was necessary; hence the large number of outlaws."[19] In fact, a minor theft was punishable by hanging, and the victim's family lost all claim to his property. Those who escaped legal apprehension turned to a life of wandering and crime either in cities and towns or the forests.

Other often enumerated factors in adding numbers to the vagrant bands were engrossing of farms, enclosures, and sheep grazing—all three ejected yeomen from the land thus forcing them to lead lives of vagabondage. The disbanding of feudal retainers often receives citation as another cause of the wandering mob. Then there are the monasteries to consider and, since their relationship to vagrancy received full treatment earlier in this study, a brief summary will suffice here. Some historians have assigned a double role to them in causing an increase in begging and vagabondage. Firstly, they are blamed for "promiscuous" alms distribution (that is, equal distribution to all beggars without consideration of merit), thus adding to the ease of a life of beggary and, consequently, to the numbers of beggars. Secondly, though the religious houses are not directly to blame for this, the dissolution of the monasteries not only removed a primary source of alms to many of the poor but added to their numbers by the eviction of the inmates of the houses into the secular life. Then there were the "Popish" vagabonds or priests, mendicants, and monks who reportedly wandered about the realm seditiously plotting how best to overthrow the Tudor government and Protestantism. The hordes of vagabonds furnished fertile soil for such activity for, "their ranks contained political, religious, and social malcontents and agitators."[20] A bit of source information confirming part of the above argument and adding yet another cause of vagrancy is contained in the 1537 letter of Norfolk to Cromwell. "The alms they have in religious houses is the great occasion thereof, and the slackness of the justices in doing their duty." In addition to this letter, there is a circular from Norfolk to the governors of the religious houses of a certain riding of Yorkshire forbidding them to give alms to the sturdy beggars.[21]

In view of the fact that religious malcontents worked busily among the vagabond class, did Henry VIII perhaps seek to break up an alliance between these two factions by establishing a separate system of charity and control for the vagrants along with the dissolution of the monasteries? An affirmative answer to this question is possible. And while on the subject of the religious orders, it is needless to say that mendicant friars have received more than their share of blame for contributing to beggary and vagabondage.

Insofar as "slackness" of the justices is concerned in the letter of Norfolk to Cromwell, this is only one of many charges by the Tudor government against local officials throughout the sixteenth century. If one believed the fulminations of monarchs and privy councils, this furnished the cause célèbre of vagrancy. The prevalence of corrupt brokers, especially in London, who bought stolen merchandise furnished another contemporary complaint as a cause of crime. This, too, added to the crime-does-pay aspect of roguery and to the numbers so engaged. This type of concern appears in "A Letter from the Lord Mayor and Aldermen about Corrupt Brokers in London, 1601." There was another prevalent complaint that London tenements or "pennyrents" furnished breeding grounds for the continuous supply of beggars and vagrants.[22]

The problem of the realm's discharged military men furnishes the final and major contributing factor to roguery and vagabondage. Considerable attention has been given earlier to this matter of the army as a breeding ground for vagrants, so those items will not need further elucidation at this point. But because it is such an important part of the subject, ex-military roguery needs additional consideration.

Sir John Cheke writing in 1549 vouched for the multitude of vagabonds, especially those returning from wars. Concerning the graveness of the problem, he says,

And after warres it is communelye sene, that a great number of those whiche wente out honest, returne home againe like roisters and as though they were burnt to the warres botome, they have all their lyfe after an unsavery smacke thereof, and smel stil towarde daieslepers, purse pikers, highwaie robbers, quarelmakers, ye and bloudsheders to. Do we not se comunely in thende of warres more robbing more begging more murdering then before, and those to stand in the high wai to aske their almes whom ye be afraied to say nai unto honestly, lest they take it awaye from you violentlye, and have more cause to suspecte their strength, then pitie their nede.[23]

William Harrison about 1587 also attests to the large number of vagrants. He says that warfare produced such men. After serving over-seas they considered it a disgrace to work for a living. They posed a great danger to the nation, even to the out-of-the-way places.[24]

Another contemporary account, *The Life and Death of Gamaliel Ratsey* . . . (author unknown), tells the story of this famous thief who suffered public execution at Bedford on March 26, 1605. He served as a soldier in the Irish campaign, and upon his return to England he led a robber band and for almost two years ruled as England's most notorious criminal. With such gang leaders on the prowl, one can understand Tudor concern. Nevertheless, their own policy—not only of using the "press gang" for forcing vagrants into military service, but the fact that even criminals condemned to death had their sentences commuted to service in the wars overseas—was greatly responsible for this state of affairs. Such an arrangement provided excellent opportunities for crimi-nal soldiers of fortune of Ratsey's caliber. In the years 1592 and 1596 at least three criminals awaiting execution received such pardons.[25]

In addition to this usage of the most hardened variety of criminal, "press gangs" forced thousands of rogues, vagabonds, and sturdy beg-gars to serve in overseas campaigns. When discharged, most of them returned to the old way of life as better trained criminals because of the nature of sixteenth-century warfare. In 1545 vagrants in and about Lon-don were impressed as galley slaves; in 1596 London received orders to furnish 50 such men. On July 12, 1597, London, Middlesex, Surrey, and Kent were ordered to levy 700 men in this manner: "which will be a great ease and good to the country to be rid of those kind of people." On July 16, 1597, the lord mayor of London and his council reluctantly de-cided to provide clothing for 80 impressed, "naked sort" of men before sending them overseas. Year, 1601, Surrey, Middlesex, and London or-dered to press the masterless men for service at Ostend. "And good the countrey shall finde by being disburthened of so many unprofitable persons." Year, 1601, Middlesex, Kent, Surrey, and London: masterless men to be pressed for the Low Countries. Year, 1601, London: masterless men to be pressed for the Ostend campaign. In the years 1602-03 orders went out for the impressing of masterless men from eighteen counties in one case and from Surrey, Middlesex, Essex, and Kent in another.[26]

The major reason the Tudors had problems with vagrancy and poverty was because they developed a short-sighted policy in dealing with the socioeconomic problems of the poor. They did not attack the situation logically by using diplomacy and planning. Instead, they depended on repressive measures. Such maladroitness is shown in the impressment of vagrants for military service with the words already quoted, "and good the countrey shall finde by being disburthened of so many unprofitable persons." Perhaps the government was pleased to free itself of this "naked sort" of riffraff, but the day of reckoning came when these men returned home bringing with them the lessons learned on the battlefield. The poor people of England knew by its attitude and actions toward them that the government looked upon them as the scum of the earth, and they often proceeded to act out the role. Certainly more than one brawling ruffian must have uttered words in similar vein to the blasphemous and resounding ejaculation of Perot the tailor when he angrily exclaimed "a turde for the King"—and meant it too.[27]

CHAPTER VIII

Did Tudor Social Legislation Get at the Roots of the Poverty and Vagrancy Problems?

Queen Elizabeth's reign saw the enactment of the definitive form of poor-law legislation, and it served England until nineteenth-century reform ended the older system. The introduction to the 1562-63 legislation is to the point. It states the confirmation of the statutes of Henry VIII except as amended, "to the intent that idle persons and valiant beggars may be avoided, and the impotent, feeble and lame, which are the poor in very deed, should be hereafter relieved and well provided for."[1] This act supplied innovations: it ordered officials, priests, and church-wardens to appoint collectors of alms who would also distribute them to the poor. Donations for alms were made compulsory with imprisonment facing the "obstinate" person.

In spite of this legislation, many problems remained unsolved, for John Stow reports that in 1572 the whole of England overflowed with rogues, vagabonds, and sturdy beggars to the extent that they committed murders, thefts, and other crimes.[2] In any case parliament saw fit to pass further legislation in the same year, and the statute states similar conditions as those mentioned by Stow. The punishment and restrictions were drawn tighter.[3]

Legislation in 1575-76 stipulated that officials should acquire stocks of wool, hemp, flax, and iron in order to provide employment in manufacturing for the able-bodied poor. The make-work provision is a noteworthy innovation in that for the first time the law distinguished between the sturdy beggar who would work and his counterpart who refused employment. Another novel feature in this legislation required the construction of houses of correction in each county in order to provide both punishment and work.[4] Following this, the poor-law statute of 1601 served as a summation of all previous Tudor legislation and provided the future shape of English poverty care.

As mentioned in Chapter VI, certain towns had experimented (before Elizabethan legislation in this respect) with the idea of providing stores of materials for creating jobs and houses in which to work. Also, individuals had had thoughts along these lines, for as early as 1550 Robert Crowley in his "Epigrammes" decided that many people begged because they could not find work. He expressed his social concerns in the form of a question to the officials:

> Ye Aldermen and other,
>   that take Allaye [alley] rente,
> Why bestowe ye not the riches,
>   that God hath you sente,
> In woule or in flaxe,
>   to finde them occupied,
> That nowe lye and begge
>   by everye highe waye side?[5]

Apparently the legislation of Elizabeth to provide stores of materials and houses of correction or workhouses in which to work them reflected sound reasoning and humanitarian concern for the poor. But does the implementation of the program warrant this assumption? Philip Stubbes gave a negative answer in 1583. He acknowledged the goodness of the laws but denounced the inadequate execution of them because this produced vagrants and disturbances. When asked concerning the provision of hospitals, almshouses, and houses of correction for the poor, one of two characters in a dialogue replied, "yes there are some such in cities, townes, and some other places, wherein manie poore are releeved, but not the hundred part of those that want."[6]

Edward Hext, justice of the peace for Somersetshire, wrote to the lord treasurer in 1596 to inform him that vagrancy increased because the houses of correction "are put down in most parts of England," hand branding faded, and local officials failed to enforce laws.[7]

The above examples deal with the situation during the reign of Elizabeth when the implementation of her poor-law legislation supposedly flourished. The following illustrations deal with the continued ineffectiveness of these laws after her lifetime.

The years 1613-14 provide the setting for the first case. The privy council wrote to the justices of Middlesex concerning the increase of vagrancy in London and neighborhood and warned that the officials should properly provide for night watches, searches, and building of a house or houses of correction according to provisions of the Elizabethan statute.[8] After all these years the legislation of the late queen still remained a dead item outside the halls of parliament and the privy council, even at the realm's nexus.

Secondly, the period is the reign of James I, and the information comes from an anonymously written tract called "Stanleyes Remedy, or The Way how to reform wandring Beggars, Theeves, High way Robbers and Pick Pockets." The "Remedy" represented that old Tudor pill for curing vagrant problems "by the means of workhouses, in all Cities, Market-townes, and all able parishes in the Kingdome."[9] What a shame that no one bothered to inform him that this stupendous work had already been accomplished, supposedly, by the philanthropic Protestant ethic of Queen Elizabeth's reign and the enactments of her parliaments.

Tudor poor laws did not provide rehabilitation but called for repressive control. A privy council letter to the lord keeper in 1592 about the trial and sentences of certain rogues and vagabonds substantiates this: "We cold have wished the same to have been more seaveare." Apparently the judgments were never "severe" enough to suit the government, for a royal proclamation complained of the many vagabonds, especially about London and the court, and proclaimed the following action: "Therefore the Queen, to cut off such offences in the beginning, will appoint a provost marshal, with power to execute them upon the gallows without delay."[10] The severity of such measures guaranteed the satisfaction of the queen's penchant for judgments to serve "an example for others."

Perhaps the queen performed a charitable act after all in decreeing death for certain vagrants, for life in a Tudor prison equaled a state of living death itself. "I see also a pytyful abuse of presoners. Oh Lord God, their lodging is to bad for hoggys, and as for their meate, it is evyl inough for doggys, and yet, the Lord knoweth, thei have not inough thereof!" Prisoners often remained incarcerated for years without trial. Philip Stubbes, while walking by the prisons, complained of hearing the despairing cries and complaints of the poor prisoners therein. Some suffered there during a lifetime of exposure to inadequate, loathsome food and filthy conditions. They could only long for death to ease their pains. Many of them did not wait long, for they often met death as the penalty for petty theft. When such a person received execution he forfeited his possessions to the state, and this often reduced his family to poverty and begging. The Tudor manner of treatment and punishment of vagrants continued under the Stuart monarchy. John Taylor, the Water Poet, in "The Whip of Pride" described the 1630 conditions quite trenchantly.[11]

The historian can attain a greater understanding of the nature of the Tudor social program by asking: to what extent were the laws enforced? All evidence points to the conclusion that suppressive and punitive aspects of legislation operated more efficiently than measures designed for aid and comfort. There were plenty of things the government could have planned and enforced if it had not been so anxious to shun positive responsibility by passing it off to the intermittent implementation of local communities. John Taylor told the town of Salisbury that their wood for fuel was carted a great distance and was too expensive for the poor people; therefore, they had to steal from and deplete the nearby forests to the detriment of all. A simple remedy would solve the problem, for it only required the clearing of the river in order to bring in cheap coal by barge.[12] Essential ideas such as this could have made a great difference in the solution of the social problems of England had the government been receptive to planning, legislating, enforcing, and supporting them on a nationwide basis. Moreover, as stated earlier, Tudor England had plenty of socially conscious men with such ideas; a likewise socially conscious government dedicated to giving coordination to such schemes could have solved many of the problems.

Even in cases where the local community expressed concern for the poor, the Elizabethan government refused to cooperate if the proffered aid cost it anything. This attitude appears explicitly in 1579 (to use an example cited earlier in another context) when the crown challenged the bailiff and jurats of the island of Guernsey for taking the fines of the court "belonging to Her Majesty" and using them to aid the poor. The magistrates replied that this special fine levied on anyone caught blaspheming God served the specific purpose of aiding the poor. The crown replied in the negative for, as the queen's advocate reiterated, "under colour of paying the poor these fines, they also pay them the fines due to the Prince, thus bringing the revenues to nothing." The Tudors demanded their revenues regardless of the cost in human misery. The dynasty dedicated itself to alms-based gratuities for the poor because this relieved the crown of the cost of a governmentally involved mode of operation. For one area of confirmation of this, and there are many others, one need only examine the large number of charity briefs or licenses to beg issued by the privy council. In addition, implementation of the poor laws devolved upon the parishes, and they were neither equipped nor inclined to carry out the task. Frederick G. Marcham states that local officials showed contempt for the poor, regarding them as burdens, misfits, and a disgrace to society.[13]

An inspection of some of the sources for the period provides further indication of this attitude. In one case the petitioner to the justices of Wiltshire complained that though he was born and bred in Stockton, the parish would not allow his newly acquired wife to enter, "saying we would breed a charge among them"—a charge the parish might have to maintain in view of the provisions of current poor-law legislation. In addition, the parish in which the man's wife lived would not have her either. He ended his request with the plea: "I most humbly crave your good aid and help in this my distresse, or else my poor wife and child are like to perish without the doors. . . . I do humbly crave, that by your good help and order to the parish of Stockton I may have a house there to bring my wife and child unto, that I may help them the best I can."[14]

In another case, a brother abandoned his aged sister, and the parish of Eldersfield charged her with begging and sent her to the parish of her birth, but that parish returned her to Eldersfield. One other case will complete the picture. A father abandoned his child, and the parish questioned its responsibility. "The parishioners desire to know whether they may not avoid keeping the child." Also, they desired to seize goods left behind by the father.[15]

There is an additional element that needs consideration. In the foregoing analysis of governmental poor-law and vagrancy policy it appears that proper collection and usage of alms and care of the needy are the least successful aspects of the system. Success appears in the machinery of repression and control. It is not part of the monastic system of alms-giving but represents the policy of the religiously conservative Tudors, especially Elizabeth, of combining various elements in order to achieve comprehension. So, while one can say that Elizabeth continued to use the old system relative to alms dispersal by the Church, she combined with this the strictly governmental and therefore secular direction from above insofar as such direction was needed as a means of attempting to maintain the social, economic, and political status quo.

Housing for the poor, especially in London and environs, attracted governmental attention as one of the areas in which direction from above manifested itself. The attempt apparently failed, because the government reiterated the same statutes, proclamations, and directions from the privy council forbidding expansion of slum housing areas. Opposition to expansion derived from the spread of the plague, overcrowding, and fear that these housing conditions attracted vagrants. Why did this type of building continue to develop in spite of legislation to the contrary? A major cause was, as in other areas of attempted social control, lack of law enforcement by local officials. The problems continued unabated into the Stuart era.

Maintenance of the realm's grain and food supply for the poor furnishes another area in which control measures met with similar results. In 1527 grain became scarce in England, especially in London, and many died. The king sent supplies to London and the Steelyard also supplied grain. People were so famished that grain entering the City needed an escort. Grain speculators made the situation worse by buying up all available grain and selling it at inflated prices. The government made some attempt to control the activities of these men, but even local officials sometimes involved themselves in the speculative transactions.

The privy council in 1598 considered a case accusing the mayor of Dartmouth of selling to the grain speculators and keeping for himself part of the grain consigned for aid to the hungry poor of that city.[16] Again, the old problem, its effective treatment still unresolved, carried over to become a concern of the Stuart monarchs.

The Stuart government proved itself more efficient than its predecessor in the area of planning. The Stuart monarchy recognized problems of the City's population growth, anticipated the probability of poor harvests and famine and, beginning in 1608, built twelve new granaries and two storehouses. More plans for concerted action on the problem reveal themselves in the royal proclamation of 1623 for storing and furnishing of grain for the realm. The scope and imagination of this proposal are greater than any plans envisioned by Tudor monarchs. "It would be well to have magazines of corn to find food in bad times, and keep up the price in time of plenty. They may be erected in London, Dover, Portsmouth, Southhampton, Bristol, Excester, Plymouth, Ipswich, Linne, Yarmouth, Hull, Yorke, Newcastle, Chester, Lerpoole, Haverford West, and all the shire-towns."[17] Perhaps an ounce of Stuart prevention might effectively outweigh several pounds of Tudor spur-of-the-moment legislation, proclamations, and haranguing by the privy council.

The major shortcomings of Tudor social legislation resided in its lack of foundation upon comprehensive and integrated planning and the necessity of passing it to the local institutions for implementation. When these bodies did not carry out their legal instructions, the government failed its law enforcement obligation. The Tudors caused the problem by their dependence upon overburdened, amateur, and largely unpaid local officials who operated without assistance from the central government. Local institutions neither progressed nor broke down—they simply failed to move in a majority of instances.

Evidence of Tudor inability to secure enforcement of their many laws and regulations is plentiful. Aydelotte says that despite the Elizabethan poor-law legislation of 1572—and this was the mold of all such legislation—the social situation of lower-class England continued to decline. London remained in a state of social unrest at this time. The mayor in 1594 blamed the crowded tenements for this situation. Aydelotte asserts that vagrancy control provided the subject of one of Elizabeth's last proclamations before her death and contained instructions to the justices for enforcing the laws of the realm. Aydelotte admits that Elizabeth's social legislation did not bring reform, and he includes here the laws of 1572, 1575, 1597, and 1601. Then he contradicts this by stating: "But many things show that conditions gradually improved in the latter part of Elizabeth's reign." How could he maintain the truth of this when he had just stated that the laws of 1597 and 1601, certainly passed in the "latter part" of Elizabeth's reign, did not bring about any immediate reform. This would also include the laws of 1572 and 1575 by association, for Aydelotte himself said that the Laws of 1597 and 1601 "only carried out the principles of the statutes of 1572 and 1575."

As further proof that conditions were improving during the latter part of the queen's reign, Aydelotte offers the statement that, "there are fewer orders from the Privy Council to justices concerning vagabonds, fewer precepts about them in London." This simply is not true as the sources indicate for, contrary to Aydelotte, problems of vagrancy were increasing. The present writer counted in Appendix III four statutes, nineteen proclamations, and eighty-one cases either at law or before the privy council relative to the problem of vagrancy—the count was made on the assumption that anything from 1585 to Elizabeth's death would fall within the range of the "latter part" of her reign. Here is another paradox of Aydelotte's argument: just two pages before defending the progress of the latter part of the queen's reign, he says, "the task of instructing the Justices of the Peace and Overseers of the Poor in their duties and of making them feel a responsibility to the Privy Council for performing them was not adequately performed until 1630-1." He then adds the weak defensive statement that Queen Elizabeth had, after all, begun this task.[18]

Why devote so much effort to refuting Aydelotte's interpretation? It is necessary in order to demonstrate that a major portion of textbook history derives from this sort of mythology. This happens because Aydelotte and other historians go to the most obvious source, the *Statutes of the Realm*, read the magnificent pronouncements contained therein, and come away feeling that progress certainly took place under a government that enacted such a body of laws. Thus the myth is born, and it continues on the strength of the pronouncements of the original authorities on the subject while the potential revelations of forgotten "petty" documents remain unresearched. An examination of these documents often exposes the falsity of myths such as the one maintaining that the poor-laws of Queen Elizabeth solved much of the poverty problems of her era. It also exposes the irrelevance of statements such as Aydelotte's when he says that the vagrancy problem was diminishing during the latter part of Elizabeth's reign. It is the same as saying, to repeat an earlier illustration, that you cannot determine the true constitution of a country by reading the glowing language of the document.

Facts of the constitution reveal themselves when the researcher answers the question: how do the people live? The concern expressed here has not been with Aydelotte as a historian but with the continued propagation of the school of historical mythology that bases its interpretations upon obvious surface features of evidence rather than probing the extent of the social conglomeration consisting of the commonality. It is true that under the Tudors, especially Elizabeth, the famous poor laws were passed, but during that dynasty's reign the most obvious extent of this legislation was its enrollment with other statutes. It looked good on paper. The real test of effectiveness came with its enforcement at the local level and here it largely failed. What do contemporaries say about it? "The Highway to the Spital-House" of Robert Copland (1535-36) observed that the laws sufficed to control vagabondage if properly executed. Latimer, in his sixth sermon to Edward VI, accused justices of the peace of not doing their duty. Stephen Gosson's work (published 1579) asserts that laws were not enforced but that Puritans demanded their enforcement. The period underwent rapid change, and Puritans looked back with nostalgia to the good old days of a lawful England and bewailed crime in their own era. George Whetstone who published *Touchstone for the Time* in 1584 and Samuel Rowlands who published *Greenes Ghost* in 1602 examined London's vice and decided that only enforcement of existing laws would effect reform.[19]

What do contemporary documents say about law enforcement? A privy council letter to London's aldermen in 1569 bewailed the fact that they had not carried out statutory regulations for control of vagabonds.

A report to the privy council in 1591 mentioned that lack of enforcement of laws for punishment of vagrants and care of the poor caused an increase in the numbers of these people. Provost marshals ignored their duties, and for this reason vagrants swarmed back into Middlesex and London according to a privy council report of 1596. The title of a 1601 statute reveals another problem of enforcement—"An Acte to redresse the Misemployment of Landes Goodes and Stockes of Money heretofore given to Charitable Uses." On account of a state of social upheaval in those areas, parliament passed in 1601 "An Acte for the more peaceable Government of the partes of Cumberland Northumberland Westmorland and the Bishopricke of Durham."[20]

The problems of law enforcement continued after Elizabeth's reign. In 1603 James I issued a proclamation for vagrancy control containing the statement that, "whereas the Act of 39 Eliz. has been of late not put in execution, the Privy Council hath by an order assigned places beyond the seas for incorrigible Rogues, etc., and the Law is now to be put into full exercise." This proclamation further stated that owing to laxity of certain justices of the peace, vagabonds "swarm everywhere more frequently than in times past." For that reason, the new punishment of transportation, originally ordained in Elizabeth's act just mentioned, should receive full implementation. There followed this proclamation in 1609-10, a statute for vagrancy control and building houses of correction. It confirmed statutes already in effect but called for their due and full execution, for "the said Howses of Correccion have not beene buylte according as was intended." The statute further charged that, in addition to laxity in building houses of correction, other statutes relating to vagrancy control remained unenforced. This statute called for their immediate execution, and it also called for the construction of enough houses of correction so that every county in the realm would contain one or more. The words of Latimer's sermon to King Edward VI sum up the failure of Tudor social legislation. "We have good statutes made for the commonwealth, as touching commoners and inclosers; many meetings and sessions; but in the end of the matter there cometh nothing forth."[21] And if there "cometh nothing forth," the later state of the realm remained worse than the earlier, for it had witnessed a rising tide of expectations only to receive disappointment.

Evidence for inefficiency in the Tudor system ranges from the serious as just cited to comic opera as in the case of four overseers of the poor at West Bromwich, three of whom lodged a complaint that the fourth member had added to their problems by fathering two bastard children whom he refused to support.[22]

Robert Hitchcock, author of the "Politic Plat" (1580), realized that lack of work or "Idleness" caused vagabondage. He saw that laws had failed to help the situation. "Idleness," he said, increased the realm's ruin, and "all these laws, so circumspectly made, could not, nor cannot banish that pestilent canker out of this common weal by any degree."[23] He offered a partial solution to the problem in his aforementioned fleet of fishing vessels to provide work for the unemployed.

Early in Tudor times Sir Thomas More denounced the Tudor system of social control as a failure. In *Utopia* he condemned laws that hanged for petty theft. "This way of punishing thieves is neither just in itself nor good for the public. The remedy is not effectual because the severity is too great. . . . No punishment however severe is sufficient to restrain a man from robbery who can find no other livelihood." It would suffice, he felt, to provide work for men instead of forcing them to steal because of hunger and then sending them to the gallows. This policy defeated itself. In reference to vagabonds, More added, "we have passed many laws against them, but have produced no effect as yet." Then he sums up his position with the observation that "a bondman's labor is worth more to the state than his death."[24]

Contemporaries knew that the problem's solution rested in the hands of the government. Henry Brinklow implored God and the Holy Spirit to "open the earys" of king and parliament that they might hear the desperate cries of the poor for help. Latimer, in his second sermon before Edward VI, delivered much the same message. That is the king should look to matters pertaining to the poor; and to judges Latimer adds the admonition that God has commanded that they listen to the pleas of the poor as well as the rich.[25] Added to these voices calling royal attention to its responsibility is that of Sir William Forrest's *Pleasaunt Poesie of Princelie Practise*. The poet enumerated all the adverse conditions under which the poor suffered and then in the following verse struck the target on center.

Thus thorowe Rentes reysinge and pillinge the poore,
Povertie regnethe and is induced muche:
compelled to begge nowe from doore to doore:
as (tyll owre tyme) hathe not beene herde of suche.
Your highnes, o prince, this case dothe sore tuche,
for chieflie youre Crowne to this intent yee weare,
wronge to reforme that *Equite* may rule beare.

Later in the poem he warned the king that equity and justice guarantee
peace while "*Division* by grudge" produces the opposite; again, he informed the king that this is his responsibility. The warning voice said
that the strength of a king resides in the many and not the few.
Therefore, the monarch should see to the welfare of the poor commons
for when they receive wealth the king can never be poor.[26]

Robert Crowley took a slightly different tack. He emphasized the
responsibility of gentlemen rather than that of the king, though he probably would have included the king with such eminent men. Crowley's
poem of about 1550 titled "The Gentleman's Lesson" called upon these
persons to walk upright, punish vice, defend the innocent poor, and
help the wicked to reform. Above all, gentlemen should not raise rents.
This reflects a note of irony, for these were the things, except raising the
rents, that the gentlemen of the age were notorious for not doing.
Stephen Gosson, writing prior to 1579, gathered the current ideas of
responsibility and made everyone responsible for everyone else. That
is, the "meane" should serve the "mighty" who in turn must protect the
"meane." Subjects should obey the king who must look after the
welfare of his poor subjects.[27]

Enough sermonizing on how kings and gentlemen *should* conduct
themselves. The question is: did they act in a manner conducive to the
welfare of the poor? Philip Stubbes in 1583 published "Gluttonie and
drunkennesse in Alig[na]." It tells what he thinks about "gentlemen."
Gluttony and drunkenness are their fashion at hospitality among themselves, while the poor receive nothing but the worst of leavings. Some
receive instead, "whipping cheer to feed them withall." Twelve years
later Thomas Churchyard affirmed this judgment in a poem that lamented the lack of charity during his time. Finally, a royal proclamation
of 1605 adds more information to the grimness of the gentlemen's
ledger: "A Proclamation to redresse the misimployment of Lands,

Goods, and other things given for Charitable uses."[28]

The foregoing were the attitudes of the monarch and gentlemen who legislated and administered the poor-law measures. They were mainly interested in controlling and fleecing the unruly commons. Sir Frederic Morton Eden says this was the case because vagrants threatened society and probably participated in every disturbance. He then says, "the Poor Law in its origin, therefore, was purely a matter of police regulation and the desire to succour those in distress merely an unavoidable corollary, imposed by necessity, and not dictated by philanthropy." Even in connection with levying the poor-rate, he states that directions for its usage in providing work operated haphazardly, if at all, and the money went indiscriminately to those who applied for relief. That is, if the poor rate was even collected in the first place, for as Eden continues, "the author of the pamphlet entitled 'Bread for the Poor' (p. 25) says indeed that no rates were levied in many places for twenty, thirty, or even forty years after the Act of Elizabeth." Eden then cites Henry Fielding's observation that Elizabethan overseers of the poor, in buying supplies for the provision of work, had received orders to carry out this program and no instructions for its accomplishment. Even allowing for an honest attempt, the poor rate was difficult to collect, and the assessments often ridiculously low. This provided, as Eden states, relief so meager that many died of starvation. Eden cites the 1622 pamphlet by M. S. London titled "Greevous Grones for the Poor. . . ." The author found the poor-law statutes adequate but unenforced while the poor increased without receiving benefit of a collection for seven years in many parishes.[29]

During Elizabeth's reign, therefore, her statutes, proclamations, and other procedures accomplished nothing toward reducing vagrancy and poverty; this legacy she passed to the Stuarts. Ribton-Turner reports on a 1616 privy council letter to London's mayor complaining of increasing vagrancy in the city and adjoining areas and requesting the appointment of provost marshals for their control. Then in 1618 the king wrote to Sir Thomas Smyth, who became governor of the Virginia Company in 1619, concerning "idle young people" at court whom the monarch desired to have transported to Virginia and there put to work. They had no employment, had received punishment, but still followed the court. In a subsequent letter Smyth asked permission of the king to hold and work these "idle young people" or "children," as they were called in another letter, in Bridewell until a ship could transport them to Virginia.[30] Transportation provided a severe sentence for youngsters whose only crime was the inability to find employment.

Peter Laslett presents indictment of the Tudor legacy to their successors, for he says that vagabonds like those found in Stuart times supplied a perennial feature of England "and most noticeable under the Tudors." He further supports this criticism by means of a statistical study of the register of the church at Greystoke in Cumberland. Laslett is here presenting facts to support his theory that many of the deaths of Tudor-Stuart times resulted not from plague and famine but from starvation—either immediate or as a result of years of malnutrition. For this study, Laslett worked out an annual average of about 37 deaths, but in the year 1623 the number of burials increased to 161 at Greystoke— over four times the statistical average. Then he pins his statistics to the worst months for deaths, September to November, 1623, when there were 62 funerals reported, and demonstrates that 10 resulted from starvation by admission of entries in the register. As Laslett admits, his is only a small sampling, for no one has yet attempted to isolate hunger deaths from those caused by disease for a parish throughout a particular extended period of history. He feels that such a study might prove possible in the near future. In order to present the truly "melancholy" nature of these entries in the Greystoke parish record relative to people who died of starvation, Laslett's interesting compilation for 1623 is here presented in full.

Extracts from the Register of Greystoke 1623

29th January: 'A poor fellow destitute of succour and was brought out of the street in Johnby into the house of Anthony Clemmerson, constable there, where he died.'

27th March: 'A poor hungerstarved beggar child, Dorothy, daughter of Henry Patteson, Miller.'

28th March: 'Thomas Simpson, a poor hungerstarved beggar boy and son of one Richard Simpson of Brough by Nandgyes house in Thorp.'

19th May: At night 'James Irwin, a poor beggar stripling born upon the borders of England. He died in Johnby in great misery.'

12th July: 'Thomas, child of Richard Bell, a poor man, which child died for very want of food and maintenance to live.'

11th September: 'Leonard, son of Anthony Cowlman, of Johnby, late deceased, which child died for want of food and maintenance to live.'

12 September: 'Jaine, wife of Anthony Cowlman, late deceased, which woman died in Edward Dawson's barn of Greystoke for want of maintenance.'

27th September: 'John, son of John Lancaster, late of Greystoke, a waller by trade, which child died for want of food and means.'

[The register tells us that he was baptized on October 17, 1619, so he was four years old.]

4th October: 'Agnes, wife of John Lancaster, late of Greystoke, a waller by trade, which woman died for want of means to live.'

27th October: 'William child of Lancelot Brown, which Lancelot went forth of the country [the district] for want of means.'[31]

The many examples of this type demonstrate the lack of Tudor poverty care both during the Tudor era and in the years immediately thereafter.

E.M. Hampson also finds the Tudor poor-law system inadequate. He basically agrees with Eden in that he too feels that the Tudor government's main interest was to control rather than develop the welfare of the poor. The privy council, he says, primarily concerned itself with controlling vagrancy and supplying markets with reasonably priced grain. The latter concern merely furnished a control rather than a philanthropic measure, for hungry men could soon become dangerous mobs. Hampson admits that cities and towns both influenced and were influenced by the royal government without, however, becoming accustomed to the many laws of the latter. Therefore, at the end of the sixteenth century care of the poor remained principally the responsibility of local institutions and "only by stringent settlement regulations can the towns, without the backing of Government hope to achieve any measure of success."[32] In other words, the crown demanded that they make progress against poverty in spite of rather than with the aid of central government.

Tawney agrees that Tudor relief measures attempted to prevent social upheaval caused by socioeconomic changes of the era. And, he adds, in spite of this massive effort for social control at the lower-class level, the Tudors failed. The government only reluctantly accepted its role of succoring the poor, for "Governments made desperate efforts for about one hundred years to evade their new obligations."[33]

The intent behind Tudor social legislation demanded control of the masses and did not stem from Christian or humanitarian motivation.

Being shallow it failed to get at the roots of vagrancy and poverty problems. Ironically, therefore, it did not secure the social control that Tudor monarchs craved. This two-fold failure of governmental policy furnished the Stuarts a legacy of growing popular anger. The Civil War leaders surely must have known that they could depend upon such social discontent as a major force in their successful bid to overthrow the monarchy.

Appendixes

APPENDIX I

A chronology of revolts, rebellions, riots, and other disturbances:*

1536-37 Pilgrimage of Grace. Stow, pp. 572-73.

1537 Bigott's Rebellion. *RP*, 166.

1541 Conspiracy in northern England by "certain priests and gentlemen." *CSP*, 1531-47, XVI, 733, 852, 1131.

1548 Enfield, a riot, *APC*, II, 219.

1548 Cornwall, rebels. *APC*, II, 554.

1549 Somersetshire and Lincolnshire, enclosure riots. Stow, p. 596.

1549 Norfolk, enclosure riot, Kett's Rebellion. Heylyn, I, 158-61; *APC*, II, 316.

1549 "Western rebels." *APC*, II, 313.

1549 Kent, rebels. *APC*, II, 314.

1549 Rebellion widespread in England. *APC*, II, 330-31.

1549 Devonshire and Cornwall, rebellion: enclosure and religion. Heylyn, I, 156; *RP*, 360.

1549 Yorkshire, rebellion. Heylyn, I, 161.

1549 Sussex, Wiltshire, Hampshire, Gloucestershire, Suffolk, Warwickshire, Essex, Hertford, Leicestershire, Worcestershire, Rutlandshire, Oxfordshire, rebellions over enclosure and religion. Burnet, II, 208-209.

1549 Order issued for controlling imminent disturbances in cos. Oxford, Berks, and Bucks. *CSP*, I, 8:9.

1550 Suffolk, man urging rebellion. *APC*, III, 18.

*In presenting this rather long list of disturbances, and in future chronological lists of this type, it will be practical to give the source in abbreviated form immediately following each citation. These materials are included in the bibliography and footnotes. See the table of abbreviations, p. viii.

1550   Nottinghamshire, attempted disturbance. *APC*, III, 31.

1550   Kent and Sussex, conspiracy for disturbance. *APC*, III, 35.

1550   Oxfordshire, enclosure riot. *APC*, III, 181.

1550   London, conspiracy to rebellion. *APC*, III, 256-57.

1551   Guernsey, attempted rebellion. *APC*, III, 263.

1551   western rebels. *APC*, III, 368.

1551   Essex riot. *APC*, III, 410.

1552   Buckinghamshire, rent rebellion. Cheyney, p. 100.

1553   Thetford, rebellion. *APC*, IV, 293.

1553   Town of Sutton, rebellion. *APC*, IV, 301.

1553   Norfolk, seditious tumult. *APC*, IV, 371.

1553   Leicestershire, attempted seditious tumult. *APC*, IV, 371.

1553   Norfolk and Suffolk, revolts. *APC*, IV, 426.

1554   Ipswich, attempted disturbance. *APC*, V, 70.

1554   Salisbury, fray. *APC*, V, 71.

1554   Wyatt's Rebellion, centered in Kent. Mackie, pp. 538-39.

1554   Essex, religious disturbance. *APC*, V, 34.

1555   Sussex, a tumult. *APC*, V, 120.

1555   Sussex, unlawful assembly. *APC*, V, 115.

1555   Sussex, a tumult. *APC*, V, 155.

1555   Sussex, a conspiracy. *APC*, V, 157.

1555   Essex and Suffolk, a conspiracy. *APC*, V, 165.

1555   Essex and Norfolk, a conspiracy. *APC*, V, 171.

1556   Western counties, conspiracy. *CSP*, 1547-80, I, 9:15.

1556   Suffolk and Essex, conspiracy. *APC*, V, 310.

1556   Westminster, a fray. *APC*, V, 319.

1557-58   Wales, riot. *APC*, VI, 236.

1558   Rye, seamen's disorder. *APC*, VI, 319.

1558   Lincolnshire, rising. *APC*, VI, 336.

1558   Northern England, disorder. *APC*, VI, 360.

1558-59   Wales, disorders. *APC*, VII, 60, 67.

1564   Yorkshire, riot. *APC*, VII, 175.

1569   Northumberland and Westmorland, rebellion. Stow, pp. 662-64.

1569   Yorkshire, rebellion. *CSP*, 1547-80, VII, 17:16.

1569   Co. of Durham, rebellion. *CSP*, 1547-80, VII, 17:14.

1569   Richmondshire, rebellion. *CSP*, 1547-80, VII, 17:14.

1571   Bromyard, riot against bishop of Hereford. *APC*, VIII, 33.

1571   Nantwich, religious riot. *APC*, VIII, 40.

1571-72   Harwich, rebels. *APC*, VIII, 70-71.

1574   Gloucestershire, riots. *APC*, VIII, 218-19.

1575   Wales, disorders. *APC*, IX, 41, 66.

1575-76   Wales, serious disorders. *APC*, IX, 94-95.

1577   Essex, riot over a chapel. *APC*, X, 12, 16, 34.

1577   Wales, disorders. *APC*, X, 101.

1577   London, bearing of arms and disorderly assemblies. *APC*, X, 120.

1577   London, riots. *APC*, X, 117.

1577-78   Oxfordshire, enclosure riot. *APC*, X, 155.

1578   London, disorders. *APC*, X, 215, 218.

1578   Staffordshire, riot—"A very great riot"—*APC*, X, 324, 333, 336, 338, 344, 349, 352-53, 396-97.

1578   Wales, riot. *APC*, X, 376.

1578   Oxford, riot. *APC*, X, 433-34.

1578   Enclosure riot in the Marches. *APC*, X, 399.

1579   Staffordshire, riot. *APC*, XI, 203.

1579   Hertfordshire: enclosure riot. *APC*, XI, 95-96, 99, 103, 106, 110, 113, 169.

1580   Chester, mutiny of troops. *APC*, XII, 286, 298, 303.

1580-81   Dorsetshire, riot. *APC*, XII, 338.

1581   Chester and Liverpool, mutiny of troops. *APC*, XIII, 64, 96, 98, 123, 280.

1581   Abergavenny, riots. *APC*, XIII, 115.

1581   Wales, riot. *APC*, XIII, 139.

1581   Suffolk, riot. *APC*, XIII, 143.

1581   Welsh Marches, disorders. *APC*, XIII, 246.

1585-86   Monmouthshire, riots and disorders. *APC*, XIV, 6-7.

1586   Southamptonshire, rioting: grain and unemployment. *APC*, XIV, 91.

1586   Welsh Marches, disorders: religious and otherwise. *APC*, XIV, 124-25.

1586   Ipswich, food riot. *APC*, XIV, 128, 134.

1586   Gloucestershire, food riot. *APC*, XIV, 133.

1586   Bristol, food riot. *APC*, XXIV, 159-60.

1587   London, mutiny of troops. *CSP*, 1547-80, II, 202:8.

1588   Cumberland: enclosure riot. *APC*, XVI, 116.

1589   Earl of Desmond's Rebellion. *APC*, XVII, 384.

1589   London, Drake's seamen causing disturbances. *APC*, XVII, 416.

1590   London, apprentices rioting. *APC*, XIX, 476-77.

1590   Herefordshire, riot. *APC*, XX, 114-16.

1591   Lincolnshire, rioting and lawlessness. *APC*, XXI, 121.

1591   London, riot. *APC*, XXI, 297, 299, 300.

1592   London (Southwark), riotous apprencies. *APC*, XXIII, 19-20, 24, 28-29; XXII, 549-51.

1592   London (Holborne), riot. *APC*, XXIII, 242-43.

1592   London, riotous seamen. *APC*, XXIII, 342.

1592   Kent, riot. *APC*, XXII, 588.

1592   Yorkshire: enclosure riot. *APC*, XXII, 527.

1592-93   Nottinghamshire, disorders. *APC*, XXIV, 77, 78, 128.

1594   Wales, Roman Catholics planned a rebellion and the death of the queen. *CSP*, 1591-1625, III, 249:4.

140 Thorns on the Tudor Rose

1595 London, riots. *EJ*, II, 28-29; *RP*, 873.
1595 London, youth riot on Tower Hill. *EJ*, II, 31.
1596 Oxfordshire: conspiracy to commit enclosure riot discovered. *APC*, XXVI, 364-66, 373-74, 383, 398, 412-13, 455, 483.
1596 Kent, grain riot. *APC*, XXV, 334.
1596 Chester, mutiny of troops. *APC*, XXV, 331-33.
1596 Somersetshire, disorders. *APC*, XXV, 410.
1596 Oxfordshire, enclosure rebellion planned. *EJ*, II, 156, 161.
1596-97 Southamptonshire, riots. *APC*, XXVI, 533.
1597 Kent and Sussex, grain riots. *APC*, XXVII, 555-56.
1597 Norfolk, grain riots. *APC*, XXVII, 88-89.
1597 Sussex, grain riots. *APC*, XXVII, 92-93.
1598 Plymouth, disorder. *APC*, XXVIII, 391.
1598 London, mutiny of troops. *EJ*, II, 315.
1598 London, lawlessness near. *EJ*, II, 307.
1598 Cardiff (Glamorganshire), riots. *CSP*, 1591-1625, V, 267:56-57.
1599-1600 Bristol, mutiny of troops. *APC*, XXX, 137-38.
1599-1600 Chester, mutiny of troops. *APC*, XXX, 155-56.
1600 Chester, mutiny of troops. *APC*, XXXI, 52.
1600 Somersetshire, grain riot. *APC*, XXX, 386-87.
1600 Merionethshire, disorders. *APC*, XXX, 611-12.
1600 London, disorder. *APC*, XXX, 203-204.
1600 Wales, disorderly troops. *EJ*, III, 74.
1601 Staffordshire, widespread disorder. *APC*, XXXII, 102-104.
1601 Denbigshire, election riot. *APC*, XXXII, 342-43.
1605 Five men and five women were fined in Star Chamber for enclosure riot. *JJ*, p. 250.
1607 Northamptonshire: enclosure riots. *RP*, 1041.
1607 Northamptonshire: enclosure riots still persist in spite of *RP*, 1041. *RP*, 1042.
1607 Northamptonshire, Warwickshire, Leicestershire, enclosure rebellion. Stow, p. 889.
1615 Norfolk, rioting by Ellen Pendleton and her followers. *APC*, XXXIV, 204-205, 278-83, 312-13.
1631 Rutlandshire, grain and unemployment riots. Bland, pp. 390-91.
1641 London, riotous assemblies. *RP*, 1911.

APPENDIX II

A chronology of statutes against rumors and sedition:
1378 "The Penalty for telling slanderous Lyes of the Great Men of the Realm." *SR*, II, 2 Rich. II. 1. C. 5.
1545 "An Acte against slanderous Billes." *SR*, III, 37 Hen. VIII. C. 10.

1554-55 "An Acte against sedityous Woordes and Rumours." *SR*, IV, Pt. I, 1 & 2 Phil. & Mar. C. 3.

1554-55 "An Acte for the punishement of Traterous Woordes against the Queenes Matie." *SR*, IV, Pt. I, 1 & 2 Phil. & Mar. C. 9.

1558-59 "An Acte for the explanacon of the Statute of sedytyous Woordes and Rumours." *SR*, IV, Pt. I, 1 Eliz. C. 6.

1558-59 "An Acte to continue Thacte made against Rebellyous Assemblyes." To continue Mary's act. *SR*, IV, Pt. I, 1 Eliz. C. 16.

1562-63 "An Act agaynst fonde and phantasticall Prophesyes." *SR*, IV, Pt. I, 5 Eliz. C. 15.

1580-81 "An Acte against sedicious Wordes and Rumors uttered againste the Queenes most excellent Majestie." *SR*, IV, Pt. I, 23 Eliz. C. 2.

A chronology of royal proclamations against rumors and sedition:

1321 "Against slandering the king." *RP*, p. clxii.

1346 "Against false rumors." *RP*, p. clxv.

1403 "Against false reports." *RP*, p. clxxi.

1405 "Against false rumors." *RP*, p. clxxi.

1436 "Against false rumors and seditious writings." *RP*, p. clxxiv.

1450 "Against seditious libels posted on church doors. . . ." *RP*, p. clxxv.

1453 "Against heretical and seditious libels posted up." *RP*, p. clxxv.

1486-87 "for the suppressing of forged tydings . . . and seditious Rumors." *RP*, no. 7.

1525 "for the punishment . . . of Conspirators, Riotours, and Libellers in the Citie of Coventry." *RP*, no. 99.

1547 Against "tale tellers." *RP*, no. 306.

1549 Against "tale tellers." *RP*, no. 350.

1549 Against "tale tellers." *RP*, no. 358.

1550 Against "Sowers of sedition." *RP*, no. 379.

1554 "for suppressing of seditious Rumours and Libells." *RP*, no. 451.

1556 "The Select Council to King Philip. . . . Orders against players and pipers strolling through the Kingdom, disseminating seditions and heresies." *CSP*, 1547-80, I, 8:50.

1558 "for suppressing of seditious Rumours." *RP*, no. 491.

1567 "Speech of the Lord Keeper in the Star Chamber before the Council and others" Against the bringing of seditious books into the realm. *CSP*, 1547-80, I, 44:52.

1570 "Proclamation against harbouring seditious persons and rebels, and from bringing in traitorous books and writings from abroad." *CSP*, 1547-80, I, 74:33.

1573 "Lord Keeper . . . Observations relative to the proclamation against seditious books and libels." *CSP*, 1547-80, I, 92:26.

1579 "Proclamation by the Queen for the calling in of 'a lewde seditious booke' [The Gaping Gulfe] . . . against the Duke of Anjou and Her Majesty's intended marriage." *CSP*, 1547-80, I, 132:11, 26-36.

1586   "The new decrees of the Star Chamber for the better regulation . . . of printing in London, Oxford, and Cambridge." *CSP*, 1581-90, II, 190:48.

1586-87   "[Against seditious rumours.]" *RP*, no. 792.

1597   Rumor that the mayor of London was keeping grain prices up and selling own grain at high prices. The queen issued a proclamation denouncing such tales. *EJ*, II, 207.

1600   "A Proclamation against Those Spreading Rumours." *EJ*, III, 86-87.

1601   Proclamation against seditious libels. *APC*, XXXI, 266.

1603   "A minute of letters to all the Judges of the land to take order at their several Assises for the punishing such as do libell and spread and raise slanderous reports of Privie Councillors, etc." *APC*, XXXII, 502.

1605-1606   A proclamation "[To appease a rumour.]" A rumor of an accident to the king resulted in a calling to arms by the constables. *RP*, no. 1030.

A chronology of persons, and areas charged with rumors and sedition:

1528   "Seditious Preaching" He called the king and other officials "the strongest thieves in England" who robbed the poor. *CSP*, 1509-30, IV, 4040.

1534   "against Margaret Cowpland for calling the King an extortioner, knave and traitor, and queen Anne a strong harlot." *CSP*, 1531-47, VII, 1609.

1535   "Treasonable words" by women of Suffolk against king and queen. *CSP*, 1531-47, VIII, 196.

1536   A gentleman and a fuller accused of speaking against the king. *CSP*, 1531-47, XI, 140.

1536   Person accused of speaking against the king. *CSP*, 1531-47, XI, 190.

(1536)   Suffragan bishop of diocese of Chichester accused of speaking against king and religion. *CSP*, 1531-47, XI, 300.

1537   A "glover" of Southwark accused of spreading rumors relative to northern problems. *CSP*, 1531-47, XII, Pt. I, 62.

1537   A priest and the "master of Manton" accused of seditious words against king. *CSP*, 1531-47, XII, Pt. I, 126.

1537   A tailor accused of "tedious and unsitting words" *CSP*, 1531-47, XII, Pt. I, 589.

1537   A poor beggar accused of speaking against the king. *CSP*, 1531-47, XII, Pt. I, 797.

1537   Vagabond spreading seditious reports. *CSP*, 1531-47, XII, Pt. II, 918.

1537   "Seditious songs" by an itinerant fiddler. *CSP*, 1531-47, XII, Pt. I, 424. In this volume (XIII) there are many other references to rumors and sedition too numerous to list. Many of them refer to the Pilgrimage of Grace and the dissolution of the monasteries.

1538   Priest accused of "teaching young folks seditious songs" *CSP*, 1531-47,

XIII, Pt. I, 1054.

1538   Man accused of attempting to have a minstrel sing a song against Cromwell. *CSP*, 1531-47, XIII, Pt. I, 1370.

1538   Man accused of advocating a common revolt in the "South Country." *CSP*, 1531-47, XIII, Pt. II, 1129.

1539   A "parson" sent to gaol for "railing words." *CSP*, 1531-47, XIV, Pt. I, 542.

1540   Man pilloried for seditious words. *CSP*, 1531-47, XV, 318.

1540   Norfolk man accused of seditious speeches. *CSP*, 1531-47, XV, 748.

1541   London man sent to Fleet prison for printing seditious books. *CSP*, 1531-47, XVI, 435.

1542   Yarmouth: man charged with seditious words. *CSP*, 1531-47, XVII, 181.

1543   Man pilloried for "lewd words." *CSP*, 1531-47, XVIII, Pt. I, 469.

1545   Man to be pilloried for slandering the council. *CSP*, 1531-47, XX, Pt. I, 1140.

1545   Man accused of seditious words. *CSP*, 1531-47, XX, Pt. I, 1281.

1546   Carpenter accused of speaking against the king. *CSP*, 1531-47, XXI, Pt. I, 608.

1549-50   Man accused of seditious words—sentence: pillory and loss of an ear, "and then dismisse him with a good lesson." *APC*, II, 385.

1550   Report of conspiracy for sedition in Sussex. *APC*, III, 131.

1550   Inquiry: "seditious billes." *APC*, III, 138.

1550-51   Seditious preacher. *APC*, III, 217.

1550-51   Seditious preacher at Oxford. *APC*, III 237.

1551   "Bookes and billes of sklanderouse devises against the Counsaill to move the people to rebellion." *APC*, III, 262.

1551   Sheriffs of London to punish two men for sedition, *APC*, III, 404.

1552   Man called king "poore child" to be pilloried. *APC*, IV, 4.

1552   Seditious conspiracy in Hampshire. *APC*, IV, 45.

1552   Pillory for a seditious man. *APC*, IV, 69.

1552   Man sentenced to pillory, loss of both ears and imprisonment for "lewde and slanderous woordes." *APC*, IV, 110.

1552   Man sentenced to pillory for being a transmitter of slanderous reports. *APC*, IV, 121.

1552   Six men to receive pillory and loss of ears for advocating sedition and spreading false rumors. *APC*, IV, 168.

1552   Priest accused of writing "seditious bills." *APC*, IV, 163.

1552-53   Man released from prison after serving time for speaking against royal coinage. *APC*, IV, 200-201.

1552-53   Man sentenced to the pillory and loss of both ears for "lewde and slaunderous woordes." *APC*, IV, 211.

1553   Man and two women sentenced to pillory and prison for spreading rumors of the king's death. *APC*, IV, 266-67.

1553   Man sentenced to pillory, loss of ears and prison for "Lewde and Sediscious Woordes" against king and state. *APC,* IV, 278.

1553   Man imprisoned for seditious words. *APC,* IV, 320.

1553   Shipmaster accused of seditious words. *APC,* IV, 257.

1553   Two preachers accused of sedition, three other seditious preachers imprisoned and a man accused of seditious behavior. *APC,* IV, 321-22.

1553   A preacher and another man accused of speaking against the queen. *APC,* IV, 330.

1553   Woman: seditious words against the queen. *APC,* IV, 332.

1553   Preacher accused of sedition. *APC,* IV, 333.

1553   Two seditious preachers. *APC,* IV, 338.

1553   Archbishop of Canterbury sent to Tower for sedition and causing tumult. *APC,* 347.

1553   Man imprisoned for leading a seditious movement at Maidstone. A seditious preacher released. *APC,* IV, 375.

1553   Two men sent to prison for writing a "lewde bill." *APC,* IV, 390.

1553-54   Two men charged for saying King Edward still alive. *APC,* IV, 384.

1553-54   Hastings fisherman sentenced to pillory and loss of one ear for "certaine leawde woordes." *APC,* IV, 402.

1554   Man accused of speaking against queen. *APC,* V, 11.

1554   Man to pillory for speaking against the queen. *APC,* V, 30.

1554   Man to pillory for slander. *APC,* V, 33.

1554   Manservant of Lady Elizabeth to prison for speaking against the state. *APC,* V, 50.

1554   Yeoman of the guard imprisoned for dispensing "lewd and seditious" books. *APC,* V, 52.

1554   Man accused of seditious words. *APC,* V, 64.

1554-55   Seditious preacher. *APC,* V, 88.

1554-55   Man to pillory for singing a seditious song. A parson to the Tower for slanderous bill against king and queen. *APC,* V, 89.

1555   Man to pillory for lewd words. *APC,* V, 121.

1555   Three seditious preachers. *APC,* V, 110.

1555   A seditious book. *APC,* V, 153.

1555   Seditious bills sent to Northamptonshire. *APC,* V, 161.

1555   A seditious bill. *APC,* V, 181.

1555   Man charged with speaking against king. *APC,* V, 186.

1555-56   Man to Tower for bill asserting King Edward still alive. *APC,* V, 221.

1555-56   Persons accused of false rumors and seditious letters. *APC,* V, 226.

1555-56   Man spreading rumor that King Edward still alive. *APC,* V, 228.

1555-56   Man to Tower for traiterous letter. *APC,* V, 235.

1555-56   Man charged with distributing seditious book. *APC,* V, 243.

1555-56   Seditious bills in Sussex. *APC,* V, 245.

1556   Carpenter charged with speaking against queen. *APC,* V, 265.

1556   Spreaders of false rumors apprehended. *APC*, V, 323.

1556   Spreaders of seditious rumors apprehended. *APC*, V, 333.

1556-57   Man to prison for writing a "lewd" and seditious book. *APC*, VI, 62.

1556-57   Two men accused of writing a "lewde" book. *APC*, VI, 63.

1557   Man charged with writing a "leude" and seditious book. *APC*, VI, 76.

1557   Yeoman of the guard imprisoned for "lewde" and seditious words against queen. *APC*, VI, 139.

1557   Five men of London accused of writing and spreading "lewde" and seditious books. *APC*, VI, 144-45.

1557   Canterbury: lewd play and players. *APC*, VI, 148.

1557   Lewd play in London. *APC*, VI, 168.

1557-58   Man charged with lewd words. *APC*, VI, 251.

1558   Man pilloried for false and slanderous words. *APC*, VII, 18.

1558   Sexton of Chichester Cathedral accused of using lewd words. *APC*, VII, 19.

1558   Archdeacon of Canterbury accused of sedition. *APC*, VII, 53-54.

1558   Queen ordered man to pillory for seditious words. *CSP*, 1547-80, I, 74:33.

1558-59   Priest: seditious preaching at Canterbury. *APC*, VII, 63.

1558-59   Spanish priest: seditious preaching at Bristol. *APC*, VII, 63.

1558-59   Priest: "lewde" and seditious words—pillory, loss of an ear and prison. *APC*, VII, 71.

1559   Man accused of having called the queen a rascal. *CSP*, 1547-80, I, 3:50.

1559   Man: pillory for lewd and slanderous words. *APC*, VII, 94.

1560   Clergyman accused of speaking against queen. *CSP*, 1547-80, I, 12:51.

1560   Certain persons of Essex accused of slandering the queen. *CSP*, 1547-80, I, 13:21.

1563   Man jailed for slandering queen. *CSP*, 1547-80, I, 27:25.

1565   Man: pillory for words against the state. *APC*, VII, 218-19.

1567   Man: pillory for lewd and seditious speaking. *APC*, VII, 348.

1570   Man accused of slander of nobility and pillory proposed. *APC*, VII, 402.

1570   Northern fairs: "a great bruit raised of the fall of money." *CSP*, 1547-80, VII, 18:75 (Addenda).

1571   London butcher accused of speaking against queen and others at court. *CSP*, 1547-80, I, 80:9.

1571   Libellous matter being spread in London. *CSP*, 1547-80, I, 80:15.

1572-73   Man accused of speaking against queen. *APC*, VIII, 88.

1573   Concerning libel against Burghley. *CSP*, 1547-80, I, 92:29.

1573   Libels of Roman Catholics against Burghley. *CSP*, 1547-80, I, 92:33.

1573   Man of Wales accused of seditious speaking. *APC*, VIII, 147.

1575-76   Seditious writings in Sussex. *APC*, IX, 85.

1576   Man of Northampton with treasonable documents. *APC*, IX, 124, 128.

1576-77   Two "Masters of Arte" of Christ College, Oxford, accused of speaking against queen. *APC,* IX, 300.

(1577)   Libels against Leicester and Burghley. *CSP,* 1547-80, I, 113:30.

1577   Seditious bills at Oxford. *APC,* IX, 354.

1577   Oxford man accused of seditious speeches. *APC,* IX, 368.

1577   Man persistent in speaking against the queen; imprison him or cut out his tongue. *CSP,* 1547-80, I, 118:27.

1577   Man of Southamptonshire accused of speaking against the privy council. *APC,* X, 41, 42, 48.

1577   Man of Dover accused of speaking against privy council, sentenced to pillory. *APC,* X, 61.

1577   Leicester man accused of seditious speeches and possession of seditious book against queen. *APC,* X, 108.

1577-78   Sarum man: speaking against realm. *APC,* X, 170.

1578   Hastings man in Tower for seditious speeches. *APC,* X, 234.

1578   York man accused of speaking against queen and being leader of other rebels, including a priest. *APC,* X, 382.

1578   Chicester man for speaking against queen to be pilloried and bound to good behavior for one year. *APC,* X, 392-93.

1578   Marlborough man accused of speaking against the queen. *APC,* X, 394.

1578   Wiltshire man: speaking against queen. *APC,* X, 406.

1578   York man: speaking against queen. *APC,* X, 407-408.

1578   Staffordshire man: speaking against privy council—pillory and prison. *APC,* X, 413-14.

1578   Several prisoners in Chesters for speaking against queen. *APC,* X, 421-22.

1578   Man: speaking against members of privy council. *APC,* X, 425-26.

1578-79   Cos. of Salop and Stafford: man accused of delivering prophecies. *APC,* XI, 49.

1578-79   Man of St. Albans accused of speaking against queen for saying that she "should have been shot at with a gun." *APC,* XI, 75.

1578-79   Colchester: libellers and "slaunderous rymers." *APC,* XI, 78.

1579   Two men: speaking to stir up tummult. *APC,* XI, 108.

1579   Northampton man: speaking against queen. *APC,* XI, 132.

1579   Man of Kent: for speaking against the proclamation against carrying of "dagges." *APC,* XI, 295.

1579-80   Preacher: sermon against the queen. *APC,* XI, 368.

1579-80   "Clerke": carrying a "pocket dagg"—to be punished. *APC,* XI, 403.

1579-80   Essex man: speaking against the queen. *APC,* XI, 405.

1581   Three men and others of Hertfordshire accused of seditious speeches. *APC,* XIII, 67.

1581   Seditious persons who made a rescue at Smithfield: try, whip, pillory and cut or nail their ears. *APC,* XIII, 131.

1581   Sarum man: speaking against queen. *APC*, XIII, 180.

1581   Herefordshire: two men, speaking against queen and secret religious meetings—one a gentleman and other the mayor of Hereford. *APC*, XIII, 245.

1581-82   Three men of Oxford charged with seditious libel before Star Chamber—scourage and bind to good behavior or banish from the university. *APC*, XIII, 350-52.

1582   Two yeomen of Essex: seditious speeches on behalf of a traitor. *APC*, XIII, 407.

1582   A seditious book. *CSP*, 1581-90, II, 152:72.

(1582?)   "Libels lately dispersed in the town of Hythe." *CSP*, 1581-90, II, 157:72, 177:45.

1582   Rumors, slanderous pamphlets and seditious libels. *CSP*, 1581-90, II, 152:91.

1582   Information on disaffected persons and a seditious pamphlet. *CSP*, 1581-90, II, 154:53.

1583   Defence against slanders and libels of the queen. *CSP*, 1581-90, II, 164:85.

1584   Norfolk man: publication of a seditious book. *CSP*, 1581-90, II, 170:48.

1586   A leather dresser: speaking against the queen. *CSP*, 1581-90, II, 190:56.

1586   Possession of unlawful books. *APC*, XIV, 144.

1586   Seditious literature. *APC*, XIV, 210.

1586-87   Wates man: speaking against government—pillory prescribed. *APC*, XIV, 277.

1586-87   Canterbury shoemaker: possession of seditious literature. *APC*, XIV, 322-23.

1586-87   Somersetshire man and others accused of seditious rumors. *APC*, XIV, 366-67.

1589   Wiltshire man: speaking against queen. *APC*, XVII, 124-25.

1589   Gloucester: seditious letters and libels. *APC*, XVIII, 287.

(1590?)   "Dissertation on the evils . . . of seditious writings." *CSP*, 1581-90, II, 235:81.

1590   London man: traitorous speeches. *APC*, XX, 28-29.

1591   Sarum man: speaking against queen. *APC*, XXI, 184.

1591   Welsh man: speaking against queen. *APC*, XXI, 218.

1591   Northern man: speaking against queen—nail ears to pillory, etc., and imprisonment. *APC*, XXI, 323-24.

1591   Herefordshire man: speaking against queen. *APC*, XXI, 346.

1591   Kent man and woman: speaking against queen. *APC*, XXII, 35.

1591   Two men: seditious speaking. *APC*, XXII, 77.

1591-92   Lincolnshire woman: speaking against queen. *APC*, XXII, 317.

1592   Man of Ireland: speaking against queen. *APC*, XXII, 376.

1592   Man: speaking against queen. *APC*, XXII, 410.

1592   Three Devonshire men: speaking against queen. *APC*, XXII, 439-40.

1592   Welsh man: seditious speaking. *APC*, XXII, 475-76.

1592-93   Devonshire schoolmaster: speaking against religion and queen. *APC*, XXIV, 7-8.

1592-93   Clergyman: speaking against Earl of Leicester. *APC*, XXIV, 28-29.

1593   Certain Cornwall persons: speaking against queen. *APC*, XXIV, 158-59.

1593   A justice of the peace: speaking against queen. *APC*, XXIV, 189.

1593   London: seditious placard posted—find authors and punish. *APC*, XXIV, 222.

1593   Hampshire vicar: speaking against government. *APC*, XXIV, 268-69.

1593   Man: slander of queen's religion. *CSP*, 1591-1625, III, 245:31.

1594   London: rumor that queen had died. *EJ*, I, 286.

(1595?)   A seditious book concerning the succession. *CSP*, 1591-1625, IV, 255:76.

1596   Several men accused of sedition and seditious words. *CSP*, 1591-1625, IV, 259:16.

1596   Man: bringing of seditious literature from abroad—examine and torture. *APC*, XXVI, 10.

1597   Isle of Guernsey man: speaking against queen. *APC*, XXVIII, 26.

1597   Oxfordshire man: traitorous speaking—apprehend and send to us. *APC*, XXVIII, 28-29.

1598   Uxbridge innkeeper: disloyal speaking. *APC*, XXIX, 186-87.

1598   Dorsetshire man: speaking against queen. *CSP*, 1591-1625, V, 269:22, 270:105 (1599).

1599   The Lord Keeper's, Lord Treasurer's and other speeches in Star Chamber against libellers. *CSP*, 1591-1625, V, 273:35.

1600-1601   Monmouthshire man accused of writing seditious song and others helped him disperse it. *APC*, XXXI, 138-39.

1600-1601   Several persons of Wales accused of seditious libel. *APC*, XXXI, 208.

1601   A London servant accused of seditious speaking. *APC*, XXXI, 367.

1601   Two men of Wales: seditious speeches against queen and state. *APC*, XXXI, 466.

1601   Four men: publishing seditious books—keep them in prison and try them. *APC*, XXXII, 85.

APPENDIX III

A chronology of statutes concerning vagrancy:

1285   Statute of Winchester: against vagrancy and crime. *SR*, I, 13 Edw. I.

1331   Statute against vagrancy and crime. *SR*, I, 5 Edw. III. C. 14.

1349   Statute regulating begging. *SR*, I, 23 Edw. III. C. 7.

1360-61   Statute for punishment of fugitive laborers—imprison and brand with an "F" on forehead. *SR*, I, 34 Edw. III. C. 10.

1383   Statute against vagrancy and crime. *SR*, II, 7 Rich. II. C. 5.

1383   Statute against vagrancy and crime. *SR*, II, 7 Rich. II. C. 6.

1388   Statute against vagrancy. *SR*, II, 12 Rich. II. C. 7-10.

1495   For moderating the statute against vagrancy. *SR*, II, 11 Hen. VII. C. 2.

1503-1504   For moderating the statute against vagrancy. *SR*, II, 19 Hen. VII. C. 12.

1511-12   For moderating the statute against vagrancy. *SR*, III, 3 Hen. VIII. C. 9.

1530-31   Statute against "Egiptians" (Gypsies). *SR*, III, 22 Hen. VIII. C. 10.

1530-31   Statute against vagrancy. *SR*, III, 22 Hen. VIII. C. 12.

1535-36   Statute against vagrancy: first provision for alms and work. *SR*, III, 27 Hen. VIII. C. 25.

1536   Statute against vagrancy. *SR*, III, 28 Hen. VIII. C. 6.

1539   Statute against vagrancy. *SR*, III, 31 Hen. VIII. C. 7.

1541-42   Statutes for continuing former vagrancy and poor laws. *SR*, III, 33 Hen. VIII. C. 10; 33 Hen. VIII. C. 17.

1545   Statute for continuing former vagrancy and poor laws. *SR*, III, 37 Hen. VIII. C. 23.

1547   Statute for punishment of vagrancy and relief of the poor. *SR*, IV, Pt. I, 1 Edw. VI. C. 3.

1549-50   Statute for punishment of vagrancy. *SR*, IV, Pt. I, 3 & 4 Edw. VI. C. 16.

1551-52   Statute against vagrancy. *SR*, IV, Pt. II, 5 & 6 Edw. VI. C. 21.

1551-52   Statute against vagrancy in churchyards. *SR*, IV, Pt. I, 5 & 6 Edw. VI. C. 4.

1551-52   Statute for poor relief and against vagrancy. *SR*, IV, Pt. I, 5 & 6 Edw. VI. C. 2.

1554-55   Statute for punishment of Gypsies. *SR*, IV, Pt. I, 1 & 2 Phil. & Mary. C. 4.

1562-63   Statute for punishment of Gypsies. *SR*, IV, Pt. I, 5 Eliz. C. 20.

1572   Bill read relative to vagrancy control and poor relief. *JHL*, I, 14 Eliz.

1572   Second reading of bill relative to vagrancy control and poor relief. *JHC*, I, 14 Eliz.

1572   Statute for punishment of vagrants and relief of the poor. *SR*, IV, Pt. I, 14 Eliz. C. 5. During this session of parliament England was "exceedinglie pestered" by vagrants and crimes. A bill was enacted for control of this. Holinshed, *Chronicles*, pp. 265-66.

1592-93   Statute for relief of soldiers. *SR*, IV, Pt. II, 35 Eliz. C. 4.

1592-93   Statute for London: against new buildings for the poor. *SR*, IV, Pt. II, 35 Eliz. C. 6.

1597-98   Statute against vagrants. *SR*, IV, Pt. II, 39 Eliz. C. 17.

1597-98   Statute for control of vagrancy. *SR*, IV, Pt. II, 39 Eliz. C. 4.

1601   Statute relative to Cumberland, Northumberland, Westmoreland, and bishopric of Durham: crime, lawlessness, and vagrancy. *SR*, IV, Pt. II, 43 Eliz. C. 13.

1601   Statute relative to vagrancy, vandalism and thievery in rural areas. *SR*, IV, Pt. II, 43 Eliz. C. 7.

1601   Statute for relief of soldiers. *SR*, IV, Pt. II, 43 Eliz. C. 3.

1603-04   To continue Elizabeth's statute on vagrancy. *SR*, IV, Pt. II, 1 Ja. I. C. 7.

1609-10   An act for proper execution of former vagrancy statutes. *SR*, IV, Pt. II, 7 Ja. I. C. 4.

1627   An act for continuing certain poor-law and vagrancy statutes. *SR*, V, 3 Ch. I. C. 5.

A chronology of royal proclamations, the problem in general and cases at law concerning vagrancy:

1487   Against vagrancy and crime. *RP*, 7a.

1492-93   Against vagrancy and crime. *RP*, 22.

1516-17   Enforcement of statutes against vagrancy and crime. *RP*, 74.

1526   Vagrants excluded from court. *CSP*, 1509-30, IV, 1943.

1527   Enforcement of statutes against vagrancy and crime. *RP*, 110.

1530   Vagrants to leave court. *CSP*, 1509-30, IV, 258 (Appendix).

1530   For punishing vagrants. *RP*, 121.

1530   Against vagrancy. *CSP*, 1509-30, IV, 6485 (Appendix).

1531   Vagrants to leave London. *RP*, 125.

1531   Vagrants to leave London. *RP*, 126.

1533   Enforcement of statutes against vagrants. *RP*, 132.

1533   Vagrants to leave court. *RP*, 135.

1535-36   Against vagrant pardoners. *RP*, 155.

1535-36   Against vagrancy. *RP*, 156.

1537   Norfolk to Cromwell: he is following king's orders in suppressing vagrancy. *CSP*, 1531-47, XII, Pt. II, 14.

1537   Letter of Duke of Suffolk: he is following king's orders in suppression of vagrancy. *CSP*, 1531-47, XII, Pt. II, 364.

1537   Order for arrest of certain Gypsy criminals. *CSP*, 1531-47, XII, Pt. II, 1008:23.

1537   Letter: seditious vagabonds executed in York. *CSP*, 1531-47, XII, Pt. II, 1076.

1537   Cromwell to bishop of Chester: compel the Gypsies to leave the realm. *CSP*, 1531-47, XIII, Pt. II, 1173.

(1538)   Letter on increase of vagrancy. *CSP*, 1531-47, XIII, Pt. II, 1229.

1538   Beggar whipped and sent to place of birth. *CSP*, 1531-47, XIII, Pt. I, 269.

1538   Former monk in vagabond guise imprisoned. *CSP*, 1531-47, XIII, Pt. I, 549.

1538   King's circular to justices of the peace thanking them for suppression of vagrancy, etc. *CSP*, 1531-47, XIII, Pt. II, 1171.

(1538)   Provision of work for beggars. *CSP*, 1531-47, XIII, Pt. II, 1.

1539   Sheriff of Staffordshire to Cromwell: what shall be done with arrested Gypsies? *CSP*, 1531-47, XIV, Pt. I, 204.

(1539)   Concerning arrest and punishment of Gypsies. *CSP*, 1531-47, XIV, Pt. II, 287.

(1539)   Concerning Gypsy problem. *CSP*, 1531-47, XIV, Pt. II, 425.

(1539)   Concerning Gypsy problem. *CSP*, 1531-47, XIV, Pt. II, 427.

(1539)   Concerning Gypsy problem. *CSP*, 1531-47, XIV, Pt. II, 494.

(1539)   Concerning Gypsy problem. *CSP*, 1531-47, XIV, Pt. II, 781.

1539   Letter: what shall be done with arrested Gypsies of Romney Marsh? *CSP*, 1531-47, XIV, Pt. II, 74.

1539   Citation of excellency of vagrancy and poor laws. *CSP*, 1531-47, XIII, Pt. I, 402.

1540   Privy council: four "tapsters" to the pillory for following the court and causing food prices to increase. *CSP*, 1531-47, XVI, 10.

1540   Ordinances for repression of vagrancy in city of Chester. *CSP*, 1531-47, XV, 141.

1540   Nicholas Robertson to Cromwell: problems with Gypsies in Boston and other places. *CSP*, 1531-47, XV, 696.

1541   Privy council: man to pillory and ear nailed for forgery. *CSP*, 1531-47, XVI, 907.

1541   Letter to justices of the peace for suppression of vagrancy, Roman Catholics, seditious rumors. *CSP*, 1531-47, XVI, 945.

1541   Against vagrants at court. *RP*, 196.

1542-43   Deportation of certain Gypsies. *APC*, I, 88.

1543   Deportation of certain Gypsies. *APC*, I, 106.

1543   Gypsy problem. *APC*, I, 128.

1543   Privy council: letter to two men (justices?) to suppress certain Gypsies. *CSP*, 1531-47, XVIII, Pt. I, 190.

1543   Privy council: passport for twenty-four Gypsy families to leave the realm. *CSP*, 1531-47, XVIII, Pt. I, 372.

1543   Privy council: certain Gypsies to be deported. *CSP*, 1531-47, XVIII, Pt. I, 515.

1543   Three proclamations: 1. enforcement of statute 33 Hen. VIII against vagrancy; 2. vagrants to leave court; 3. justices to enforce statutes against vagrancy. *CSP*, 1531-47, XVIII, Pt. II, 542.

1544   Wriothesley to the council relative to ridding Calais of Gypsies. *CSP*, 1531-47, XIX, Pt. II, 206.

1544   Privy council: deport Gypsies caught at Huntingdon. *CSP*, 1531-47, XIX, Pt. II, 207.

1545 For punishment of vagrants. *RP*, 273.

1545 London vagrants to be impressed for king's galleys. *CSP*, 1531-47, XX, Pt. I, 812.

1545-46 Justices to enforce vagrancy laws. *RP*, 297.

1545-46 Passport to deport Gypsies. *APC*, I, 320.

1546 Deportation of Gypsies. *APC*, I, 358.

1546 Deportation of Gypsies. *APC*, I, 555.

1546 Privy council: deportation of certain Gypsies from London. *CSP*, 1531-47, XXI, Pt. I, 103.

1546 Privy council: letter to officials at Dover to either release or deport certain Gypsies. *CSP*, 1531-47, XXI, Pt. I, 467.

1546 Privy council: provision of a ship to deport Gypsies. *CSP*, 1531-47, XXI. Pt. II, 504.

1550 Letters to justices for execution of vagrancy laws. *APC*, II, 431.

1550 Vagrants to be driven from London. *APC*, III, 27.

1551 Against vagrancy and vagrants to be driven from London. *RP*, 395.

1552 Deportation of Gypsies at Donstable. *APC*, IV, 18.

1552 Deportation of Gypsies found anywhere. *APC*, IV, 59.

1552 London: "seditious vagabond" to be pilloried and whipped. *APC*, IV, 70.

1552 Man charged with making plays released. *APC*, IV, 73.

1552 Letter for deportation of certain Gypsies. *APC*, IV, 166.

1553 Vagrants to leave the court. *RP*, 437.

1554 Vagrants to leave the court. *RP*, 455.

1555 For deportation of Gypsies of shires of Norfolk, Sussex, and Suffolk. *APC*, V, 185.

1555-56 Gypsies to be deported from shires of Norfolk and Suffolk. *APC*, V, 231.

1556 For arrest and punishment of minstrels. *APC*, V, 323.

1557 London: censorship of plays and players. *APC*, VI, 102.

1557 Canterbury: certain players committed "to ward." *APC*, VI, 110.

1557 Order in Star Chamber to all justices to suppress players. *APC*, VI, 119.

1558 Bristol and Bedford: problem of military deserters. *APC*, VI, 312.

1558 Against vagrants in London and Westminster. *RP*, 490.

1559 Letter on problem of Gypsies. *CSP*, 1547-80, I, 6:50.

(1559) Certificate: Gypsies in Gloucestershire. *CSP*, 1547-80, I, 7:20.

(1559?) To Sussex and Surrey: punish vagrants. *CSP*, 1547-80, VI, 9:42.

1559 Birminghamshire: crime and restriction on "goonne or dagge." *APC*, VII, 101.

1559 Great number of Gypsies arrested. *CSP*, 1547-80, I, 6:31.

1559 Dorchester: trial of Gypsies from Scotland. *CSP*, 1547-80, I, 6:39.

1560 Banishment of Anabaptists. *RP*, 529.

1561 Vagrants to leave the court. *RP*, 549.

1561   Commission in York: punish vagrancy. *CSP*, 1547-80, VI, 11:10.

1562   Letters to shires of Southampton, Devon, Cornwall, Hereford, Stafford, Chester, Berks, Bucks, and Oxon to control vagrancy. *APC*, VII, 116.

1562   London: city watch to be observed. *APC*, VII, 107.

1562   Oxfordshire: deal with Gypsies. *APC*, VII, 112.

1562   Oxfordshire: Gypsies to be tried. *APC*, VII, 125.

1565   London: begging licenses being forged. *APC*, VII, 257.

1565   London: man counterfeiting licenses to beg: punish as a "terror and example" to others. *APC*, VII, 257.

(1566?)   Cecil: definition of a vagabond. *CSP*, 1547-80, I, 41:76.

1569   Yorkshire: laws against vagrancy duly executed. *CSP*, 1547-80, VII, 14:79.

1569   Winwicke: reasons for delay in making return on vagrants—names of vagrants whipped. *CSP*, 1547-80, I, 51:11.

1569   Norfolk: vagrancy and sedition repressed. *CSP*, 1547-80, I, 60:1.

1569   Cornwall: punishment of vagrants. *CSP*, 1547-80, I, 60:27.

1570   Northampton: proceedings in search of vagrants. *CSP*, 1547-80, I, 67:45.

(1571)   Bill for punishment of remaining Gypsies. *CSP*, 1547-80, I, 77:60.

1571   Sussex: punishment of vagrants. *CSP*, 1547-80, VII, 19:70.

1571   Surrey: proceedings in vagrant search. *CSP*, 1547-80, I, 81:49.

1571   Cheshire: proceedings in vagrant search. *CSP*, 1547-80, I, 81:58.

1571   Certificates to the privy council relative to searches, arrests, punishment, etc., of vagrants (the certificates cover the whole shire and/or certain hundreds, towns, etc., within the respective shires): Co. Essex, 7 certificates; Co. Nottingham, 4 certificates; Co. Gloucester, 6 certificates; Co. Oxford, 17 certificates; Co. Kent, 2 certificates; Co. Surrey, 9 certificates; Cirencester and seven adjacent hundreds, 2 certificates; Hundred of Wootton, 1 certificate; Co. Worcester, 1 certificate; Co. Northampton, 5 certificates; Co. Hereford, 1 certificate; Co. Leicester, 5 certificates; Co. Stafford, 8 certificates. *CSP*, 1547-80, I, 80, 81.

1571   Certificates of searches for Cos. Cambridge and Huntingdon and for 15 other hundreds plus the Isle of Ely of vagrants arrested and punished. *CSP*, 1547-80, I, 83:36.

1571   London: problem of beggars. *APC*, VIII, 52-53.

1571-72   London: problem of beggars. *APC*, VIII, 72-73.

1572   Yorkshire: order being duly kept. *CSP*, 1547-80, VII, 21:111.

1572   Surrey: certificates for punishment of vagrants in several hundreds—stocked and whipped. *CSP*, 1547-80, I, 86:9.

1572   Lincolnshire: keeping watch for vagrants. *CSP*, 1547-80, I, 86:12.

1572   Oxfordshire: 15 certificates for all the hundreds relative to arrest and punishment of vagrants. *CSP*, 1547-80, I, 86:16.

1572   During this session of parliament England was "exceeding pestered" by vagrants and crimes. Stow, p. 671.

1572   Middlesex: a number of vagrants arrested and punished. *CSP*, 1547-80, I, 86:21.

1572   Northampton: certificates for several hundreds relative to arrested and punished vagrants. *CSP*, 1547-80, I, 86:22.

1572   Buckinghamshire: certificates for vagrants arrested and punished in six hundreds. *CSP*, 1547-80, I, 86:27.

1572   Middlesex: vagrants punished. *CSP*, 1547-80, I, 86:28.

1573   Kent: problem of unemployed soldiers. *APC*, VIII, 100.

1574   Order for investigation of runagates. *APC*, VIII, 249.

1574   Southants: unlawful religious assemblies. *APC*, VIII, 257.

1574   Co. Norfolk: A "Bridewell"-type house to be built. *APC*, VIII, 328.

1575   License to beg to merchant due to his losses at sea and sickness. *CSP*, 1547-80, I, 9:59.

1576   London and Westminster: crime rate high—vagrants banned. *RP*, 714.

1576   Letter to mayor of London urging him to put vagrants to work. *APC*, IX, 247.

1576-77   Re license to beg for York man. *APC*, IX, 247.

1576-77   Berkshire: ten Gypsies to be punished as example. *APC*, IX, 304.

1576-77   Oxfordshire: Gypsies to be punished. *APC*, IX, 311.

1577   Berkshire: certain Gypsies accused of high treason. *APC*, IX, 312.

1577   Gypsies to trial. *APC*, IX, 314-15.

1577   Middlesex, Kent, Essex, Hartford, Bucks, Barks, and Surrey: suppress vagrants. *APC*, IX, 99.

(1577?)   London: order for poor relief to avoid begging. *CSP*, 1547-80, I, 120:50.

1578   Re license to beg for York man. *APC*, X, 285.

1578   London: vagrants to be driven out. *APC*, X, 215.

1578-79   A reissue of *RP*, 714 (1576). *RP*, 735.

(1579?)   Council to Norfolk: control vagrants and build a Bridewell-type house of correction. *CSP*, 1547-80, I, 133.

1579-80   Wales: forty Gypsies to trial. *APC*, XI, 362.

1580   Against the Family of Love. Holinshed, p. 432.

1582   London: rules for plays and players. *APC*, XIII, 404.

1582   Winchester: funds raised for employment of vagrants. *CSP*, 1581-90, II, 153:16.

1582   Winchester: orders for control of vagrants and poor relief. *CSP*, 1581-90, II, 153:17.

1582   Winchester: whip and set vagrants to work in house of correction. *CSP*, 1581-90, II, 153-24.

1583   Kent: certain servants accused of playing at interludes. *CSP*, 1581-90, II, 160:48.

1583   London: Irish beggars arrested and to be sent back to Ireland. *CSP*, 1581-90, II, 164:80.

1583   Smithfield: ten horse thieves hanged. Holinshed, p. 508.

1586   Cos. Chester and Lancaster: re collection of poor rate. *APC*, XIV, 187-88.

1586   London and Middlesex: punish sturdy beggars and aid needy ones. *APC*, XIV, 253.

1586   London: re control of vagrancy. *CSP*, 1581-90, II, 188:54.

1587   London: re control of vagrancy. *CSP*, 1581-90, II, 205:5.

1587   Re soldiers deserting in Netherlands and returning to England. *APC*, XV, 154-55.

1587   Surrey, Middlesex, Essex: control vagrants. *APC*, XV, 256.

1588   London: control vagrancy. *APC*, XVI, 136.

1588   Re vagrant discharged soldiers. *APC*, XVI, 261.

1588   London: press vagrants in military. *APC*, XVI, 291-92.

1588   London and environs: control vagrancy. *APC*, XVI, 336.

1588   Shires of Dorset, Somerset, Hampton, Devon, Cornwall, Wilts: to employ houses of correction against vagrancy. *APC*, XVI, 416.

1589   Against vagrant soldiers and others—apply martial law. *RP*, 818.

1589   Hertfordshire: re control of vagrancy. *CSP*, 1581-90, II, 228:22.

1589   Hertfordshire: re use of provost marshal there. *CSP*, 1581-90, II, 228:23.

1589   All shires: Lords Lieutenant to appoint provost marshals to control vagrants. *CSP*, 1581-90, II, 228:10.

1589   Burghley to appoint provost marshals in his lieutenacy for vagrancy control. *CSP*, 1581-90, II, 228:17.

1589   London: vagrants pressed for military. *APC*, XVII, 161.

1589   Herefordshire: get rid of Gypsies. *APC*, XVII, 279.

1589   London: problem with discharged soldiers. *APC*, XVII, 453-54.

1589   London: control vagrancy. *APC*, XVIII, 266.

1589   London: problem of unpaid mariners in state of mutiny. *APC*, XVIII, 48.

1589   London: problem of riotous discharged soldiers. *APC*, XVIII, 54-55.

1589   Cos. Surrey, Kent, Essex: problem of riotous discharged soldiers. *APC*, XVIII, 55-56.

1589   London: pressing of vagrants. *APC*, XVIII, 123.

1589   Cos. Middlesex, Essex, Surrey and city of London: suppress vagrant soldiers. *APC*, XVIII, 214.

1589   London: censorship of plays. *APC*, XVIII, 214-15.

1589   Lords Lieutenant to appoint provost marshals for control of vagrancy. *APC*, XVIII, 221-22.

1589   Southamptonshire: apply martial law to vagrants. *APC*, XVIII, 236-38.

1589   Irish widow: license to beg returning to Ireland. *APC*, XVIII, 219.

1589   Hertfordshire: re control of vagrancy. *CSP*, 1581-90, II, 229:21.

1590   Man and family travelling: license to beg for one year. *APC*, XIX, 103.

1590   Man travelling: license to beg for one month. *APC*, XIX, 159.

1590   Man travelling: license to beg. *APC*, XIX, 160.

1590   Man travelling: license to beg. *APC*, XIX, 165-66.

1590   Man travelling: license to beg. *APC*, XIX, 187.

1590   Man and wife travelling: license to beg. *APC*, XIX, 194.

1590   Irishman and family: license to beg travelling to Ireland. *APC*, XIX, 211.

1590   Irishman: license to beg travelling to Ireland. *APC*, XIX, 302.

1590   Man and wife travelling: license to beg. *APC*, XIX, 452.

1590   Poor man licensed to beg. *APC*, XX, 51.

1590   Poor man licensed to beg. *APC*, XX, 86.

1590   Wales dweller: license to beg for three years to reestablish his estate. *APC*, XX, 131.

1590   Hertfordshire: continue use of provost marshal to control vagrancy. *CSP*, 1581-90, II, 231:24.

1590   Essex: similar to *CSP*, 1581-90, II, 231:24. *CSP*, 1581-90, II, 231:25.

1590   London: press vagrants for Netherlands service. *APC*, XIX, 183.

1590   London: press vagrants for Ostend service. *APC*, XX, 69.

1590   London: curfew for vagrants. *RP*, 826.

1590   Passport and license to beg to disabled soldier until almsroom vacant in Cambridge. *APC*, XX, 10-11.

1590-91   Passport and license to beg to poor, disabled soldier until he receives almsroom at Cathedral Church in Worcester. *APC*, XX, 249.

1590-91   Poor, disabled soldier: license to beg until almsroom in Cathedral Church in Norwich available. *APC*, XX, 241.

1590-91   Two poor, disabled soldiers: licenses to beg until almsrooms available at Cathedral Churches of Westminster and Norwich.

1591   Three poor, disabled soldiers: licenses to beg until almsrooms available. *APC*, XXII, 35.

1591   Poor, disabled soldier: license to beg until almsroom available at Peterborough. *APC*, XXII, 75.

1591   Poor, disabled soldier: license to beg until almsroom available at Christchurch College. *APC*, XXII, 117.

1591   Three poor, disabled soldiers: licenses to beg while awaiting almsrooms. *APC*, XXII, 117.

1591   Poor, disabled soldier: license to beg for three months. *APC*, XXI, 120-21.

1591   Warwickshire: poor, disabled soldier given license to beg until almsroom ready. *APC*, XXI, 389.

1591   Sailor given license to beg. *RP*, 835.

1591   Many wanderers pretending to be soldiers: officials to aid the true needy soldiers and punish the false ones. *CSP*, 1591-25, III, 240:60.

1591   Two persons given license to beg travelling to Ireland. *APC*, XXI, 248.

1591   Irish woman: license to beg. *APC*, XXI, 280.

1591   Irishman and family: license to beg. *APC*, XXI, 359.

1591   Case of a Gypsy. *CSP*, 1591-1625, III, 240:103.

1591   Shires to appoint provost marshals for control of vagrancy. *CSP*, 1591-1625, III, 240:59.

1591   Control of discharged soldiers. *CSP*, 1591-1625, III, 240:76.

1591   Lancashire and Cheshire: vagrants go unpunished and poor go without provision. *CSP*, 1591-1625, III, 240:138.

1591   For control of Gypsies. *APC*, XXI, 62-63.

1591   London: vagrants pressed for Ostend service. *APC*, XXII, 129.

1591   London and Kent: vagrants pressed for Ostend service. *APC*, XXII, 129.

1591   Four men sentenced to hanging. *EJ*, I, 22.

1591   Re vagrant vs. deserving soldiers. *CSP*, 1591-1625, III, 240:60.

1591   Surrey, Sussex, Kent, Essex, Hertfordshire: re vagrants. *CSP*, 1591-1625, III, 240:68.

1591   Against vagrant soldiers. *RP*, 840.

1591   Against unlawful assemblies in London and vicinity. *RP*, 845.

1591-92   London: against vagrant soldiers. *RP*, 849.

1591-92   London and vicinity: look into situation of wandering soldiers: aid those in need and punish those pretending to be soldiers and the able-bodied not in need. *APC*, XXII, 295-96.

1592   Suffolkshire: poor, disabled soldier given license to beg for six months. *APC*, XXII, 534.

1592   Woman and children: license to beg returning to Ireland. *APC*, XXII, 572.

1592   Hertfordshire: problem of vagrant soldiers. *EJ*, I, 150.

1592   London: vagrant Irish problem—send them back to Ireland. *APC*, XXIII, 99-100.

1592   Newgate sessions: re vagrants. *APC*, XXIII, 157-58.

1592   Problem of Gypsies. *APC*, XXIII, 290-91.

1592   London: vagrant Irish to be deported. *EJ*, I, 150.

1592   Criminals used as soldiers. *EJ*, I, 156.

1592   "Cozener" pilloried and lost one ear. *EJ*, I, 140.

1593   Man and family: license to beg returning to Scotland. *APC*, XXIV, 424.

1593   Man: license to beg returning to Scotland. *APC*, XXIV, 488.

1593   London: re vagrancy and poverty problems. *APC*, XXIV, 193-96.

1593   Commission appointed to deal with vagrant soldiers. *EJ*, I, 221.

1593   London and Westminster: about 100 poor, disabled soldiers receiving aid from parliament. Do not allow them to beg or they will lose their allowance and suffer punishment. *APC*, XXIV, 178-79, 191-93.

1593   London: rogues and vagabonds to be removed or punished and poor, disabled soldiers to receive relief. *APC*, XXIV, 193-96.

1593   London and vicinity: re control of vagrants. *RP*, 858.

1593-94   Expel vagrants from court. *RP*, 867.

1594   Northamptonshire: certificate of vagabonds arrested and punished. *CSP*, 1591-1625, III, 248:104.

1594   Case of three Gypsies. *CSP*, 1591-1625, III, 249:126.

1594   London and vicinity: conference on problem of vagrants. *EJ*, I, 334-36.

1594   London, Middlesex, Surrey, Kent, Essex, etc.: re control of vagrancy. *APC*, XXV, 520.

1595   London and vicinity: re control of vagrants. *RP*, 874.

1595-96   London: re pressing of vagrants for Plymouth service. *APC*, XXV, 250-51.

1595-96   Somersetshire: re vagrancy control. *APC*, XXV, 312-13.

1595-96   "West Country" plus Norfolk and Suffolk: re control of vagrancy. *APC*, XXV, 316-17.

1595-96   Somersetshire: re vagrancy control. *APC*, XXV, 314.

1596   Southwarke: appoint provost marshal for vagrancy control. *APC*, XXV, 324.

1596   London: problem of vagrants at court. *APC*, XXV, 330.

1596   Norfolk and other shires: re control of vagrants. *APC*, XXV, 333-34.

1596   Problem of vagrants with forged passports. *APC*, XXV, 343-45.

1596   London and Middlesex: re control of vagrants. *APC*, XXVI, 23-24.

1596   Problem of Blackamoors in London. *EJ*, II, 109.

1596   London: problem of alehouses and vagrancy. *EJ*, II, 104.

1596   London: problem of passport counterfeiters. *EJ*, II, 83-84.

1596   Condemned prisoners pardoned for military service. *EJ*, II, 73, 79.

1596   London: vagrants pressed for Plymouth service. *EJ*, II, 79.

1596   Somersetshire: vagrancy and crime rampant. *EJ*, II, 136-37.

1596   Soldier given license to beg for one year until almsroom in Westminster available. *APC*, XXVI, 24.

1596   Problem of impersonators and counterfeiters of documents. *RP*, 882.

(1596?)   London and the court: re control of vagrancy and crime. *CSP*, 1591-1625, IV, 261:70.

1597   London, Middlesex, Surrey, Kent: impress vagrants for Picardy service. *APC*, XXVII, 290-91.

1597   London and environs: re censorship of plays and playhouses. *APC*, XXVII, 313-14.

1597   London: certain players imprisoned. *APC*, XXVII, 338.

1597   Middlesex, Surrey, Kent: re pressing of vagrants for Picardy service. *EJ*, II, 198-99.

1598   London: vagrants, etc., in tenements. *EJ* II, 274-75.

1598   London: Two bawds "carted," imprisoned and fined. *EJ*, II, 251-58.

1598   Problem of discharged soldiers. *CSP*, 1591-1625, V, 266:3.

1598   London, Middlesex, Surrey, Kent: re vagrancy and crime problem. *APC*, XXIX, 128-30.

1598   London and vicinity: vagrancy and crime. *APC*, XXIX, 140-42.

1598   Re suppression of vagrancy and unlawful assemblies. *RP*, 899.

1598-99   Bristol: re pressing of vagrants. *APC*, XXIX, 487.

1599   Essex: certificate of vagrants punished. *CSP*, 1591-1625, V, 272:96.

1600   Oxfordshire: watch made but no vagrants found. *CSP*, 1591-1625, V, 275:129.

1600   Playhouses restrained due to disorders. *APC*, XXX, 395-98, 411.

1600   Middlesex: press vagrants for Ireland. *APC*, XXX, 567-68.

1600-1601   London and vicinity: re vagrant problem. *APC*, XXXI, 164-65.

1600-1601   London: vagrancy and crime: martial law. *RP*, 916.

1601   License to beg to woman in Ireland. *APC*, XXXII, 33.

1601   Suffolkshire: merchant had losses at sea and given license to collect (beg) for one year. *APC*, XXXII, 430-31.

1601   Two women tried and found guilty of consorting with Gypsies: one hanged and the other reprieved due to pregnancy. *EJ*, III, 155.

1601   Surrey, Middlesex and London: vagrants pressed for Ostend service. *APC*, XXXII, 27.

1601   Middlesex, Kent, Surrey: vagrants pressed for Netherlands service. *APC*, XXXII, 74.

1601   London: vagrants pressed for Ostend service. *APC*, XXXII, 145-46.

1601   London, Middlesex, Surrey: disorders at playhouses but they were not suppressed—why not? *APC*, XXXII, 466-69.

1602   Re new buildings in London (against). *EJ*, III, 282-83.

1602-1603   Letters to eighteen shires: re impressment of vagrants for Netherlands campaign. *APC*, XXXII, 492.

1602-1603   London, Middlesex, Surrey: re restraint of plays. *APC*, XXXII, 492.

1603   Chester, Liverpool, Bristol, Barnstable and Haverford West: ships not to bring more vagabonds from Ireland. *APC*, XXXII, 502.

1603   Re use of the press gang. *CSP*, Venetian, 1592-1603, IX, 1136.

1603   Vagrancy and crime increasing—places for transportation provided. *APC*, XXXII, 503-504.

1603   Re great increase of vagrancy: statutes against vagrants to be enforced and areas for transportation provided. *RP*, 971.

1603   Man licensed to beg. *RP*, 978.

1603-1604   Lancastershire: re proposal to build house of correction. *APC*, XXXII, 507-508.

1613   Problem of English subjects returning from the Continent: prisons full—send them back from whence they came. *APC*, XXXIII, 183-84.

1613-14   Middlesex: much vagrancy, especially London: build a house of correction. *APC*, XXXIII, 392-93.

1616   Man given collection permit due to fire loss. *RP*, 1186.

1616   Against vagrants—punishment by martial law. *RP*, 1188.

1618   Restrictions on certain itinerant trades. *RP*, 1214, 1215.

1618   Vagrants to leave court. *RP*, 1224.

1619-20   Man given collection permit due to illness. *RP*, 1277.

1620   Man given collection permit due to fire loss. *RP*, 1293.

1620   Several persons given collection permit due to fire loss. *RP*, 1294.

1620   Man given collection permit due to fire loss. *RP*, 1295.

1620-21   Man given collection permit due to fire loss. *RP*, 1298.

1620-21   Widow given collection permit. *RP*, 1299.

1620-21   Man given collection permit due to fire loss. *RP*, 1300.

1620-21   Needy man given collection permit. *RP*, 1301.

1620-21   Man given collection permit due to fire loss. *RP*, 1305.

1621   London: re vagrancy and crime. *RP*, 1313.

1622   Needy man given collection permit. *RP*, 1329.

1623-24   Two needy women given collection permit. *RP*, 1369.

1625   Re prevention of disorder at court. *RP*, 1428.

1625   Re prevention of disorder at court. *RP*, 1431.

1627-28   For execution of statutes against vagrancy. *RP*, 1538.

1628   Re problem of discharged soldiers. *RP*, 1563.

1629   Re problem of discharged soldiers. *RP*, 1593.

1629   Send Irish beggars back to Ireland and execute laws against English vagrants. *RP*, 1583.

1629   Execute laws for putting poor to work. *RP*, 1584.

1629   Use of collection permits to be limited. *RP*, 1591.

1630   Against various crimes. *RP*, 1613.

1630   Relieve the poor and suppress vagrants. *RP*, 1602.

1630   Relieve the poor and suppress vagrants. *RP*, 1623.

1633-34   Send Irish beggars back to Ireland and execute laws against English vagrants. *RP*, 1670.

1641   Re problem of discharged soldiers. *RP*, 1894.

1641   Re problem of discharged soldiers. *RP*, 1896.

1642-43   Against crime and vagrancy. *RP*, 2390.

1643   Re problem of discharged soldiers. *RP*, 2513.

1646-47   Execute laws against vagrants. *RP*, 2682.

1655   Re loose social conditions. *RP*, 3057.

1661   For applying statutes relative to vagrancy and poor relief. *RP*, 3300.

1661   Discharged soldiers to leave London and Westminster. *RP*, 3339.

1664   Repetition of *RP*, 3339. *RP*, 3403.

1668   Against highwaymen and robbers. *RP*, 3522.

1670   Precautions against arson to be taken in London. *RP*, 3538.

APPENDIX IV

A chronology of statutes and proclamations relating to arms and the peace of the realm:

1487   Against weapons, making of affrays, etc. *RP*, 8.

1511-12   Act against crossbows. *SR*, III, 3 Hen. VIII. C. 13.

1514-15   Act against crossbows and handguns. *SR*, III, 6 Hen. VIII. C. 13.
1523   Act against crossbows and handguns. *SR*, III, 14 Hen. VIII, C. 7.
1524   Against carrying weapons in the king's palace at Westminster. *RP*, 94.
1526   Against crossbows and handguns. *RP*, 100.
1528   Against crossbows and handguns. *RP*, 113.
1533-34   Act against crossbows and handguns. *SR*, III, 25 Hen. VIII. C. 17.
1536-37   Against crossbows and handguns. *RP*, 164.
1539   No one to carry a sword in king's place of habitation. *RP*, 181.
1541-42   Act against crossbows and handguns. *SR*, III, 33 Hen. VIII. C. 6.
1542   Against crossbows and handguns. *RP*, 205.
1554   Against handguns and other weapons. *RP*, 452a.
1556-57   Against long rapiers and swords, use of other than bladed weapons, and fighting in churchyards. *RP*, 472.
1559   Against, due to their use in crime, handguns and "dags" (pistols). *RP*, 511.
1561   Against using weapons in churchyards. *RP*, 553.
1575   Against "dags" and pistols. *RP*, 701.
1579   Against "dags," handguns, "Harquebuzes, Colliers, and Cotes of Defence." Also, no shooting within two miles of the queen. *RP*, 739.
1594   Against "dags" and "great disorders." *RP*, 871.
1598   Against lawlessness near London, especially by use of handguns. *EJ*, II, 307 (source: *APC*, XXIX, 128, 140).
1600   Against, due to criminal usage, "dags," fowling pieces and other guns. *RP*, 910.
1612-13   Against "pocket-dags." *RP*, 1125.
1616   Against handguns. *RP*, 1184.

APPENDIX V

A chronology of enclosure, rack-renting, and engrossing of land: statutes, royal proclamations, enclosure disturbances and disputes:

1514   Counties adjoining London: proclamation to take action against those destroying husbandry. *CSP*, 1509-30, I, 121 (Addenda).
1514-15   Act against destruction and decay of towns. *SR*, III, 6 Hen. VIII. C. 5.
1515   Act against destruction and decay of towns. *SR*, III, 7 Hen. VIII. C. 1.
1518   Decree in Chancery by Cardinal Wolsey against enclosures. *CSP*, 1509-30, II, 53 (Appendix).
1526   To East Anglia: against enclosures. *RP*, 103.
1526   Persons charged with enclosure to appear in Chancery. *RP*, 107.
1526   Persons charged with enclosure to appear in Chancery. *RP*, 106.
1528   Re names of those guilty of enclosure and engrossing. *RP*, 111.
1528-29   Enclosures to be destroyed. *RP*, 115.

1533-34   An act to regulate sheep farming and to prevent enclosure. *SR*, III, 25 Hen. VIII. C. 13.

1535-36   Against decay of houses and enclosures. *SR*, III, 27 Hen. VIII. C. 22.

1537   Instructions for the Duke of Norfolk: enclosures and excessive fines were one cause of the late Pilgrimage of Grace. *CSP*, 1531-47, XII, Pt. I, 98.

1539   Dr. London to Cromwell: Northamptonshire in state of decay due to high rents and enclosures. *CSP*, 1531-47, XIV, Pt. I, 42.

1539   Enclosure offences in three shires. *CSP*, 1531-47, XIV, Pt. I, 1350.

1548   Against enclosures. *RP*, 333.

1549   Reissue of *RP*, 333. *RP*, 352.

1549   For repressing persons who, using the proclamation against enclosures as an excuse, have created disturbances by destroying enclosures. *RP*, 353.

1549   Letter against destruction of enclosures by the people. *CSP*, 1547-80, I, 7:31.

1549   Instructions to commissioners on enclosures. *CSP*, 1547-80, I, 8:10.

1549   Protector Somerset: against enclosures. *CSP*, 1547-80, I, 8:11.

1549   Instructions to commissioners for an inquiry and survey of enclosures. *RP*, 359.

1549   For repressing persons who, using the proclamation against enclosures as an excuse, have created disturbances by destroying enclosures. *RP*, 356.

1549   Letter: more power needed by the Commission on Enclosures. *CSP*, 1547-80, I, 8:24.

1549   Instructions for commissioners on enclosure. *CSP*, 1547-80, I, 8:25.

1551   Man imprisoned for engrossing farms. *APC*, III, 346.

1553   Ten men guilty of tearing down enclosures: they must rebuild them. *APC*, IV, 377.

1555   Re enclosures on Scottish borders. *CSP*, 1547-80, I, 6:82.

1562-63   Women and boys: destroying enclosures. *APC*, VII, 137.

1566   Letter: re enclosures in Birminghamshire. *CSP*, 1547-80, I, 39:31.

1566   Enclosure problem in Buckinghamshire still pending. *CSP*, 1547-80, I, 39:31.

1568-69   For maintenance of tillage. *RP*, 637.

1573-74   Enclosure dispute in Worcestershire. *APC*, VIII, 195, 240-41, 243-45, 313.

1576   Enclosure complaint by "the pore men of the Peke." *APC*, IX, 127.

1576   Middlesex: re fence destroyers. *APC*, IX, 160.

1576   Poor men's petition to prevent enclosure of a park. *APC*, IX, 167.

1577   Buckinghamshire and Oxfordshire: common people petition against enclosures. *APC*, IX, 323.

1577   Petition by "poor women" against enclosure in the north. *APC*, IX, 382.

1578   Kent: enclosure dispute. *APC*, X, 374.

1578   Enclosure dispute in Saxendale. *APC*, X, 412.

1579   Cambridge: enclosure dispute. *APC*, XI, 111, 129.

1579   Derbyshire: enclosure dispute. *APC*, XI, 154, 178.
1579   Wales: enclosure dispute. *APC*, XI, 191.
1579   Worcestershire: enclosure dispute. *APC*, XI, 320.
1580-81   Monmouthshire: enclosure dispute. *APC*, XII, 309.
1580-81   Lincolnshire: enclosure dispute. *APC*, XII, 334.
1581   Lincolnshire: enclosure dispute. *APC*, XIII, 257-58, 336-37, 345.
1585-86   Lincolnshire: enclosure dispute. *APC*, XIV, 12.
1586   Cambridgeshire: enclosure dispute. *APC*, XIV, 201.
1586-87   Somersetshire: enclosure dispute. *APC*, XIV, 305.
1587   Bedfordshire and Buckinghamshire: enclosure dispute. *APC*, XV, 85-86, 106.
1589   Norfolkshire: enclosure dispute. *APC*, XVII, 244-45.
1589   Wiltshire: enclosure dispute. *APC*, XVII, 303-304.
1590   Bedfordshire: enclosure dispute. *APC*, XIX, 213, 310.
1590   Montgomeryshire: enclosure dispute. *APC*, XIX, 327-28.
1590   Montgomeryshire: enclosure dispute. *APC*, XX, 109-10, 290.
1590-91   In the north: enclosure dispute. *APC*, XX, 249-50.
1591   Norfolk: enclosure dispute. *APC*, XXI, 331-32.
1591-92   Town cf Bath: enclosure dispute. *APC*, XXII, 360, 370-71.
1596-97   Somersetshire: enclosure dispute. *APC*, XXVI, 548-49.
1597   "A Motion in Parliament against Inclosures." Also, "against forestallers, regrators and ingrossers." *EJ*, II, 230-31.
1597   "Shipton": Enclosure dispute. *APC*, XXVII, 129.
1597-98   "An Acte againste the decayinge of Townes & Howses of Husbandrye." *SR*, IV, Pt. II, 39 Eliz. C. 1.
1597-98   "An Acte for the maintenance of Husbandrie & Tillage." *SR*, IV, Pt. II, 39, Eliz. C. 2.
1598   Derbyshire: enclosure disorder. *APC*, XXVIII, 442-43.
1598-99   Town of Warwick: enclosure disorder. *APC*, XXIX, 652.
1604   Re "A Book Against Enclosures." *JJ*, p. 119.
1618   Certain persons granted "pardons and dispensations" for converting land from tillage to pasture. *RP*, 1231.
1618   Same as *RP*, 1231. *RP*, 1232.

APPENDIX VI

Naworth estate alms-giving:

September, 1648-May, 1649 (presented in the order in which given in this record):

Mar. 27   to a poor soldier, 2s. 6d.
Sept. 10   wine cakes and sugar to about 40 injured soldiers, 19s.
Oct. 4   wine to the poor, 3s. 6d.
Nov. 20   "paid the poore," 4d.

Sept. 20   to 5 injured soldiers, 2s. 6d.
Oct. 15   to 60 hungry prisoners, 2 pounds.
Nov. 2   to the poor, 10s.
Feb. 12   to begging soldier, 2s. 6d.
Feb. 12   to the guard and the poor, 3s. 6d.
Mar. 15   to the poor, 9d.
Apr. 2   to the poor, 2s. 6d.
Apr. 3   to a poor woman, 6d.
Apr. 8   to a begging soldier, 1s. 6d.
Apr. 12   to the poor, 1s.
Apr. 30   to a poor woman and man, 1s. 6d.
Oct. 15   to 2 women to buy bread for one month, 4s.
NE, I   pp. 1-57.

May   1650-April, 1651:
Dec. 25   to the poor, 12d.
Mar. 5   to workmen, the poor, and servants, 9s.
Apr. 16   to workmen and the poor, 4s. 6d.
May 15   to servants, 9s. 6d.
June 10   to a poor man, 6d.
June 26   to the poor, 2s. 6d.
July 24   to the poor, 7s.
Aug. 14   to the poor, 6d.
Oct. 16   aid to sick people, 5s.
Dec. 4   aid to the poor, 4s.
NE, II   pp. 58-110.

December, 1651-March, 1652:
Jan. 27   to a soldier, 5s.
Mar. 3   to a man who cut his foot, 2s. 6d.
Mar. 8   to a man who cut his leg, 2s. 6d.
NE, III   pp. 111-30.

February-December, 1653:
Mar. 9   paid doctor's fee for treating 3 persons, 2 pounds.
Apr. 3   paid doctor's fee for a woman, 10 pounds.
NE, IV   pp. 131-69.

February, 1658-February, 1659:
June 30   to the poor, 2s. 6d.
Feb. 2   paid doctor's fee for treatment of a man, 3 pounds.
July 7   paid to a schoolmaster, 2 pounds 10s.
Aug. 11   to a poor minister, 10s.
Nov. 17   paid to a schoolmaster, 2 pounds 10s. paid to another schoolmaster, 1 pound.
NE, V   pp. 170-206.

APPENDIX VII

A chronology of statutes pertaining to the relief of the poor:

1349   Re regulation of begging. *SR*, I, 23 Edw. III. C. 7.

1391   At the appropriation of a church, money shall be set aside annually for the care of the poor. *SR*, II, 15 Rich. II. C. 6.

1541-42   Act for continuing former vagrancy and poor laws. *SR*, III, 33 Hen. VIII. C. 10.

1541-42   Act for continuing former vagrancy and poor laws. *SR*, III, 33 Hen. VIII. C. 17.

1545   Act for continuing former vagrancy and poor laws. *SR*, III, 37 Hen. VIII. C. 23.

1547   For punishment of vagrancy and relief of the poor. *SR*, IV, Pt. I, 1 Edw. VI. C. 3.

1551-52   For poor relief and against vagrancy. *SR*, IV, Pt. I, 5 & 6 Edw. VI. C. 2.

1555   Re poor relief. *SR*, IV, Pt. I, 2 & 3 Phil. & Mar. C. 5.

1562-63   Act for poor relief. *SR*, IV, Pt. I, 5 Eliz. C. 3.

1572   Bill read relative to vagrancy control and poor relief. *JHL*, I, 14 Eliz.

1572   Second reading of bill relative to vagrancy control and poor relief. *JHC*, I, 14 Eliz.

1572   For punishment of vagrants and relief of the poor. *SR*, IV, Pt. I, 14 Eliz. C. 5.

1575-76   Act for poor relief. *SR*, IV, Pt. I, 18 Eliz. C. 3.

1592-93   "An acte for Relief of Souldiours." *SR*, IV, Pt. II, 35 Eliz. C. 4.

1592-93   London: against new buildings for the poor. *SR*, IV, Pt. II, 35 Eliz. C. 6.

1597   Act for establishing certain land in Berks for poor relief and other causes. *JHL*, II (Nov. 24 & Dec. 1).

1597-98   Act to continue and explain former act (35 Eliz. C. 4) for relief of soldiers and sailors. *SR*, IV, Pt. II, 39 Eliz. C. 21.

1597-98   Act for poor relief. *SR*, IV, Pt. II, 39 Eliz. C. 3.

1597-98   For establishing hospitals and workhouses. *SR*, IV, Pt. II, 39 Eliz. C. 5.

1601   For relief of soldiers. *SR*, IV, Pt. II, 43 Eliz. C. 3.

1601   Act for poor relief. *SR*, IV, Pt. II, 43 Eliz. C. 2.

1601   Act to correct misuse of charitable funds. *SR*, IV, Pt. II, 43 Eliz. C. 4.

1603-1604   Poor relief act for plague victims. *SR*, IV, Pt. II, 1 Ja. I. C. 31.

1623-24   Act for establishing hospitals and workhouses. *SR*, IV, Pt. II, 21 Ja. I. C. 1.

1627   Act for continuing certain poor-law and vagrancy statutes. *SR*, V, 3 Ch. I. C. 5.

A chronology of royal proclamations, acts of the privy council, and other measures for the relief of the poor:

1509   Henry VII's will: 2,000 pounds for distribution as alms. *CSP*, 1509-30, I, 1.

1509   Henry VII's funeral: alms distributed to the poor on two days. *CSP*, 1509-30, I, 19.

1509   Goods of felons "*de se*" and "*deodands*" to augment king's alms. *CSP*, 1509-30, I, 257 (31).

1511   License to the guild of the Virgin Mary and St. George of Southwark to collect alms for one year. *CSP*, 1509-30, I, 833-54.

1511   License to a monastery in Leicestershire to declare indulgences and collect alms due to decay and fire within the buildings. *CSP*, 1509-30, I, 924:2.

1511   King's gift of a corrody. *CSP*, 1509-30, I, 709.

1513   Disbursement of king's alms. *CSP*, 1509-30, I, 2295.

1513   Disbursement of king's alms. *CSP*, 1509-30, I, 2380.

1514   Goods, etc., of "felons *de see*" and "*deodands*" to augment the king's alms. *CSP*, 1509-30, I, 3499: (51).

1514   License to St. Mary Axe, London, to collect alms to repair the building. *CSP*, 1509-30, I, 2862: (4).

1537   Disbursement of king's alms. *CSP*, 1531-47, I, 1284 (Addenda).

1537   John Parkyns to Cromwell proposing almshouses for "impotent priests and others" and free grammar schools for poor children. *CSP*, 1531-47, XII, 261.

1539   Goods, etc., of suicides and deodands to augment king's alms. *CSP*, 1531-47, XIV, 619.

1539   Cites excellency of vagrancy and poor law. *CSP*, 1531-47, XIII, Pt. I, 402.

1543   License to the proctor of a house of lazars to gather alms for the inmates. *CSP*, 1531-47, XVIII, Pt. II, 535.

1545-46   Three wounded soldiers to become the king's almsmen. *APC*, I, 337.

1546-47   Widow received life pension from the crown. *APC*, II, 447.

1546-47   Re king's alms. *APC*, II, 62.

1547-48   Re king's alms. *APC*, II, 174.

1547-48   Re distribution of king's alms. *APC*, II, 174.

1548   Re distribution of king's alms. *APC*, II, 230.

1549   Seventeen wounded soldiers given two months pay and promised future care by the Church. *APC*, II, 313.

1550   Re king's alms. *APC*, III, 127.

1551   Re king's alms. *APC*, III, 332.

1552   Co. of Bucks: letter for application of recent statute for relief of the poor. *APC*, IV, 161-62.

1553   Re king's alms. *APC*, IV, 243.

Appendixes 167

1553 Certain bishop to aid three poor vicarages. *APC*, IV, 256-57.

1553 Two men making provision for distribution of alms before their execution. *APC*, IV, 359.

1554 Re queen's alms. *APC*, IX, 247.

1554 Distribution of queen's alms. *CSP*, 1547-80, I, 2:1.

1560 Will of Thomas Trepe of Warburton: bequeathal of refreshments to the poor at his funeral. *CSP*, 1547-80, VI, 9:83.

1560 Permission for a hospital and collection in Wales. *RP*, 535.

1563 Collection taken in the House of Commons for poor relief. *JHC*, I.

1565 London: begging licenses being forged. *APC*, VII, 257.

1565 London: man counterfeiting licenses to beg: punish as a "terror and example" to others. *APC*, VII, 257.

1571 Certain fines of the House of Commons to go to the poor-box. *JHC*, I.

1571 London: problem of beggars. *APC*, VIII, 52-53.

1571-72 London: problem of beggars. *APC*, VIII, 72-73.

1573 Permit for public collection for a church and hospital at Bath. *RP*, 680.

1574 Queen's instructions to the Council of the North to look into and redress any cases of oppression of the poor so that they do not take things into their own hands. *CSP*, 1547-80, VII, 23:59 (Addenda).

1574 Norfolkshire: a "Bridewell"-type house to be built. *APC*, VIII, 328.

1575? License to beg to merchant due to his losses at sea and sickness. *CSP*, 1547-80, I, 106:77.

1576 Letter to mayor of London urging him to put vagrants to work. *APC*, IX, 247.

1576 Estimate of repairs required for fourteen of the queen's almshouses. *CSP*, 1547-80, I, 108:64.

1576-77 Re license to beg for York man. *APC*, IX, 301.

1577? London: order for provision of poor relief to avoid begging. *CSP*, 1547-80, I, 120:50.

1578 Re license to beg for York man. *APC*, X, 285.

1579 Re ecclesiastical collection to provide stock of goods for work in house of correction in Winchester. *APC*, XI, 300.

1579 House of correction in Winchester working prisoners at making felt hats. *CSP*, 1547-80, I, 131:71.

1579 Queen's attorney for Island of Guernsey: inquiry as to why the queen's revenues are being used for poor relief. *CSP*, 1547-80, VII, 26:24: VI (Addenda).

1579? Council to Norfolk: control vagrants and build a "Bridewell"-type house of correction. *CSP*, 1547-80, I, 133.

1579-80 Preceding ecclesiastical collection (1579, *APC*, XI, 300) unsuccessful, so establish a committee to take care of the collection. *APC*, XI, 417.

1580 Petition of poor man relative to alleged wrongs suffered. *APC*, XII, 263.

1580 Letter to Gloucestershire re collection (previously ordered without results) for gaol prisoners. *APC,* XII, 272-73.

1580-81   Lynne (Norfolkshire): successful in raising funds for building a workhouse. *APC,* XII, 336.

1580-81   Dean of Canterbury shall see that an old soldier receives a pension. *APC,* XII, 344.

1581   Letter to all bishops to turn in all relief money collected for town of Portsmouth. *APC,* XIII, 276.

1581   Letter to Gloucestershire: money collected shall immediately be used for relief of gaol prisoners there. *APC,* XIII, 278.

1581?   Will of Sir William Cordell: property given for maintenance of a hospital or almshouse in Suffolk already established there by Sir Wm.

1582   Winchester: re funds raised for employment of vagrants. *CSP,* 1581-90, II, 153:16.

1582   Winchester: orders made for control of vagrants and poor relief. *CSP,* 1581-90, II, 153:17.

1582   Winchester: vagrants to receive work and whipping in the house of correction. *CSP,* 1581-90, 153:24.

1582?   Petition of disabled soldier for a pension. *CSP,* 1581-90, II, 157:70.

1583   Letter of Katherine Barthram to Walsingham requesting that the queen grant her an almsroom. *CSP,* 1581-90, II, 163:40.

1583   London: Irish beggars arrested and to be sent back to Ireland. *CSP,* 1581-90, II, 164:80.

1584?   Report on the estate of St. John's Hospital in Northampton formerly endowed by the earl of Northampton. *CSP,* 1581-90, II, 163:40.

1585   Petition by Christ's Hospital of Sherbourne. House to expand from sixteen to thirty inmates. *CSP,* 1581-90, II, 176:67.

1586   Privy council meeting for the purpose of signing orders for relief of the poor and for providing corn for the markets. *CSP,* 1581-90, II, 195:71.

1586   Re collection for Leicestershire town destroyed by fire. *APC,* XIV, 148.

1586   Cos. Chester and Lancaster: re collection of poor rate. *APC,* XIV, 187-88.

1586   London and Middlesex: punish sturdy and aid needy beggars. *APC,* XIV, 253.

1586   Re collection for Nottinghamshire town destroyed by fire. *APC,* XIV, 160-61.

1586-87   London: re protection of the funds for orphans. *APC,* XIV, 356-57.

1586-87   London: re cause of three orphans and aid for a poor woman. *APC,* XIV, 314.

1587   Cos. Norfolk and Suffolk: re collection for prisoner maintenance. *APC,* XV, 198.

1587-88   Gloucestershire: difficulty of collecting taxes for support of gaol prisoners. *APC,* XIV, 342-43.

1588 Suffolkshire: re aid needed for gaol prisoners. *APC*, XVI, 133-34.

1588 Shires of Dorset, Somerset, Hampton, Devon, Cornwall, Wilts: requested to employ houses of correction against vagrancy. *APC*, XVI, 146.

1589 Irish widow: license to beg returning to Ireland. *APC*, XVIII, 219.

1589 Order given that widow and children of Essex soldier receive poor relief. *APC*, XVIII, 209.

1589-90 Bristol: letter demanding protection for orphans. *APC*, XVIII, 408-409.

1590 Man granted an almsroom for life in Christ Church, Oxford. *CSP*, 1581-90, II, 232:29.

1590 Passport and license to beg to disabled soldier until almsroom vacant in Cambridge. *APC*, XX, 10-11.

1590 Norwich man: license to beg until almsroom vacant in Cathedral Church. *APC*, XX, 51.

1590 Poor, sick man given license to beg. *APC*, XX, 86.

1590 Wales: man given license to beg for three years to reestablish his decayed estate. *APC*, XX, 131.

1590 Man and family travelling: license to beg for one year. *APC*, XIX, 103.

1590 Man travelling: license to beg for one month. *APC*, XIX, 159.

1590 Man travelling: license to beg. *APC*, XIX, 159.

1590 Man travelling: license to beg. *APC*, XIX, 165-66.

1590 Man travelling: license to beg. *APC*, XIX, 187.

1590 Man and wife travelling: license to beg. *APC*, XIX, 194.

1590 Irishman and family: license to beg while travelling to Ireland. *APC*, XIX, 211.

1590 Irishman: license to beg. *APC*, XIX, 302.

1590 Man and wife travelling: license to beg. *APC*, XIX, 452.

1590 Poor man: license to beg. *APC*, XX, 51.

1590 Poor man: license to beg. *APC*, XX, 86.

1590 Wales dweller: license to beg for three years to reestablish his estate. *APC*, XX, 131.

1590-91 Poor, disabled soldier: passport and license to beg until he receives almsroom at Worcester Cathedral Church. *APC*, XX, 249.

1590-91 Poor, disabled soldier: license to beg until almsroom in Norwich Cathedral Church available. *APC*, XX, 241.

1590-91 Two poor, disabled soldiers: licenses to beg until almsrooms ready at Cathedral Churches of Westminster and Norwich. *APC*, XX, 296.

1590-91 London: orphans of a brewer being cheated. *APC*, XX, 310.

1591 Cos. Suffolk and Lancaster: letters to justices requesting aid for two poor, disabled soldiers. *APC*, XXII, 23.

1591 Kent: give aid to poor, disabled soldier until his almsroom available in Canterbury. *APC*, XXII, 28.

1591   Three poor, disabled soldiers: licenses to beg until almsrooms available. *APC*, XXII, 35.

1591   Poor, disabled soldier: provide for his relief. *APC*, XXII, 13.

1591   Poor, disabled soldier: license to beg until almsroom available at Peterborough. *APC*, XXII, 75.

1591   Poor, disabled soldier: license to beg until almsroom available at Christchurch College. *APC*, XXII, 117.

1591   London: soldier given job in a hospital. *APC*, XXI, 65.

1591   Cathedral of Durham: we have formerly asked that you aid these three men—see to it. *APC*, XXI, 79.

1591   Cathedral of Durham: rebuke for not caring for three men formerly recommended—see to it. *APC*, XXI, 92.

1591   Canterbury Cathedral: one man: provide for him. *APC*, XXI, 79.

1591   Canterbury Cathedral: aid this man and no more procrastination. *APC*, XXI, 93.

1591   St. Thomas Hospital: treat this man's wounds until he is able to accept almsroom at Canterbury. *APC*, XXI, 151.

1591   Kent: man formerly recommended: try to aid him until his almsroom ready. *APC*, XXI, 451-52.

1591   Three poor, disabled soldiers: licenses to beg while awaiting almsrooms. *APC*, XXII, 117.

1591   Warwickshire: poor, disabled soldier—provide for him. *APC*, XXII, 66.

1591   London: two poor, disabled soldiers needing aid until almsroom vacant—see to it. *APC*, XXII, 131.

1591   London: provide for a poor, disabled soldier. *APC*, XXII, 168.

1591   London: give employment to a poor, disabled soldier. *APC*, XXI, 292.

1591   Poor, disabled soldier: given passport and license to beg for three months. *APC*, XXI, 120-21.

1591   Two persons: given passports and licenses to beg on way to Ireland. *APC*, XXI, 248.

1591   Three Irish women given passports and licenses to beg on way to Ireland. *APC*, XXI, 280.

1591   Irishman and family given passport and license to beg on way to Ireland. *APC*, XXI, 359.

1591   Warwickshire: poor, disabled soldier given license to beg until almsroom ready. *APC*, XXI, 389.

1591   Sailor given license to beg. *RP*, 835.

1591   Royal proclamation: many wanderers pretending to be soldiers. Officials to aid the real soldiers and punish the false ones. *CSP*, 1591-1625, III, 240:60.

1591   Two persons: license to beg travelling to Ireland. *APC*, XXI, 248.

1591   Irish woman: license to beg travelling to Ireland. *APC*, XXI, 280.

1591   Irishman and family: license to beg travelling to Ireland. *APC*, XXI, 359.

1591-92   London and vicinity: look into the situation of wandering soldiers. Aid those in need and punish those pretending to be soldiers and other able-bodied persons not in need. *APC*, XXII, 295-96.

1591-92   Norfolkshire: provide for a poor disabled soldier until almsroom ready at Christ Church, Norwich. *APC*, XXII, 323-24.

1591-92   Letter to dean of Chester: provide for a poor, disabled soldier until his almsroom ready at the Chester almshouse. *APC*, XXII, 343.

1591-92   Area not given: provide for poor, disabled soldier. *APC*, XXII, 356.

1591-92   Devonshire: poor, disabled soldier—provide for until almsroom is ready in Cathedral Church, Gloucester. *APC*, XXII, 228.

1591-92   Kent: poor, disabled soldier—you ignored our first request for his aid—see to it. *APC*, XXII, 272.

1592   London: provide for poor, disabled soldier. *APC*, XXII, 446.

1592   Suffolkshire: poor, disabled soldier given license to beg for six months. *APC*, XXII, 534.

1592   Ireland, Lord Deputy: provide for a poor, disabled soldier. *APC*, XXII, 558.

1592   Letter to dean at Worcester: provide for poor, disabled soldier and family until almsroom is vacant at Cathedral Church, Worcester. *APC*, XXIII, 207.

1592   Letter to mayor of London: send money for poor, disabled soldiers that was collected in London for that purpose. *APC*, XXII, 468.

1592   Lincoln Castle prisoners suffering starvation. *APC*, XXIII, 339-40.

1592   Re queen's alms. *APC*, XXIII, 382.

1592   Woman and children: license to beg returning to Ireland. *APC*, XXII, 572.

1592-93   Lincolnshire: provide for soldier. *APC*, XXIV, 46.

1592-93   Rochester: provide for soldier and family. *APC*, XXIV, 46.

1592-93   Rochester: same case as *APC*, XXIV, 46—order that they be given an almsroom. *APC*, XXIV, 132.

1593   Letter to dean of Chester: you failed to provide for soldier as requested—see to it. *APC*, XXIV, 149-50.

1593   Dean of Norwich: provide for a soldier. *APC*, XXIV, 168.

1593   Letter to mayor of London: an earlier letter requested that money that had been collected for wounded soldiers be sent to the council. It has not been sent—send it at once. *APC*, XXIV, 170-71.

1593   London and Westminster: about 100 poor, disabled soldiers being provided for by parliament. Do not allow them to beg or they will lose their allowance and be punished. *APC*, XXIV, 178-79, 191-93.

1593   Sheriffs and justices of the realm to provide relief for wounded soldiers according to provisions of recently passed statute. *APC*, XXIV, 298-301.

1593   Dean of Chester: provide for soldier. *APC*, XXIV, 184.

1593   Huntingdon: provide for soldier. *APC*, XXIV, 293.

1593   Kent: provide for soldier. *APC*, XXIV, 293.

1593   Salop: soldier: provide for his care. *APC*, XXIV, 468.

1593   Lords Lieutenant to provide for wounded soldiers until the recent act of parliament can be put into execution. *EJ*, I, 233 (source: *APC*, XXIV, 178).

1593   London: rogues and vagabonds to be either removed or punished and poor, disabled soldiers to receive relief. *APC*, XXIV, 193-96.

1593   Commission appointed to examine soldiers claiming to be wounded. *EJ*, I, 221 (source: *APC*, XXIV, 159).

1593   House of Lords to make a contribution to aid wounded soldiers. *EJ*, I, 221-22 (source: D'Ewes' *Journals*, p. 463; Townshend, p. 42).

1593   Man and family: license to beg returning to Scotland. *APC*, XXIV, 424.

1593   Man given license to beg returning to Scotland. *APC*, XXIV, 488.

1593   London: re vagrant and poverty problems. *APC*, XXIV, 193-96.

1593-94   London: money from butchers' licenses to be used for relief of poor, disabled soldiers. *APC*, XXV, 515.

1594   Letter to hospitals about provision for poor, disabled soldiers. *APC*, XXV, 520.

1594   License to Sir John Hawkins for building of a hospital in Kent for ten or more mariners. *CSP*, 1591-1625, III, 249:23.

1595   Cornwall and other counties: collection made to relieve those who suffered as a result of the recent invasion of Cornwall. *EJ*, II, 67 (source: *APC*, XXV, 129).

1595   Lancastershire: letter to justices to levy a heavier rate on the parishes for aid to poor, disabled soldiers. *APC*, XXV, 9.

1595   Shires Pembroke and Hartfordwest: provide for one soldier. *APC*, XXV, 12.

1595   Suffolk: provide for one soldier. *APC*, XXV, 16-17.

1595   Warwickshire: soldier not cared for as formerly requested—see to it. *APC*, XXV, 119-20.

1595   Bristol: taxes for support of almshouse not being paid. *APC*, XXV, 10-11.

1595   Pension to a soldier wounded in warfare. *CSP*, 1591-1625, IV, 251:21.

1595-96   Brecknockshire: care for this soldier. *APC*, XXV, 142.

1595-96   Cornwall: care for this soldier. *APC*, XXV, 148.

1595-96   Staffordshire: care for this soldier to whom you formerly refused aid. *APC*, XXV, 182.

1595-96   Northumberland: care for this soldier. *APC*, XXV, 188.

1595-96   Letter to Lord Deputy of Ireland re failure to consider a soldier's claim. *APC*, XXV, 199.

1595-96   Letter to Lord Deputy of Ireland: provide pension for this soldier. *APC*, XXV, 247.

1595-96   Monmouthshire: renew this soldier's pension which you failed to do previously. *APC*, XXV, 249-50.

1595-96   Oxon: care for this soldier. *APC*, XXV, 291.

1595-96   Monmouth: care for this soldier. *APC*, XXV, 291.

1595-96   London: care for this soldier. *APC*, XXV, 291.

1596   Order for aid to a poor man. *APC*, XXV, 357.

1596   Permit for public collection for prisoners in the Marshalsea. *RP*, 887.

1596 and 1602   Devonshire: two towns suffered loss by fire—justices levied collections and quartered the homeless on other parishes. Rowse, p. 350.

1596   Pension granted to an old soldier. *CSP*, 1591-1625, IV, 260:112.

1596   Grant to a wounded soldier of an almsroom at Durham Cathedral. *CSP*, 1591-1625, IV, 261:25.

1596   Letter to Lord Deputy of Ireland: against sending soldiers from Ireland to England for care—care for them there. *APC*, XXV, 386-87.

1596   Soldier given license to beg for one year until almsroom in Westminster available. *APC*, XVI, 24.

1596   Hartfordshire: soldier recommended for aid by previous letter—see to it. *APC*, XXVI, 74-75.

1596   Lord Deputy of Ireland: soldier sent to England being sent back to Ireland for relief. *APC*, XXVI, 77.

1596   Newcastle: care for this soldier. *APC*, XXVI, 115.

1596   Radnorshire: care for this soldier. *APC*, XXVI, 117-18.

1596   Dean of Durham: provide for this soldier and give him an almsroom. *APC*, XXVI, 153-54.

1596   Berkshire: soldier denied payment of pension—why? *APC*, XXVI, 168.

1596   Leicestershire: soldier denied payment of his pension—why? *APC*, XXVI, 201.

1596   "Brecnock": soldier denied aid—check into this and give him relief. *APC*, XXVI, 265.

1596   Monmouthshire: continue the pension of this soldier which you have discontinued. *APC*, XXVI, 317.

1596   Shires Denbigh, Radnor, Worcester: aid these four soldiers. *APC*, XXVI, 343.

1596   Letter to Lord Deputy of Ireland: keep own soldiers and care for them—do not send them to England. *APC*, XXV, 391-92.

1596   Area not identified: care for seaman's wife in need while he is at sea. *APC*, XXV, 355.

1596   Suffolkshire: soldier's relief money still due—pay it to his widow. *APC*, XXV, 407-408, 412.

1596   Merionethshire: why was this soldier's pension stopped? *APC*, XXVI, 348.

1596   Lincolnshire: care for this soldier. *APC*, XXVI, 404.

1596-97   Warwickshire: you refused this soldier aid—care for him. *APC*, XXVI, 463-64.

1596-97   Kent: soldier denied his pension—see to it. *APC*, XXVI, 436.

1596-97   Devonshire: soldier's pension to be paid to his representative. *APC*, XXVI, 513.

1596-97   Lincolnshire: see to the care of a blind sailor whom you refused to aid. *APC*, XXVI, 513-14.

1596-97   London: care for this soldier. *APC*, XXVI, 526-27.

1596-97   Bedfordshire: care for this soldier. *APC*, XXVI, 556-57.

1597   Grant to poor soldier of an almsroom in Canterbury. *CSP*, 1591-1625, IV, 262:18.

1597   Soldier who received a pension in 1594 now granted one for life. *CSP*, 1591-1625, IV, 264:38.

1597   Almsroom in Peterborough to a wounded soldier. *CSP*, 1591-1625, IV, 264:38.

1597   Will of the Lord Warden of the Five Ports and Chamberlain (Lord Cobham): part of estate to be used for maintenance of the poor at Cobham and for the erection of a college for the poor. *CSP*, 1591-1625, IV, 262-48.

1597   City of Hereford: care for this soldier. *APC*, XXVII, 5.

1597   Dean of Rochester: give this soldier his almsroom without further ado. *APC*, XXVII, 125-26.

1597   Wiltshire: soldier refused relief—aid him or give reason why not. *APC*, XXVII, 147.

1597   Salopshire: restore this soldier's pension without fail. *APC*, XXVII, 211.

1597   Berkshire: resume paying this soldier's pension. *APC*, XXVII, 289-90.

1597   Dean of Durham: pay this soldier what is due him or show cause why not. *APC*, XXVII, 303.

1597   West Riding, Yorkshire: restore this soldier's pension. *APC*, XXVII, 339.

1597   Town of "Barwick": provide for this soldier. *APC*, XXVII, 339-40.

1597   Essex: provide for this soldier. *APC*, XXVII, 364.

1597   Worcester dean: care for this soldier. *APC*, XXVIII, 101.

1597   Monmouthshire: soldier complains that one-half of pension withheld. *APC*, XXVIII, 102.

1597   Staffordshire: man's pension taken away—why? *APC*, XXVIII, 150.

1597   Staffordshire: restore this man's withheld pension. *APC*, XXVIII, 172.

1597   London: care for this man. *APC*, XXVIII, 173.

1597   Staffordshire: care for this soldier. *APC*, XXVIII, 181.

1597   Norfolk: care for this soldier. *APC*, XXVIII, 199.

1597   London: care for this soldier. *APC*, XXVIII, 205-206.

1597-98   Herefordshire: man's pension revoked—why?—restore it. *APC*, XXVIII, 229-30.

1597-98   Devonshire: why has this man's pension been denied?—see to it. *APC*, XXVIII, 266.

1597-98   Northamptonshire: why did you refuse this worthy man? *APC*, XXVIII, 323.

1597-98   London: provide for these three mariners. *APC*, XXVIII, 341.

1597-98   Essex: provide for this soldier. *APC*, XXVIII, 352.

1597-98   Denbighshire: provide for this man. *APC*, XXVIII, 356.

1597-98   Salop: provide for this man. *APC*, XXVIII, 356-57.

1597-98   Glamorgan: provide this man's pension that was withdrawn. *APC*, XXVIII, 365.

1597-98   Salop: this man denied care—see to it. *APC*, XXVIII, 372.

1598   Yorkshire: continue this revoked pension. *APC*, XXVIII, 381.

1598   Radnor: continue this revoked pension. *APC*, XXVIII, 382.

1598   Norfolk: provide for this soldier. *APC*, XXVIII, 393.

1598   Kent: provide for this seaman. *APC*, XXVIII, 394.

1598   Devonshire: provide for this man. *APC*, XXVIII, 403.

1598   Denbigh: provide for this man. *APC*, XXVIII, 404.

1598   Surrey: provide for these two men. *APC*, XXVIII, 409.

1598   "Hartfordshire": provide for this man. *APC*, XXVIII, 412.

1598   London: provide for this man. *APC*, XXVIII, 417.

1598   Staffordshire: provide for this man and pay back relief due him. *APC*, XXVIII, 417.

1598   Surrey: provide for this man. *APC*, XXVIII, 423.

1598   Northamptonshire: provide for this man. *APC*, XXVIII, 490.

1598   Berkshire: place this man in the almshouse there in the vacancy that was previously refused him because it had been sold by the former occupant before his death. The present man has wife and children. *APC*, XXVIII, 633.

1598   "License to erect a hospital in Buckingham for 36 maimed unmarried soldiers dwelling in the town or three hundreds of co. Bucks, and to purchase lands for their maintenance, not exceeding 2001. a year." *CSP*, 1591-1625, V, 266:34.

1598   "Grant to . . . a maimed soldier, of an alms-room in Worcester." *CSP*, 1591-1625, V, 268:54.

1598   Re collection for town of Tiverton due to fire loss. *APC*, XXVIII, 452.

1598   License to build a hospital in Buckingham for thirty-six disabled soldiers. *CSP*, 1591-1625, V, 266:34.

1598   Disabled soldier: almsroom granted in Worcester. *CSP*, 1591-1625, V, 268:54.

1598   Hertfordshire: this soldier referred to you several times—see to his care. *APC*, XXIX, 235-36.

1598   Letter to bishop of Durham: aid this soldier. *APC*, XXIX, 261-62.

1598   Devonshire: aid this soldier. *APC*, XXIX, 264.

1598-99   Dorsetshire: seaman sent to you and refused care—see to it. *APC*, XXIX, 534-35.

1599   Co. Surrey: pay this seaman's unpaid stipend. *APC*, XXIX, 675.

1599   Carlisle: poor soldier granted almsroom. *CSP*, 1591-1625, V, 271:7.

1599   Worcester: soldier granted almsroom. *CSP*, 1591-1625, V, 271:7.

1599   Several items of payments of pensions requested and payments received from the treasurer for disabled soldiers "in 11 hundreds of Surrey West." *CSP*, 1591-1625, V, 271:42-65.

1599?   Queen's letter relative to proposed state management of Cornwall tin mines for relief of 12,000 poor families of miners. *CSP*, 1591-1625, V, 273:74.

1599   Grant of an almsroom to one born lame. *CSP*, 1591-1625, V, 270:118.

1599   Grant of an almsroom to a crippled female. *CSP*, 1591-1625, V, 270:118.

1599?   Court at Greenwich to a hospital: admit an orphan as an alms-child, despite rules to contrary, or he is likely to die. *CSP*, 1591-1625, V, 273:75.

1599   "Grant . . . maimed soldier, of an alms-room in Norwich Cathedral." *CSP*, 1591-1625, V, 271:15.

1599   "Grant . . . a maimed soldier, of an alms-room in Gloucester Cathedral." *CSP*, 1591-1625, V, 271:15.

1599   "Grant to . . . an aged soldier, of an alms-room in St. Stephen's, Westminster." *CSP*, 1591-1625, V, 270:118.

1599   "Grant to . . . an aged soldier, of an alms-room in Ely." *CSP*, 1591-1625, V, 270:118.

1599   "Grant to . . . of a pension of 6d. a day, for service in the wars." *CSP*, 1591-1625, V, 270:118.

1599   "Grant to . . . a maimed soldier, of an alms-room in Donnington, cos. Berks." *CSP*, 1591-1625, V, 270:118.

1599   "Like grant in Leicester for . . . maimed soldier." *CSP*, 1591-1625, V, 270:118.

1599   "Like grant in Chester for . . . an aged soldier of Ireland." *CSP*, 1591-1625, V, 270:118.

1599   "Like grant in St. Peter's, Westminster, for . . . service in the wars." *CSP*, 1591-1625. V, 270:118.

1599-1600   University of Oxford: remove unworthy almsmen and provide for disabled soldiers. *APC*, XXX, 175-76.

1600   Offer of Sir Richard Martin to coin small money in order to help relieve the poor. *CSP*, 1591-1625, V, 276:65.

1600   Proposals of Captain Brickwell for aid to Darlington fire refugees by means of local relief and a collection. *CSP*, 1591-1625, V, 275:44.

1600   Salopshire: pension this soldier. *APC*, XXX, 263.

1600   Norfolkshire: resume payments of this soldier's pension. *APC*, XXX, 267.

1600   Cathedral at Oxford: remove unworthy almsmen and provide for this soldier until an almsroom is vacant. *APC*, XXX, 330.

1600   Devonshire, "Brecknocke" (shire), Surrey and Anglesey: provide pensions for these soldiers. *APC*, XXX, 348.

1600   Dorsetshire: provide for this soldier. *APC*, XXX, 403.

1600 Worcestershire: pay this soldier's overdue pension payments. *APC*, XXX, 475.

1600 Shire Cardigan: provide for this soldier. *APC*, XXX, 475.

1600 Worcestershire: after several requests this soldier still has received no aid—why? *APC*, XXX, 605-606.

1600 Letter to Lord Deputy of Ireland: provide for this soldier. *APC*, XXXI, 71-72.

1600-1601 Surrey: provide for this soldier. *APC*, XXXI, 102.

1601 Collection for the poor to be taken in the House of Lords. *JHL*, II.

1601 Leicestershire and town of Leicester: you ignored our letter of appeal for this seaman's relief—see to it. *APC*, XXXII, 45-46.

1601 Oxford University: give this soldier the next almsroom vacant. *APC*, XXXII, 92.

1601 Bedfordshire: care for this sailor. *APC*, XXXII, 366.

1601 London: care for this soldier. *APC*, XXXII, 389.

1601 Devonshire: care for this soldier. *APC*, XXXII, 418.

1601 License to beg to woman in Ireland. *APC*, XXXII, 33.

1601 Suffolkshire: merchant had losses at sea and given license to collect for one year. *APC*, XXXII, 430-31.

1601 Re town of Fordham's petition for public collection due to fire loss. *APC*, XXXII, 16.

1601 Town of Walton re public collection due to fire loss. *APC*, XXXII, 179-80.

1601 Town of Bastingstoke re public collection due to fire loss. *APC*, XXXII, 420-21.

Undated Exchequer accounts of payments made to disabled soldiers in Corn wall. *CSP*, 1591-1625, VI (1601-1603), 388:36.

1603 Westminster: re problem of poor relief. *APC*, XXXII, 503.

1603 Lancastershire: re problem of collecting poor tax. *APC*, XXXII, 505.

1603 Man licensed to beg. *RP*, 978.

1603-1604 Lancastershire: re proposal to build a house of correction. *APC*, XXXII, 507-508.*

APPENDIX VIII

A chronology of grain and food: statutes, acts of the privy council, royal proclamations, etc.:

1491 Against exporting grain without license. *RP*, 18.
1521-22 Re provision of grain for London. *RP*, 80.

---

*This list could be extended through the Stuart era.

1522   Against export of grain from southern counties. *RP*, 87.

1527   Bread scarce in England, especially London, and many died. The king provided supplies of grain to London. Stow, p. 537.

1527   Against speculation in grain and for furnishing London with grain. *RP*, 110.

1529   Against speculating in grain. *RP*, 117.

1529   Against speculating in grain and for supplying grain to the markets. *RP*, 119.

1533   Re butchers. *RP*, 133.

1534   Against price fixing by butchers. *RP*, 143.

1534   Against speculating in grain. *RP*, 146.

1535   Against price fixing by butchers. *RP*, 149.

1535   Re allowing butchers to raise prices. *RP*, 154.

1536   Re allowing butchers to sell meat by retail. *RP*, 157.

1540   Privy council: food speculators at court to be pilloried. *CSP*, 1531-47, XVI, 10.

1542   Against speculating in grain. Becon, p. 253.

1543-44   Against export of grain and food. *RP*, 248.

1544   Regulation of the price of meat. *RP*, 256.

1545   Against grain speculation. *APC*, I, 259.

1545   Against grain speculation. *APC*, I, 261.

1545   Against grain speculation. *APC*, I, 283.

1545   Against grain speculation. *APC*, I, 290.

1545-46   Regulation of food exports. *RP*, 286.

1545-47   Regulation of buying and selling of food. *RP*, 298.

1548-49   Regulations on grain and food. *RP*, 342.

1550   Against export of grain and food, for supplying the markets and for price control. *RP*, 389.

1550   Same as *RP*, 389 preceding. *RP*, 390.

1550   Re lack of food in the realm and a list of certain foods not exportable. *APC*, III, 27.

1550-51   Letter directing that grain be supplied to Berwick. *APC*, III, 208.

1551   Letter directing that grain be supplied to certain areas in Suffolk. *APC*, III, 242.

1551   Against speculation in grain. *RP*, 402.

1551   Regulation of food prices. *RP*, 405.

1551   Against food speculators. *APC*, III, 318.

1561-62   Against speculation in grain. *RP*, 558.

1566   For control of pests that destroy food supplies. *APC*, IV, Pt. I, 498-99.

1576   Re scarcity of grain in London. *APC*, IX, 206.

1576   Re scarcity of grain in England. *APC*, IX, 210.

1586   Privy council orders re poor relief and for supplying grain to the markets. *CSP*, 1581-90, II, 195:71.

1586   Against grain speculation and for supplying grain to the markets at reasonable prices. Holinshed, pp. 944-45.

1586   Herefordshire: money for building house of correction to be used to buy grain for the needy people at reasonable prices. *APC*, XIV, 236-37.

1587   Hastings: grain scarce and market to be supplied for the aid of the poor. *APC*, XV, 23.

1589   Grain shortage in the realm and export of this item to cease. Also, markets to be supplied so that the poor may have grain at a fair price. *APC*, XVIII, 280-81, 284-85.

1595   Grain prices high this year; food scarce in London. *EJ*, II, 39. (source: Stow's *Annales*).

1595   Leicestershire: poor people suffering due to the high price of grain. *EJ*, II, 50. (source: *APC*, XXV, 7).

1595   Grain and food high priced in many counties due to slackness on part of the justices and the activity of the grain speculators. Grain to be made available at reasonable prices by the justices. *EJ*, II, 52-53. (source: *APC*, XXV, 25, 31).

1596   Grain in short supply and prices high. *RP*, 884.

1596   London's mayor to supervise sale and distribution of the cargo of twenty grain laden ships so that the poor may benefit and the grain not fall into the hands of the speculators. *EJ*, II, 147-48. (source: *APC*, XXVI, 281).

1596   Against grain speculation. Sheriffs and justices to alleviate the situation. Mayor of London to provide grain for the city. *EJ*, II, 127-28. (source: *APC*, XXVI, 81, 95-98).

1596   Privy council to mayor of London: avoid "excess of fare" in public and private diet due to the dearth at this time. *EJ*, II, 157-58. (source: *APC*, XXVI, 380, 383).

1596   Against grain speculators and export of grain and for supplying markets with grain. *RP*, 888.

1597   Dover: man accused of withholding grain of an almshouse ordered to give the inmates what is due them. *APC*, XXVII, 149-50.

1597   Against food speculators. *EJ*, II, 205. (source: *APC*, XXVII, 359).

1597   A bill for relief of the poor in time of grain shortage. *JHL*, II.

1598   A bill against export of grain and for purchase of the same for relief of the poor. *JHL*, II.

1598   For restraining and punishing grain speculators—they brought about the shortages. *RP*, 898.

1598   Lincolnshire: grain speculators have produced a shortage of food and discontent among the people. *EJ*, II, 286. (source: *APC*, XXVIII, 537).

1598   Dartmouth: mayor and businessmen speculating in unlawfully seized grain. *EJ*, II, 277. (source: *APC*, XXVIII, 438).

1600   Against speculation in grain. *EJ*, III, 122. (source: *APC*, XXX, 733).

1600   Against slander of the queen and against grain speculators. *RP*, 909.

1601   Against destruction of food supplies by vagrants. *SR*, IV, Pt. II, 43 Eliz. C. 7.

1604   Speculators have raised food prices and the prices shall be regulated. *RP*, 994.

1608   For preventing and remedying the shortage of grain and other food. *RP*, 1058.

1608   Twelve new granaries and two storehouses built in London. Stow, p. 907.

1612-13   Grain scarce and not to be exported. *RP*, 1126.

1622   For poor relief and remedying of high grain prices. *RP*, 1344.

1623   For storing and furnishing the realm with grain. *RP*, 1365.

1630   For preventing shortage of grain and food. *RP*, 1624.

Notes

NOTES TO CHAPTER I

1. Gilbert Burnet, *The History of the Reformation of the Church of England*, ed. N. Pocock (Oxford: Clarendon Press, 1865), III, 208.

2. Wilbur K. Jordan, *The Charities of Rural England, 1480-1660: The Aspirations and Achievements of the Rural Society* (London: George Allen & Unwin, Ltd., 1961), 377-78.

3. Public Record Office, *State Papers of King Henry VIII* (London: John Murray, 1831), IV, 489.

4. *Acts of the Privy Council, 1542-1628*, ed. John R. Dasent *et al.* (London: Eyre and Spottiswoode for Her Majesty's Stationery Office, 1890-1949), XXXIV, 204-205, 278-83, 312-13.

5. Sidney J. Herrtage (ed.), *Starkey's Life and Letters*, Pt. 1 of *England in the Reign of King Henry the Eighth* (Early English Text Society, Extra Series, Vol. X, nos. 12, 32; London: N. Trubner & Co., 1878), lxxxviii, 16, 17:106-19. From: Appendix: An extract from Sir William Forrest's *Pleasaunt Poesie of Princelie Practise* (1548).

6. David Knowles, *The Religious Orders in England*, Vol. III: *The Tudor Age* (Cambridge University Press, 1959), 247; Jordan, *The Charities of Rural England*, 360-61.

7. Thomas Starkey, *A Dialogue Between Cardinal Pole and Thomas Lupset, Lecturer in Rhetoric at Oxford*, Pt. 2 of *England in the Reign of King Henry the Eighth*, ed. J. M. Cowper (Early English Text Society, Extra Series, Vol. X, nos. 12, 32; London: N. Trubner & Co., 1878), 82, 102.

8. Alexander Savine, *English Monasteries on the Eve of the Dissolution*, Vol. I of *Oxford Studies in Social and Legal History*, ed. Paul Vinogradoff (Oxford: Clarendon Press, 1909), 231, 241; Wilbur K. Jordan, *Philanthropy in England, 1480-1660: A Study of the Changing Pattern of English Social Aspirations* (London: George Allen & Unwin, Ltd., 1959), 59.

9. Simon Fish, *A Supplication for the Beggars* (ca. 1529), ed. F. J. Furnivall (Early English Text Society, Extra Series, Vol. XIII; London: N. Trubner & Co., 1871), 2-8; Edward P. Cheyney, *Social Changes in England in the Sixteenth Century: As Reflected in Contemporary Literature*, Pt. 1: *Rural Changes* (Publications of the University of Pennsylvania Series in Philology, Literature and Archaeology, Vol. IV, no. 2, 1895), 62.

10. John Stow, and E. Howes, *The Annales . . . of England* (London: Thomas Adams, 1615), 571; George M. Trevelyan, *History of England* (London: Longmans, Green and Co., 1927), 307; George G. Coulton, *Five Centuries of Religion*, Vol. IV: *The Last Days of Medieval Monachism* (Cambridge: University Press, 1950), 714; William E. Lunt, *History of England* (Rev. ed.; New York: Harper & Brothers, 1938), 314.

11. Geoffrey Baskerville, *English Monks and the Suppression of the Monasteries* (New Haven: Yale University Press, 1937), 185.

12. Public Record Office, *Calendar of Letters and Papers, Foreign and Domestic of the Reign of Henry VIII, 1531-1547*, ed. James Gairdner (London: His Majesty's Stationery Office, 1880-1910), X (1536), 364.

13. *The Victoria History of the Counties of England, London* (London: Constable and Co., Ltd., 1909), I, 506.

14. *Letters and Papers . . . Henry VIII, 1531-1547*, X (1536), 364.

15. *Ibid.*, X (1536), 364.

16. *Ibid.*, IX (1535), 434.

17. *Ibid.*, 139, 708.

18. *Ibid.*, XIV (1539), 1189.

19. *Ibid.*, XI (1536), 1437; IX (1535), 816; XIV (1539), 161; *The Victoria History . . . London, I, 506.*

20. *Letters and Papers . . . Henry VIII, 1531-1547*, XII, Pt. 1 (1537), 192; Burnet, *The History of the Reformation*, I, 357 (paraphrasing Nicholas Sanders' account); Raphael Holinshed, *Chronicles of England, Scotland, and Ireland*, Vol. IV: *England* (New York: Ams Press, Inc., 1965), 735.

21. R. H. Snape, *English Monastic Finances in the Later Middle Ages*, (Cambridge University Press, 1926), 174; Starkey, *A Dialogue, 156.*

22. Herrtage, *Starkey's Life and Letters*, liii, lvi, lviii; *Letters and Papers . . . Henry VIII, 1531-1547*, XII (1537), 548, XIV, Pt. 1 (1539), 988; *The Statutes of the Realm* (Dawsons of Pall Mall, 1963), III, 27 Hen. VIII. C. 28; Burnet, *The History of the Reformation*, II, xiii.

23. *State Papers of King Henry VIII*, I, 125; *Journals of the House of Lords* (London: Record Publication, 1846-), II, 39 Eliz., January 14, 1598.

NOTES TO CHAPTER II

1. *SR*, III, 27 Hen. VIII. C. 28.

2. *SR*, III, 31 Hen. VIII. C. 13. (1539); *Letters and Papers . . . Henry VIII, 1531-1547*, IX (1535), 472, 622, 632.

3. *Letters and Papers . . . Henry VIII, 1531-1547*, X (1536), 1191, 1246.

4. *Ibid.*, XI (1536), 2 (Appendix).

5. *Ibid.*, XIII, Pt. 1 (1538), 547, 1117, 1384; IX (1535), 822.

6. *Ibid.*, Pt. 2 (1538), 224, 866, 911, 1036, 1153.

7. *Ibid.*, IX (1535), 472, 509, 457, 6, 160, 139.

8. *Ibid.*, XIV, Pt. 1 (1539), 269.

9. *Ibid.*, XII, Pt. 1 (1537), 4, 1172.

10. *Ibid.*, X (1536), 383.

11. *Ibid.*, IX (1535), 866, 1075.

12. *Ibid.*, XIV, Pt. 1 (1539), 161, 207.

13. *The Victoria History . . . London*, I, 506, 459.

14. *Letters and Papers . . . Henry VIII, 1531-1547*, XV (1540), 19.

15. R. W. Chambers, "Literary History Lecture: The Saga and the Myth of Sir Thomas More," *Proceedings of the British Academy*, XII (1926), 205-209.

16. For an explanation of Tudor usage of the term hospital see pages 96-97 of this text. *Letters and Papers . . . Henry VIII, 1531-1547*, XIII (1538), 492; *SR*, III, 31 Hen. VIII. C. 13. *The Victoria History . . . London*, I, 494.

17. *Letters and Papers . . . Henry VIII, 1531-1547*, XIV, Pt. 2 (1539), 391, 623, 227, Pt. 1 (1539), 323, 246, 270; XV (1540), 60, 743, 691, 695.

18. *The Victoria History . . . London*, I, 533, 536-37, 538-41, 542-45, 546-47, 550, 581, 583.

19. *Ibid.*, I, 496-97, 528, 549, 551, 553.

20. *Letters and Papers . . . Henry VIII, 1531-1547*, XV (1540), 498; *The Victoria History of the Counties of England, County of York* (London: Constable and Co., Ltd., 1913), III: 143 (pp. 315-17), 151 (pp. 321-22), 176 (pp. 336-45).

21. William Cobbett, *A History of the Protestant Reformation in England and Ireland* (New York: Benziger Brothers, Printers to the Holy Apostolic See, n.d.), p. xi (Preface by F. A. Gasquet); Baskerville, *English Monks*, 38.

22. Alfred Leslie Rowse, *The Elizabethan Age*, Vol. I: *The England of Elizabeth: The Structure of Society* (London: Macmillan & Co., Ltd., 1950), 489-90, 496-97.

23. Knowles, *The Tudor Age*, 295.

24. Keith Feiling, *England Under the Tudors and Stuarts, 1485-1688* (Oxford University Press, 1927), 56-57.

25. See 7 and 26, herein.

26. Snape, *English Monastic Finances*, 111, 117-18; Henry Brinklow, *Complaynt of Roderyck Mors* (ca. 1542), ed. J. M. Cowper (Early English Text Society, Extra Series, Vol. XVI, no. 22; London: N. Trubner & Co., 1874), 32-33.

27. Jean Adrien Antoine Jules Jusserand, *English Wayfaring Life in the Middle Ages*, trans. L. T. Smith (New York: Barnes & Noble, 1961), 60-61; Baskerville, *English Monks*, 32. George M. Trevelyan, *Illustrated English Social History*, Vol. I: *Chaucer's England and the Early Tudors* (London: Longmans, Green and Co., 1949), 105.

28. Francis A. Gasquet, *Henry VIII and the English Monasteries* (London: George Bell & Sons, 1906), 462-64. He is quoting from a document: "Brit. Mus. Cole MS., XII. Written about the year 1591." He identifies the writer as "this anonymous writer." *State Papers of King Henry VIII*, III, 273.

29. *Letters and Papers . . . Henry VIII, 1531-1547*, X (1536), 215, 858; XII, Pt. 1 (1537), 901; XIV, Pt. 1 (1539), 200.

30. Brinklow, *Complaynt*, 9, 33.

31. Savine, *English Monasteries*; Knowles, *The Tudor Age*, 264-66.

32. Frank Aydelotte, *Elizabethan Rogues and Vagabonds*, Vol. I of *Oxford Historical and Literary Studies* (Oxford: Clarendon Press, 1913), 16.

33. *SR*, III, 27 Hen. VIII. C. 25 (1535-36).

NOTES TO CHAPTER III

1. Cobbett, *A History of the Protestant Reformation*, vi-viii (Preface by F. A. Gasquet).

2. B. Kirkman Gray, *A History of English Philanthropy from the Dissolution of the Monasteries to the Taking of the First Census* (London: P. S. King & Son, 1905), 34.

3. Robert Crowley, *The Select Works of Robert Crowley*, ed. J. M. Cowper (Early English Text Society, Extra Series, Vol. XII, no. 15; London: N. Trubner & Co., 1872), 11-12: 205-44. From "Epigrammes," 1550.

4. Rowse, *The England of Elizabeth*, 196.

5. Crowley, *Works*, 7:64-76. From: "Epigrammes": "Of Abbayes."

6. W. P. Hall et al. *A History of England and the British Empire* (3rd ed.; Boston: Ginn and Co., 1953), 269-70; Brinklow, *Complaynt*, 23; Thomas Becon, *Works of Thomas*

Becon, ed. John Ayre (Parker Society, Vols. II, III; Cambridge University Press, 1843-44), III, 435. From: "The Jewel of Joy." Becon, *Works*, II, 40. From: "Prologue" of "The News out of Heaven."

7. E. Jeffries Davis, "The Transformation of London," *Tudor Studies*, ed. R. W. Seton-Watson (London: Longmans, Green & Co., 1924), 303. See also 287, 300-303. Rowse, *The England of Elizabeth*, 235.

8. Burnet, *The History of the Reformation*, I, 264.

9. Anon., *A Supplication to . . . Henry VIII*, ed. F. J. Furnivall (Early English Text Society, Extra Series, Vol. XIII; London: N. Trubner & Co., 1871), (year 1544); Anon., *A Supplication of the Poor Commons*, ed. F. J. Furnivall (Early English Text Society, Extra Series, Vol. XIII; London: N. Trubner & Co., 1871), 79 (year 1546).

10. Trevelyan, *History of England*, 284.

NOTES TO CHAPTER IV

1. *SR*, I, 5 Edw. III. C. 14. (1331); 23 Edw. III. C. 7. (1349); II, 7 Rich. II. C. 5. (1383); 12 Rich. II. C. 7-10. (1388).

2. *Ibid.*, 15 Rich. II. C. 6. (1391); 11 Hen. VII. C. 2. (1495).

3. Jordan, *The Charities of Rural England*, 226, 232, 236, 373-75.

4. *Ibid.*, 180-81.

5. Wilbur K. Jordan, *The Charities of London, 1480-1660: The Aspirations and the Achievements of the Urban Society* (London: George Allen & Unwin, Ltd., 1960), 280-81.

6. Jordan, *The Charities of Rural England*, 62; Jordan, *The Charities of London*, 9 [sic] Preface.

7. Gray, *A History of English Philanthropy*, vii.

8. Jordan, *The Charities of Rural England*, 121, 151, 159; *The Victoria History . . . London*, I, 549; Peter Laslett, *The World We Have Lost* (London: Methuen & Co., Ltd., 1965), 243-44, no. 17.

9. Jordan, *The Charities of Rural England*, 41; Frederick George Marcham, *A Constitutional History of Modern England, 1485 to the Present* (New York: Harper & Brothers, 1960), 49-50; *Acts of the Privy Council*, X (1578), 422.

10. Jordan, *Philanthropy in England*, 77, 92-93.

11. A. C. Floriano (ed.), *El monasterio de Cornellana*, Vol. I of *Coleccion de fuentes para la historia de Asturias* (Oviedo: Seminario de Investigacion Diplomatica del I.D.E.A., 1949), 13; Alexandre Bruel (ed.), *Recueil des chartes de l'abbaye de Cluny* (Paris, 1876), I, 53, 141, 283; J. Depoin (ed.), *Recueil de chartes et documents de Saint-Martin-des-Champs, monastère Parisien* (Paris, 1912), I, 34.

12. G. F. Duckett (ed.), *Charters and Records: Ancient Abbey of Cluni from 1077 to 1534* (London, 1888), I, 121, 179, 180, 212, 213, 217, 251; *The Victoria History . . . London*, I, 539; *SR*, II, 2 Hen. V. C. 1.

13. *The Victoria History . . . London*, I, 497, 547, 528.

14. Brinklow, *Complaynt*, 32-33; G. B. Harrison (ed.), *The Elizabethan Journals: Being a Record of Those Things Most Talked of During the Years 1591-1603* (Ann Arbor: University of Michigan Press, 1955), II, 68.

15. J. H. Thomas, *Town Government in the Sixteenth Century* (London: George Allen & Unwin, Ltd., 1933), 118; *SR*, IV, Pt. II, 18 Eliz. C. 3. (1575-76); A. V. Judges (ed.), *The Elizabethan Underworld* (New York: E. P. Dutton & Co., 1930), Introduction.

16. Public Record Office, *Calendar of State Papers, Domestic Series, of the Reigns of Edward VI, Mary, Elizabeth, 1547-1580*, ed. Robert Lemon (London: Her Majesty's Stationery Office, 1856-1865), VII 26:24 (Addenda, 1566-79).

17. R. H. Tawney, *The Agrarian Problem in the Sixteenth Century* (New York: Burt Franklin, n.d.), 269, 280.

18. Robert Steele, *A Bibliography of Royal Proclamations of the Tudor and Stuart Sovereigns and of Others Published under Authority, 1485-1714*, Vol. I: *England and Wales* (New York: Burt Franklin, 1967), no. 121 (1530); *State Papers . . . 1547-1580*, VII (1555-79), 23:59.

19. C. J. Ribton-Turner, *A History of Vagrants and Vagrancy and Beggars and Begging* (London: Chapman and Hall, Ltd., 1887), 150.

20. John Taylor, *Works of John Taylor, the Water Poet*, ed. Charles Hindley (London: Reeves and Turner, 1872), 22. From: "A New Discovery by Sea, with a Wherry from London to Salisbury" (1623); Henry Brinklow, *The Lamentacyon of a Christen Agaynst the Cytye of London, Made by Roderigo Mors* (1545), ed. J. M. Cowper (Early English Text Society, Extra Series, Vol. XVI, no. 22; London: N. Trubner & Co., 1874), 80-81.

21. *Acts of the Privy Council*, XXXII (1603), 503; XXXIII (1614), 597-99, 661-62; XVIII (1589-90), 408-409; Taylor, *Works*, 11. From: "Part of this Summers Travels" (n.d.).

22. Hugh Latimer, *Sermons by Hugh Latimer, Sometime Bishop of Worcester* (London: J. M. Dent & Co., 1906), 59. From: "Sermon of the Plough." Gray, *A History of English Philanthropy*, 26-27.

23. Taylor, *Works*, 22. From: "A Verry Merry-Wherry-Ferry Voyage" (1622).

24. Thomas, *Town Government*, 26; Ribton-Turner, *A History of Vagrants*, 142.

25. *SR*, III (1543-44), 35 Hen. VIII. C. 4; Public Record Office, *Calendar of State Papers, Domestic Series, of the Reigns of Edward VI, Mary, Elizabeth I, and James I, 1591-1625*, ed. Mary Anne Green (London: Her Majesty's Stationery Office, 1867-72), V (1598), 268:120.

26. Burnet, *The History of the Reformation*, II, 367-68; Public Record Office, *Calendar of Letters and Papers, Foreign and Domestic of the Reign of Henry VIII, 1509-1530*, ed. J. S. Brewer (London: His Majesty's Stationery Office, 1864-1932), I (1509), 1, 19, 20, 257:31.

27. Public Record Office, *Calendar of State Papers, Domestic Series, of the Reigns of Edward VI, Mary, Elizabeth I, 1581-1590*, ed. Robert Lemon (London: Her Majesty's Stationery Office, 1856-72), II (1581?), 151:30, (1584?), 175:99; *State Papers . . . 1547-1580*, VI (1560), 9:83; *State Papers . . . 1591-1625*, III (1594), 249:23; IV (1597), 262:48; Trevelyan, *Chaucer's England and the Early Tudors*, 106.

28. Gray, *A History of English Philanthropy*, 19.

29. Steele, *Royal Proclamations*, I, 1591 (1629).

30. Thomas, *Town Government*, 130-32; Laslett, *The World We Have Lost*, 155.

31. *State Papers . . . 1591-1625*, V (1599?), 273:74.

32. Andrew Lang (ed.), *Social England Illustrated: A Collection of XVII Century Tracts* (Westminster: Archibald Constable & Co., Ltd., 1903), IX, 67-87. Publisher's note to this volume: "The texts . . . in the present volume are reprinted with . . . slight alterations from the *English Garner* issued in eight volumes (1877-1890), London, 8 vo.) by Professor [Edward] Arber."

33. Ribton-Turner, *A History of Vagrants*, 136-39.

34. Taylor, *Works*, 32. From: "A New Discovery by Sea."

35. *Acts of the Privy Council*, XI (1578-79), 84.

36. Starkey, *A Dialogue*, 197.

37. Even during sessions of the House of Lords and the House of Commons, collections and fines were levied for poor relief. See 90 herein, for specific citation of this.

NOTES TO CHAPTER V

1. *SR*, III (1530-31), 22 Hen. VIII. C. 12.

186   Thorns on the Tudor Rose

2. *Ibid.*, (1535-36), 27 Hen. VIII. C. 25.

3. Thomas More, *Utopia*, ed. and trans. H. V. S. Ogden (New York: Appleton-Century-Crofts, 1949), 6; *Letters and Papers . . . Henry VIII, 1509-1530*, II, 3204, 4676; IV, 105, 4310; *State Papers of King Henry VIII*, IV, Pt. 4, 177; Stow and Howes, *The Annales*, 572-73, 596, 618-19, 621, 662-64, 889.

4. Stow and Howes, *The Annales*, 769.

5. See Appendix I, 137, herein.

6. Godfrey Davies, *The Early Stuarts, 1603-1660*, Vol. IX of *The Oxford History of England*, ed. Sir George Clark (15 vols.; 2nd ed. rev.; Oxford: Clarendon Press, 1959), 126-27. Quoting from *Verney Memoirs*, ii. 69 and "The Round-heads Race," appended to *The Distractions of Our Times* (1642).

7. *Ibid.*, 127. Quoting from *Verney Memoirs* (1642) ii. 69.

8. A. E. Bland *et al.* (eds.), *English Economic History, Select Documents* (London: G. Bell & Sons, Ltd., 1915), 390-91.

9. Gladys Scott Thomson, *Lords Lieutenants in the Sixteenth Century: A Study in Tudor Local Administration* (London: Longmans, Green & Co., 1923), 2; Judges, *The Elizabethan Underworld*, xxxi.

10. Jusserand, *English Wayfaring Life*, 199.

11. May McKisack, *The Fourteenth Century, 1307-1399*, Vol. V of *The Oxford History of England*, ed. Sir George Clark (15 vols.; Oxford: Clarendon Press, 1959), 408; *Letters and Papers . . . Henry VIII, 1509-1530*, II, 3204, 3218, 3230, 3233, 3244, 3259.

12. *Letters and Papers . . . Henry VIII, 1509-1530*, IV, 4310.

13. Stow and Howes, *The Annales*, 572; J. D. Mackie, *The Earlier Tudors, 1485-1558*, Vol. VII of *The Oxford History of England*, ed. Sir George Clark (15 vols.; Oxford: Clarendon Press, 1952), 387, 389; *Letters and Papers . . . Henry VIII, 1531-1547*, XI (1536), 585, 670.

14. *Letters and Papers . . . Henry VIII, 1509-1530*, II, 4676.

15. *Letters and Papers . . . Henry VIII, 1531-1547*, XI, 782, 892:3, 1246, 705; XII, Pt. 1, 302, 478.

16. Stow and Howes, *The Annales*, 573.

17. *Letters and Papers . . . Henry VIII, 1531-1547*, XI, 780. "Henry VIII, to the Duke of Suffolk."

18. M. St. Clare Byrne (ed.), *The Letters of King Henry VIII: A Selection with a Few Other Documents* (New York: Funk and Wagnalls, 1968), Pt. 3, 168-69; *Letters and Papers . . . Henry VIII, 1531-1547*, XII,1, 764; XI (1536), 780.

19. Cheyney, *Social Changes in England*, 95-96; Anon., *A Supplication of the Poor Commons*, 83.

20. Brinklow, *Complaynt*, 15.

21. Crowley, *Works*, 22:553-560 and 23:589-592. From: "Epigrammes."

22. *Letters and Papers . . . Henry VIII, 1531-1547*, XII, Pt. 1, 302.

23. *State Papers . . . 1547-1580*, IV, Pt. 1, 3-4 Edw. VI. C. 5; Steele, *Royal Proclamations*, I, 362.

24. Cheyney, *Social Changes in England*, 98. Quoting from: "Letter from Duke of Somerset, Cotton MS., Galba, B. XII, leaf 115. Printed in Ballad Soc. Pub., Vol. I."

25. *State Papers . . . 1547-1580*, VII, 15:77 (Addenda, 1566-79).

26. *Ibid.*, 17:17, 15:139 (Addenda, 1555-79), 15:132 (Addenda, 1566-79).

27. Judges, *The Elizabethan Underworld*, xvii-xviii; *State Papers . . . 1581-1590*, II (1586), 188:47. "Justices of Gloucestershire to the Council."

28. *Acts of the Privy Council*, XXV, 88-89, 334.

29. Harrison, *The Elizabethan Journals*, I, 41-43. Quoting from Richard Cosin, *The Conspiracy for Pretended Reformation*. Steele, *Royal Proclamations*, I, 873; Harrison, *The Elizabethan Journals*, II, 32-33. Quoting from "A Proclamation against Unlawful

Assemblies."

30. Rowse, *The England of Elizabeth*, 90. See also: Steele, *Royal Proclamations*, I, 1041, 1042, "[Against rioters in Northamptonshire.]"

31. Crowley, *Works*, 39:1125-1132. From: "Epigrams."

32. Jusserand, *English Wayfaring Life*, xii.

33. *Ibid.*, 112-13.

34. Taylor, *Works*, 3, 6-7, 11. From: "The Whole Life and Progress of Henry Walker the Ironmonger."

35. Holinshed, *Chronicles of England*, IV, 56.

36. *Ibid.*, 561, 580.

37. *Letters and Papers . . . Henry VIII, 1531-1547*, XII, Pt. 1, 589:2; XIV, Pt. 1 (1539), 542.

38. *State Papers . . . 1547-1580*, I (1577), 188:27; *State Papers . . . 1581-1590*, II (1582), 152:72.

39. *Acts of the Privy Council*, XXVIII, 26, 28-29.

40. See Appendix II, 140, herein.

41. Samuel Rowlands, *The Runnagates Race, or the Originall of the Regiment of Rogues* (The Hunterian Club, No. XIX; London, 1872-73). 44-60. This volume is published under the title *Martin Mark-All, Beadle of Bridewell*, another of Rowland's works. *The Runnagates Race* was first published in 1610.

42. Aydelotte, *Elizabethan Rogues and Vagabonds*, 53; Gray, *A History of English Philanthropy*, 3.

43. William Harrison, *The Description of England* (1545), ed. Georges Edelen (The Folger Shakespeare Library; Cornell University Press, 1968), 194; Harrison, *The Elizabethan Journals*, II, 136 (Source: Strype, *Annales*, IV, 290, 291).

44. *Ibid.*, II, 137 (Source: Strype, *Annales*, IV, 290, 291); Judges, *The Elizabethan Underworld*, xviii-xix (Source: Tawney and Power, *Tudor Economic Documents*, II, 341-44). This document is given in the original in Aydelotte, *Elizabethan Rogues and Vagabonds*, Appendix A, 14, 167-73.

45. Savine, *English Monasteries*, 227; *Acts of the Privy Council*, XXXII, 503-504.

46. See Appendix III, 148, herein.

47. Steele, *Royal Proclamations*, I, 8, 472, 511, 871; Harrison, *The Elizabethan Journals*, II, 307 (Source: *Acts of the Privy Council*, XXXIX, 128, 140); II, 131-32 (Source: *Proclamations*, 376).

48. See Appendix IV, 160, herein.

49. More, *Utopia*, 9-11.

50. Crowley, *Works*, 137-38, 142-45, 149; 125; 67-69. From: "The Way to Wealth," "Pleasure and Payne," and "Voyce of the Last Trumpet."

51. *Ibid.*, This quotation is from J. M. Cowper's Introduction, xxii.

52. *Ibid.*, 168: 531-51, 34:960-64, 40-41:1169-92, 41:1193-1208, 46-47: 1369-88.

53. *Ibid.*,116-17:253-80, 483:470-76.

54. *Ibid.*

55. *Ibid.*, 66:317-28, 337-44.

56. Becon, *Works*, III, 434. From: "The Jewel of Joy"; 583-84, 593-94, 601-602. From: "Fortress of the Faithful."

57. Herrtage, *Starkey's Life and Letters*, lxxxvii. (Appendix), 12, 13, 14:78-98. An extract from Forrest's *Pleasaunt Poesye of Princelie Practise* (1548).

58. Starkey, *A Dialogue*, 86 (marginal note), 171; Philip Stubbes, *Anatomy of the Abuses in England in Shakspere's Youth, A.D. 1583*, ed. Frederick J. Furnivall (The New Shakspere Society, Ser. VI, no. 4, Pt. 1; Ser. VI, no. 6, Pt. 1; Ser. VI, no. 12, Pt. 2; London, N. Trubner, 1877, 1879, 1882).

59. Latimer, *Sermons*, 215; Philip Massinger, *A New Way to Pay Old Debts*, ed. and

intro. M. St. Clare Byrne (London: Falcon Educational Books, 1949), 5 (Introduction). A comedy and his "most famous play."

60. *Letters and Papers . . . Henry VIII, 1531-1547,* XII, Pt. 1 (1537), 98; XIV, Pt. 1 (1539), 42, 1350.

61. *The Statutes,* III, 6 Hen. VIII. C. 5; 7 Hen. VIII. C. 1; 25 Hen. VIII. C. 13; 27 Hen. VIII. C. 22; IV, Pt. 2 (1597-98), 39 Eliz. C. 1, 2. See Appendix V, 161, herein.

62. More, *Utopia,* 8.

63. See 51-53, 62, 107-08, herein.

NOTES TO CHAPTER VI

1. Crowley, *Works,* 96-97:1387-1408. From: "The Voyce of the Last Trumpet." *State Papers . . . 1591-1625,* V (1600?), 276:72.

2. Jordan, *Philanthropy in England,* 82; Massinger, *A New Way,* 31, 32.

3. *State Papers . . . 1547-1580,* VII, 23:59 (Addenda); Crowley, *Works,* 57:9-20. From: "The Voyce of the Last Trumpet."

4. See 52, herein.

5. *The Statutes,* II, 12 Rich. II. C. 7-10; II, 11 Hen. VII. C. 2; 19 Hen. VII. C. 12; Coulton, *The Last Days,* 715; Starkey, *A Dialogue,* 140-42.

6. Aydelotte, *Elizabethan Rogues and Vagabonds,* 61 and Appendix A, 1: pp. 140-42.

7. Steele, *Royal Proclamations,* I, 121, 155; *The Statutes,* III, 22 Hen. VIII. C. 10, 12.

8. *The Statutes,* III, 27 Hen. VIII. C. 25.

9. *Letters and Papers . . . Henry VIII, 1531-1547,* XVI, 945; XVIII, Pt. 2, 542; *The Statutes,* III, 33 Hen. VIII. C. 10.

10. *The Statutes,* IV, 1 Edw. V. C. 3; Latimer, *Sermons,* 164. From: "Fifth Sermon before King Edward the Sixth."

11. *The Statutes,* IV, Pt. 1, 3 & 4 Edw. VI. C. 16. 2 & 3 Phil. & Mary. C. 5.

12. *Ibid.,* 5 Eliz. C. 3; *Judges, The Elizabethan Underworld,* xl (Introduction).

13. *The Statutes,* IV, Pt. 1, 14 Eliz. C. 5.

14. *Ibid.,* 18 Eliz. C. 3; Aydelotte, *Elizabethan Rogues and Vagabonds,* 69.

15. W. Harrison, *The Description of England,* 185-93; Harrison, *The Elizabethan Journals,* I, 287-88; Steele, *Royal Proclamations,* I, 874.

16. *Acts of the Privy Council,* XXVII, 313-14, 338.

17. Rowse, *The England of Elizabeth,* 348.

18. *Acts of the Privy Council,* XXIII (1592), 382; IV (1553), 359; *Letters and Papers . . . Henry VIII, 1509-1530,* I, 3499:51; 1531-1547, XIV, 619.

19. C. Roy Hudleston (ed.), *Naworth Estate and Household Accounts, 1648-1660,* CLXIII (Surtees Society; Durham, N.C., 1953). See Appendix VI, 163, herein.

20. *State Papers . . . 1591-1625,* IV, 262:48; VI (1601-1603, with Addenda, 1547-65), 9:83 (Addenda, 1560).

21. *Journals of the House of Commons* (London: Record Publication, 1846-), I (1563), 9 Eliz.; (1571), 13 Eliz. *Journals of the House of Lords,* II (1601), 43 Eliz.; *Judges, The Elizabethan Underworld,* lxiii (Introduction).

22. See 50-51 herein. *Acts of the Privy Council,* XXXII, 16, 178-80, 420-21 (See also, XXVIII, 452; XXXII, 33, 430-31). For other examples of both corporate and individual licensed collections, see Appendix VII, 165, herein.

23. *Acts of the Privy Council,* XXVIII, 452.

24. Harrison, *The Elizabethan Journals,* II, 67 (Source: *Acts of the Privy Council,* XXV, 129); Rowse, *The England of Elizabeth,* 350; *Acts of the Privy Council,* XXIII, 339-40; *Letters and Papers . . . Henry VIII, 1509-1530,* I, 2862:4.

25. Ribton-Turner, *A History of Vagrants,* 116-17. From: Harleian MSS., British Museum, no. 364.

26. *Acts of the Privy Council,* XI, 300, 417; XXXIII, 597-99, 661-62; See 48, herein.

27. Jordan, *The Charities of Rural England*, 33-34; Laslett, *The World We Have Lost*, 243-44 (no. 17); *Acts of the Privy Council*, XXV, 10-11.

28. E. M. Hampson, *The Treatment of Poverty in Cambridgeshire, 1597-1834* (Cambridge University Press, 1934), 6,11. See Appendixes VII, 165 and VIII, 177, herein.

29. George M. Trevelyan, *Illustrated English Social History*, Vol. II, *The Age of Shakespeare and the Stuart Period* (London: Longmans, Green, 1949), 32.

30. Thomas, *Town Government*, 76-77.

31. See Appendix VIII, 177, herein. *Letters and Papers . . . Henry VIII, 1531-1547*, XVI, 10; Becon, *Works*, II, 253. From: "The Policy of War."

32. Holinshed, *Chronicles of England*, IV, 944-46.

33. *Acts of the Privy Council*, XIV, 236-37; W. Harrison, *The Description of England*, 133; Harrison, *The Elizabethan Journals*, II, 39, 50, 52-53. (Sources: Stow's *Annales*, n. p.; APC, XXV, 7,25,31).

34. Harrison, *The Elizabethan Journals*, II, 157-58 (Source: APC, XXVI, 380,383); Steele, *Royal Proclamations*, I, 888.

35. Harrison, *The Elizabethan Journals*, II, 286 (Source: APC, XXVIII, 537).

36. Judges, *The Elizabethan Underworld*, 491; Steele, *Royal Proclamations*, I, 535.

37. *State Papers . . . 1591-1625*, III, 249:23.

38. *The Statutes*, IV, Pt. 1, 14 Eliz. C. 14.

39. Steele, *Royal Proclamations*, I, 535, 3762.

40. *State Papers . . . 1581-1590*, II, 176:67; *The Statutes*, II, 2 Hen. V. C. 1; *Letters and Papers . . . Henry VIII, 1531-1547*, I, 864.

41. *State Papers . . . 1547-1580*, I, 88:21; VII, 14:14; *Letters and Papers . . . Henry VIII, 1531-1547*, XI, 168; *The Victoria History . . . Yorkshire*, III, 323-26.

42. *The Victoria History . . . Yorkshire*, III, 310-12.

43. *The Statutes*, I, 23 Edw. III. C. 1-7; III, 6 Hen. VIII. C. 3.

44. *Ibid.*, IV, Pt. 1,5 Eliz. C. 4.

45. See Appendixes I, 137, and III, 148, herein. Public Record Office, *Calendar of State Papers and Manuscripts, Relating to English Affairs, Existing in the Archives and Collections of Venice, and in Other Libraries of Northern Italy*, ed. Horatio F. Brown (London: Her Majesty's Stationery Office, 1897), IX (1592-1603), 1136.

46. *State Papers . . . 1591-1625*, III, 240:60.

47. Harrison, *The Elizabethan Journals*, I, 221 (Source: APC, XXIV, 159); *The Statutes*, IV, Pt. 1, 35 Eliz. C. 4. and IV, Pt. 2, 43 Eliz. C. 3.

48. *The Statutes*, IV, Pt. 2, 39 Eliz. C. 17.

49. *Acts of the Privy Council*, XXII, 295-96; XXIV, 298-301; Harrison, *The Elizabethan Journals*, I, 245 (Source: APC, XXIV, 298); I, 233 (Source: APC, XXXIV, 178); I, 221-22 (Source: D'Ewes' *Journals*, 463 & Townshend, 42).

50. See Appendix VII, 165, herein.

51. *Acts of the Privy Council*, XXIV, 178-79, 191-93.

52. *Ibid.*, XXII, 131.

53. *Ibid.*, 468; XXIV, 170-71.

54. *Ibid.*, XXI, 79, 92-93; See Appendix VII, 165, herein.

55. *Acts of the Privy Council*, XXV, 9, 119-20, 182; XXVI, 513-14; XXIX, 235-36.

56. *Ibid.*, XXV, 386-87, 391-92; XXVI, 77.

57. Steele, *Royal Proclamations*, I, 2416, 2418, 2486.

58. Rowse, *The England of Elizabeth*, 352.

59. *Ibid.*, 353.

60. *Letters and Papers . . . Henry VIII, 1531-1547*, XII, 261.

61. Crowley, *Works*, 14:296-316, 38:1104-12. From: "Epigrammes."

62. *State Papers . . . 1591-1625*, V (1600?), 276:65; Ribton-Turner, *A History of Vagrants*, 145.

NOTES TO CHAPTER VII

1. Taylor, *Works*, 11. From: "The Unnatural Father."
2. Latimer, *Sermons*, 80, 84-85. From: "First Sermon Preached before King Edward VI."
3. Rowse, *The England of Elizabeth*, 223.
4. *Ibid.*
5. Steele, *Royal Proclamations*, I, 1972, 1974.
6. *Ibid.*, 1972.
7. Fish, *A Supplication*, 98.
8. Aydelotte, *Elizabethan Rogues and Vagabonds*, 145-47. From: Appendix A, 3, John Bayker's Letter to Henry VIII (Source: *State Papers of Henry VIII*, 141, fos. 134-35; *Calendar, Letters and Papers of Henry VIII*, II, 1229); Herrtage, *Starkey's Life and Letters*, xciv-xcv: 24-30 (Appendix).
9. Rowse, *The England of Elizabeth*, 354; Taylor, *Works*, 5-7. From: "The True Cause of the Waterman's Suit Concerning Players."
10. Gray, *A History of English Philanthropy*, 9, 11.
11. Martin Luther (ed.), *The Book of Vagabonds and Beggars: With a Vocabulary of Their Language*, trans. and intro. John Camden Hotten (London, 1860), xxviii (Introduction); John Awdeley, *The Fraternitye of Vacabondes* (1560-61), ed. Edward Viles and F. J. Furnivall (Early English Text Society, Extra Series, No. 9: London: Humphrey Milford, Oxford University Press, 1869). Citation from this volume: Thomas Harman, *A Caveat or Warening for Commen Cursetors* . . . (1567), 28; *ibid.*, Citation from this volume: Parson Haben, *A Sermon in Praise of Thieves and Thievery* (n. d.), 92.
12. Awdeley, *The Fraternitye*; Richard Head and Francis Kirkman, *The English Rogue Described in the Life of Meriton Latroon A Witty Extravagant* (New York: Dodd, Mead and Co., 1928 [1665]), 23, 24, 39ff; Rowlands, *Martin Mark-All*, 7.
13. Harrison, *The Elizabethan Journals*, II, 274-75 (Source: APC, XXVIII, 427, 435); *Acts of the Privy Council*, XXVI, 23-24.
14. Starkey, *A Dialogue*, 89.
15. Taylor, *Works*, 8.
16. Awdeley, *The Fraternitye*, 33, 78.
17. Aydelotte, *Elizabethan Rogues and Vagabonds*, 4-5.
18. Judges, *The Elizabethan Underworld*, xxvii-xxviii. He was quoting Beatrice and Sidney Webb, *English Poor Law History*, I, 26.
19. Jusserand, *English Wayfaring Life*, 143-46.
20. Aydelotte, *Elizabethan Rogues and Vagabonds*, 17. For a full presentation of the above mentioned "double role" of the monasteries see further 15-17.
21. *Letters and Papers* . . . *Henry VIII, 1531-1547*, XII, Pt. 2, 6-7.
22. Aydelotte, *Elizabethan Rogues and Vagabonds*, 164-65 (Appendix A, 12); Harrison, *The Elizabethan Journals*, II, 47 (Source: *Remembrancia*, II, 102).
23. Ribton-Turner, *A History of Vagrants*, 92-93 (Source: Sir John Cheke, "Hurt of Sedicion howe greveous it is to a commune welth." Written in 1549 and contemporary with Kett's Rebellion. See also Samuel Rowlands', *Martin Mark-All*, 16-17. In this work it is given as part of the Belman's defense and is not credited to Cheke.)
24. W. Harrison, *The Description of England*, 119, 194.
25. Anon., *The Life and Death of Gamaliel Ratsey a Famous Thief, of England* . . . (The Shakespeare Association; Oxford University Press, 1935), vi-vii; Harrison, *The Elizabethan Journals*, I, 156; II, 73, 79 (Source: APC, XXIII, 151; XXV, 182, 233).
26. *Letters and Papers* . . . *Henry VIII, 1531-1547*, XX (1545), Pt. 1, 812; Harrison, *The Elizabethan Journals*, II (1596), 79 (Source: APC, XXV, 250); II (1597), 198 (Source: APC, XXVII, 290); II (1597), 198-99 (Source: APC, XXVII, 292); *Acts of the Privy Coun-*

cil, XXXII, 27, 74, 145-46, 492, 502.
27. See 67, herein, for this quotation in context.

NOTES TO CHAPTER VIII

1. *The Statutes*, IV, 5 Eliz. C. 3.
2. Stow and Howes, *The Annales*, 671.
3. See 85-86, herein.
4. *The Statutes*, IV, 18 Eliz. C. 3.
5. Crowley, *Works*, 10:172-80.
6. Stubbes, *Anatomy of the Abuses*, VI, No. XII, Pt. 2, 41-43.
7. Ribton-Turner, *A History of Vagrants*, 124-25.
8. *Acts of the Privy Council*, XXXIII, 392-93.
9. Ribton-Turner, *A History of Vagrants*, 136-39. In addition, see 52-53, herein.
10. *Acts of the Privy Council . . .* , XXIII, 157-58; *State Papers . . . 1591-1625*, IV (1596?), 261-70.
11. Brinklow, *Complaynt*, 14, 27-28; Stubbes, *Anatomy of the Abuses*, VI, No. VI, Pt. 1, 127. See the earlier quotation from his poem, 47, herein.
12. Taylor, *Works*, 25. From: "A New Discovery by Sea."
13. *State Papers . . . 1547-1580*, VII, 26:24 (Addenda, 1566-79). See Appendix VII, 000, herein. Marcham, *A Constitutional History*, 250-51.
14. Bland et al. *English Economic History, Select Documents*, no. 10.
15. Bland et al. *English Economic History, Select Documents*, no. 9.
16. Stow and Howes, *The Annales*, 537; Harrison, *The Elizabethan Journals*, II, 277 (Source: APC, XXVIII, 438).
17. Stow and Howes, *The Annales*, 907; Steele, *Royal Proclamations*, I, 1365.
18. Aydelotte, *Elizabethan Rogues and Vagabonds*, 72-75. See Appendix III, 148, herein.
19. Judges, *The Elizabethan Underworld*, 9; Latimer, *Sermons*, 170-71; Stephen Gosson, *The School of Abuse, Containing a Pleasant Invective against Poets, Pipers, Players, Jesters . . .* (London: reprinted for the Shakespeare Society, 1841), 23; Thomas C. Izard, *George Whetstone, Mid-Elizabethan Gentleman of Letters* (New York: Columbia University Press, 1942), 141; Samuel Rowlands, *Greenes Ghost Haunting Coniecatchers* (The Hunterian Club, No. I; London, 1872), 4.
20. Aydelotte, *Elizabethan Rogues and Vagabonds*, 152 (Appendix A, 6); *State Papers . . . 1591-1625*, III, 240:138. The date 1591 is questionable. Harrison, *The Elizabethan Journals*, I, 110 (Source: APC, XXVI, 23); *The Statutes*, IV, Pt. 2, 43 Eliz. C. 4, C. 13.
21. Steele, *Royal Proclamations*, I, 971; *The Statutes*, IV, Pt. 2, 7 Ja. I. C. 4; Latimer, *Sermons*, 86. From: "First Sermon Preached before King Edward VI."
22. Rowse, *The England of Elizabeth*, 349.
23. Lang, *Social England Illustrated*, IX, 67.
24. More, *Utopia*, 7, 15, 59.
25. Brinklow, *Complaynt*, 5, 16, 51; Latimer, *Sermons*, 108-109.
26. Herrtage, *Starkey's Life and Letters*, xcvii-xcix, 12-42:477-693 (Appendix); lxxxviii-lxxxix, 16-24:105-168.
27. Crowley, *Works*, 91:1209-16, 92:1229-36. From: "Voyce of the Last Trumpet"; Gosson, *The School of Abuse*, 41.
28. Stubbes, *Anatomy of the Abuses*, VI, No. IV, Pt. 1, 105; Harrison, *The Elizabethan Journals*, II, 68 (Source: S.T.C., 5245; m.e. in A. Boswell's *Frondes Caducae*, 1817); Steele, *Royal Proclamations*, 1016.

29. Frederic Morton Eden, *The State of the Poor: A History of the Labouring Classes in England, with Parochial Reports*, ed., intro. A. G. L. Rogers (New York: E. P. Dutton, 1929), xxiii-xxv, and 25-27.

30. Ribton-Turner, *A History of Vagrants*, 142-44.

31. Laslett, *The World We Have Lost*, 114-17.

32. Hampson, *The Treatment of Poverty*, 11.

33. Tawney, *The Agrarian Problems*, 280, 269.

Bibliography

Source Materials

Acts of the Privy Council, 1542-1628. Vols. I-XXXIV (1542-1616). Edited by John R. Dasent *et al*. London: Eyre and Spottiswoode for Her Majesty's Stationery Office, 1890-1949.

Anon. *The Life and Death of Gamaliel Ratsey a famous thief, of England* (The Shakespeare Association.) Oxford University Press, 1935.

Awdeley, John. *The Fraternitye of Vacabondes* (1560-61). Edited by Edward Viles and F. J. Furnivall. (Early English Text Society, Extra Series, No. 9.) London: Humphrey Milford, Oxford University Press, 1869. Also in this volume: Harman, Thomas. *A Caveat or Warening for Commen Cursetors* (1567). Parson Haben, *A Sermon in Praise of Theives and Thievery* (n.d.). Anon. *The Groundworke of Conny-catching* (1592).

Becon, Thomas. *Works of Thomas Becon*. Edited by John Ayre. (Parker Society, Vols. II, III.) Cambridge University Press, 1843-44. Used: II, "The News out of Heaven" (1543). "The Policy of War" (1542). III, "The Fortress of the Faithful" (1550).

Bland, A. E., *et al*., eds. *English Economic History, Select Documents*. London: G. Bell & Sons, Ltd., 1915.

Brinklow, Henry. *Complaynt of Roderyck Mors* (*ca*. 1542) and *The Lamentacyon of a Christen Agaynst the Cytye of London, Made by Roderigo Mors* (1545). Edited by J. M. Cowper. (Early English Text Society, Extra Series, Vol. XVI, No. 22.) London: N. Trubner & Co., 1874.

Bruel, Alexandre, ed. *Recueil des chartes de l'abbaye de Cluny*. 5 vols. Paris, 1876.

Byrne, M. St. Clare, ed. *The Letters of King Henry VIII: A Selection with a Few Other Documents*. New York: Funk and Wagnalls, 1968.

Camden, William. *The Historie of the Most Renowned and Virtuous Princess Elizabeth, Late Queen of England.* London, 1630.

Comperta Monastica. Visitation reports for purpose of closing of the smaller monasteries. They are printed in various source collections—see especially the *Calendar of Letters and Papers Foreign and Domestic of the Reign of Henry VIII, 1531-1547* cited fully in this bibliography.

Crowley, Robert. *The Select Works of Robert Crowley.* Edited by J.M. Cowper. (Early English Text Society, Extra Series, Vol. XII, No. 15.) London: N. Trubner & Co., 1872. Consists of: "Epigrammes" (1550). "Voyce of the Last Trumpet" (1550). "Pleasure and Payne" (n.d.). "The Way to Wealth" (1550). "An informacion and Peticion agaynst the Oppressours of the pore Commons of this Realme" (n.d.).

Depoin, J., ed. *Recueil de chartes et documents de Saint-Martin-des-Champs, monastere parisien.* 3 vols. Paris, 1912.

Duckett, G. F., ed. *Charters and Records: Ancient Abbey of Cluni from 1077 to 1534.* 2 vols. London, 1888.

Fish, Simon. *A Supplication for the Beggars (ca.* 1529). Edited by F. J. Furnivall. (Early English Text Society, Extra Series, Vol. XIII.) London: N. Trubner & Co., 1871. Also in this volume: Anon. *A Supplication of the Poor Commons* (n.d.). Anon. *A Supplication to . . . Henry VIII* (1544). Anon. *The Decay of England by the Great Multitude of Sheep* (1550s).

Floriano, A. C., ed. *El monasterio de Cornellana.* Vol. I of *Coleccion de fuentes para la historia de Austurias.* Oviedo: Seminario de Investigacion Diplomatica del I.D.E.A., 1949.

Frere, Walter H., and W. P. M. Kennedy, eds. *Visitation Articles and Injunctions of the Period of the Reformation.* (Alcuin Club, XIV-XVI.) London, 1908.

Gosson, Stephen. *The School of Abuse, Containing a Pleasant Invective Against Poets, Pipers, Players, Jesters.* London: reprinted for the Shakespeare Society, 1841.

Harrison, G. B., ed. *The Elizabethan Journals: Being a Record of those Things Most Talked of During the Years 1591-1603.* 3 vols. in one. Ann Arbor: University of Michigan Press, 1955.

————, ed. *A Jacobean Journal: Being a Record of Those Things Most Talked of During the Years 1603-1606.* London: George Routledge & Sons, Ltd., 1941 (revised ed. 1946).

Harrison, William. *The Description of England* (1545). Edited by Georges Edelen. (The Folger Shakespeare Library.) Cornell University Press, 1968.

Head, Richard and Francis Kirkman. *The English Rogue Described in the Life of Meriton Latroon, a Witty Extravagant* (1665). New York: Dodd, Mead and Co., 1928.

Heylyn, Peter. *Ecclesia Restaurata; or, the History of the Reformation of the Church of England* (1661). 2 vols. Edited by J. C. Robertson. Cambridge,

1842.

Holinshed, Raphael. *Chronicles of England, Scotland, and Ireland.* 6 vols. Vols. I-IV: *England.* New York: Ams Press, Inc., 1965.

Huddleston, C. Roy, ed. *Naworth Estate and Household Accounts, 1648-1660.* (Surtees Society, Vol. CLXIII.) Durham, N.C., 1953.

Hughes, Paul L. and James F. Larkin, eds. *Tudor Royal Proclamations.* Vol. I: *The Early Tudors, 1485-1553.* Yale University Press, 1964.

Journals of the House of Commons. Vol. I. (Record Publication.) London, 1846-.

Journals of the House of Lords. Vols. I, II. (Record Publication.) London, 1846-.

Judges, A. V., ed. *The Elizabethan Underworld.* New York: E. P. Dutton & Co., 1930.

Lang, Andrew, ed. *An English Garner.* Vol. IX: *Social England Illustrated, A Collection of XVII Century Tracts.* Westminster: Archibald Constable & Co., Ltd., 1903.

Publisher's note to this volume: "The texts . . . in the present volume are reprinted with . . . slight alterations from the *English Garner* issued in eight volumes (1877-1890, London, 8 vo.) by Professor [Edward] Arber."

Latimer, Hugh. *Sermons by Hugh Latimer, Sometime Bishop of Worcester.* London: J. M. Dent & Co., 1906.

Lodge, Thomas. *The Complete Works of Thomas Lodge [1580-1623?].* 4 vols. New York: *Russell & Russell, Inc., 1963. Used: Wits Miserie, and the Worlds Madnesse,* Vol. IV.

Luther, Martin, ed. *The Book of Vagabonds and Beggars: With a Vocabulary of their Language.* Translated with an introduction by John Camden Hotten. London, 1860.

Massinger, Philip. *A New Way to Pay Old Debts.* Edited with an introduction by M. St. Clare Byrne. London: Falcon Educational Books, 1949.

More, Thomas. *Utopia.* Edited and translated by H. V. S. Ogden. New York: Appleton-Century-Crofts, Inc., 1949.

Pollard, A. F. ed. *An English Garner.* Vol. VI: *Tudor Tracts, 1532-1588.* Westminster: Archibald Constable & Co., Ltd., 1903. See annotation under Lang, Andrew above.

Public Record Office. *Calendar of Letters and Papers, Foreign and Domestic of the Reign of Henry VIII, 1509-1530.* Vols. I-IV. Edited by J. S. Brewer. London: His Majesty's Stationery Office, 1864-1932.

————. *Calendar of Letters and Papers, Foreign and Domestic of the Reign of Henry VIII, 1531-1547.* Vols. I, V-XXI. Edited by James Gairdner. London: His Majesty's Stationery Office, 1880-1910.

————. *Calendar of State Papers, Domestic Series, of the Reigns of Edward VI, Mary, Elizabeth, 1547-1580.* Vols. I-VII. Edited by Robert Lemon. London: Her Majesty's Stationery Office, 1856-1865.

————. *Calendar of State Papers, Domestic Series, of the Reigns of Edward VI,*

Mary, Elizabeth I, 1581-1590. Vol. II. Edited by Robert Lemon. London: Her Majesty's Stationery Office, 1856-72.

———. *Calendar of State Papers, Domestic Series, of the Reigns of Edward VI, Mary, Elizabeth I, and James I, 1591-1625.* Vols. III-VII, XII. Edited by Mary Anne Green. London: Her Majesty's Stationery Office, 1867-72.

———. *Calendar of State Papers and Manuscripts, Relating to English Affairs, Existing in the Archives and Collections of Venice, and in Other Libraries of Northern Italy.* Vol. IX. Edited by Horatio F. Brown. London: Her Majesty's Stationery Office, 1897.

———. *State Papers of King Henry VIII.* London: John Murray, 1831.

Rowlands, Samuel. *Greenes Ghost Haunting Coniecatchers.* (The Hunterian Club, No. I.) London: 1872. First edition, 1602.

———. *Hell's Broke Loose.* (The Hunterian Club, No. VIII.) London, 1605. Reprinted from the first edition of 1605.

———. *Martin Mark-All, Beadle of Bridewell.* (The Hunterian Club, No. XIX.) London, 1872-73. First edition, 1610. Also in this volume: *The Runnagates Race, or the Originall of the Regiment of Rogues.* First edition, 1610.

Salisbury, The Marquis of. *Calendar of the Manuscripts of the Most Hon. the Marquis of Salisbury, K. G.* (Historical Manuscripts Commission, Series IX, Parts I-XIX.) London: Her Majesty's Stationery Office, 1883-1965.

Smith, Sir Thomas. *The Commonwealth of England the Manner of Government Thereof.* London, 1640.

Starkey, Thomas. *A Dialogue Between Cardinal Pole and Thomas Lupset, Lecturer in Rhetoric at Oxford.* Part II of *England in the Reign of King Henry the Eighth.* Edited by J. M. Cowper. (Early English Text Society, Extra Series, Vol. X, Nos. 12, 32.) London: N. Trubner & Co., 1878.

The Statutes of the Realm. 11 vols. Dawsons of Pall Mall, 1963.

Steele, Robert. *A Bibliography of Royal Proclamations of the Tudor and Stuart Sovereigns and of Others Published Under Authority, 1485-1714.* Vol. I: *England and Wales.* New York: Burt Franklin, 1967.

Stow, John. *A Survey of London.* 2 vols. Edited by Charles L. Kingsford. Oxford, 1908.

Stow, John and E. Howes. *The Annales . . . of England.* London: Thomas Adams, 1615.

Stubbes, Philip. *Anatomy of the Abuses in England in Shakspere's Youth, A. D. 1583.* Edited by Frederick J. Furnivall. (The New Shakspere Society, Series VI, No. 4, Part I; Series VI, No. 6, Part I; Series VI, No. 12, Part II.) London: N. Trubner & Co., 1877, 1879, 1882.

Tawney, Richard H. and Eileen Power, eds. *Tudor Economic Documents.* 3 vols. (University of London Historical Series, No. 14.) 1924.

Taylor, John. *Works of John Taylor, the Water Poet.* Edited by Charles Hindley. London: Reeves and Turner, 1872.

Valor Ecclesiasticus. 6 vols. Edited by John Caley and Joseph Hunter.

Published by the Records Commission, 1810-34.

Results of the survey to determine the tax on spiritual benefices, 1535.

Wilson, Thomas. *The State of England, A.D. 1600.* Edited by F. J. Fisher. (Camden Miscellany, XVI, 3rd Ser. LII.) London, 1936.

Wright, Thomas, ed. *Three Chapters of Letters Relating to the Suppression of the Monasteries.* (Camden Society, Old Ser., XXVI.) London, 1843.

Wriothesley, Charles. *A Chronicle of England During the Reigns of the Tudors.* Edited by William D. Hamilton. (Camden Society, New Ser., XI, XX,) London, 1875-77.

Secondary Materials

Aydelotte, Frank. *Elizabethan Rogues and Vagabonds.* Vol. I of *Oxford Historical and Literary Studies.* Oxford: Clarendon Press, 1913.

Bainton, Roland H. *The Reformation of the Sixteenth Century.* Boston: The Beacon Press, 1956.

Baskerville, Geoffrey. *English Monks and the Suppression of the Monasteries.* New Haven: Yale University Press, 1937.

Beresford, Maurice W. "The Common Informer, the Penal Statutes, and Economic Regulation," *Economic History Review,* 2nd Ser., 10 (December, 1957), 221-38.

Bindoff, S. T. *Tudor England.* Harmondsworth, Middlesex: Penguin Books, 1950.

Black, J. B. *The Reign of Elizabeth, 1558-1603.* 2nd ed. revised. Vol. VIII of *The Oxford History of England.* 15 vols. Edited by Sir George Clark. Oxford: Clarendon Press, 1959.

Burnet, Gilbert. *The History of the Reformation of the Church of England.* 7 vols. Edited by Nicholas Pocock. Oxford: Clarendon Press, 1865. Vol. I dedicated to King Charles II and Vol. II dated 1680.

Gilbert Burnet (1643-1715), became bishop of Salisbury.

Chambers, R. W. "Literary History Lecture: The Saga and the Myth of Sir Thomas More," *Proceedings of the British Academy,* XII (1926), 179-225.

Chandler, Frank W. *The Literature of Roguery.* 2 vols. New York: Houghton, Mifflin & Co., 1907.

Cheyney, Edward P. *Social Changes in England in the Sixteenth Century: As Reflected in Contemporary Literature.* Part I: *Rural Changes.* (Publications of the University of Pennsylvania Series in Philology, Literature and Archaeology, Vol. IV, No. 2.) Philadelphia, 1895.

Cobbett, William. *A History of the Protestant Reformation in England and Ireland.* Preface by F. A. Gasquet. New York: Benziger Brothers, Printers to the Holy Apostolic See, n.d.

Coulton, George G. *Five Centuries of Religion.* Vol. IV: *The Last Days of Medieval Monachism.* Cambridge University Press, 1950.

Davies, Godfrey. *The Early Stuarts, 1603-1660.* 2nd ed. revised. Vol. IX of *The Oxford History of England.* 15 vols. Edited by Sir George Clark. Oxford: The Clarendon Press, 1959.

Davis, E. Jeffries. "The Transformation of London," *Tudor Studies.* Edited by R. W. Seaton-Watson. London: Longmans, Green & Co., 1924.

Dickens, Arthur G. "An Elizabethan Defender of the Monasteries," *Church Quarterly Review,* 130 (July-September, 1940), 236-62.
   An analysis of Michael Sherbrook's *Falle of Religious Howses.*

――――. "Sedition and Conspiracy in Yorkshire during the Later Years of Henry VIII," *Yorkshire Archaeological Journal,* 34 (Part 4, 1939), 379-98.

Eden, Frederic Morton. *The State of the Poor: A History of the Labouring Classes in England, with Parochial Reports.* Edited and introduction by A. G. L. Rogers. New York: E. P. Dutton & Co., 1929.

Elton, Geoffrey R. "Informing for Profit: A Sidelight on Tudor Methods of Law Enforcement," *Cambridge Historical Journal,* II (No. 2, 1954), 149-67.

Feiling, Keith. *A History of England.* New York: McGraw-Hill Book Co., Inc., 1948.

――――. *England Under the Tudors and Stuarts, 1485-1688.* Oxford University Press, 1927.

Gasquet, Francis A. *Henry VIII and the English Monasteries.* London: George Bell & Sons, 1906.

Gray, B. Kirkman. *A History of English Philanthropy from the Dissolution of the Monasteries to the Taking of the First Census.* London: P. S. King & Son, 1905.

Hall, W. P., *et al. A History of England and the British Empire.* 3rd edition. Boston: Ginn and Co., 1953.

Hampson, E. M. *The Treatment of Poverty in Cambridgeshire, 1597-1834.* Cambridge University Press, 1934.

Herrtage, Sidney J. ed. *Starkey's Life and Letters.* Part I of *England in the Reign of King Henry the Eighth.* (Early English Text Society, Extra Series, Vol. X, Nos. 12, 32.) London: N. Trubner & Co., 1878.
   The Appendix contains an extract from Sir William Forrest's *Pleasaunt Poesie of Princelie Practice* (1548).

Hodgett, G. A. J. "The Unpensioned Ex-religious in Tudor England," *Journal of Ecclesiastical History,* 13 (Oct. 1962), 195-202.

Hughes, Philip. *The Reformation in England.* Vol. I: *The King's Proceedings.* London: Hollis & Carter, 1950.

Izard, Thomas C. *George Whetstone, Mid-Elizabethan Gentleman of Letters.* New York: Columbia University Press, 1942.

Jordan, Wilbur K. *The Charities of London, 1480-1660: The Aspirations and the Achievements of the Urban Society.* London: George Allen & Unwin, Ltd., 1960.

――――. *The Charities of Rural England, 1480-1660: The Aspirations and*

Achievements of the Rural Society. London: George Allen & Unwin, Ltd., 1961.

_____. *The Forming of the Charitable Institutions of the West of England: A Study of the Changing Pattern of Social Aspirations in Bristol and Somerset, 1480-1660.* (Transactions of the American Philosophical Society, New Series, Vol. L, Part 8.) Philadephia, 1960.

_____. *Philanthropy in England, 1480-1660: A Study of the Changing Pattern of English Social Aspirations.* London: George Allen & Unwin, Ltd., 1959.

_____. *Social Institutions in Kent, 1480-1660: A Study of the Changing Pattern of Social Aspirations.* (Kent Archaeological Society, 1961, Vol. LXXV of *Archaeologia Cantiana.*) Kent: Headley Bros., Ltd., 1961.

Jusserand, Jean Adrien Antoine Jules. *English Wayfaring Life in the Middle Ages.* Translated by L. T. Smith. New York: Barnes & Noble, 1961.

Knowles, David. *The Religious Orders in England.* Vol. III: *The Tudor Age.* Cambridge University Press, 1959.

Laslett, Peter. *The World We Have Lost.* London: Methuen & Co., Ltd., 1965.

Leonard, E. M. *The Early History of English Poor Relief.* Cambridge, 1900.

Lunt, William E. *History of England.* Revised edition. New York: Harper & Brothers, 1938.

Mackie, J. D. *The Earlier Tudors, 1485-1558.* Vol. VII of *The Oxford History of England.* 15 vols. Edited by Sir George Clark. Oxford: The Clarendon Press, 1952. Reprinted with corrections, 1957.

McKisack, May. *The Fourteenth Century, 1307-1399.* Vol. V of *The Oxford History of England.* 15 vols. Edited by Sir George Clark. Oxford: The Clarendon Press, 1959.

Marcham, Frederick George. *A Constitutional History of Modern England, 1485 to the Present.* New York: Harper & Brothers, 1960.

Moorman, John R. H. *A History of the Church in England.* New York: Morehouse-Gorham Co., 1954.

Ribton-Turner, C. J. *A History of Vagrants and Vagrancy and Beggars and Begging.* London: Chapman and Hall, Ltd., 1887.

Rowse, Alfred Leslie. *The Elizabethan Age,* Vol. I: *The England of Elizabeth: The Structure of Society.* London: Macmillan & Co., Ltd., 1950.

Savine, Alexander. *English Monasteries on the Eve of the Dissolution.* Vol. I of *Oxford Studies in Social and Legal History.* Edited by Paul Vinogradoff. Oxford: Clarendon Press, 1909.

Smith, Lacey B. "English Treason Trials and Confessions in the Sixteenth Century," *Journal of the History of Ideas,* 15 (October, 1954), 471-98.

Snape, R. H. *English Monastic Finances in the Later Middle Ages.* Cambridge University Press, 1926.

Stone, Lawrence. "State Control in Sixteenth-century England," *Economic History Review,* 17 (No. 2, 1947), 103-20.

Tawney, R. H. *The Agrarian Problem in the Sixteenth Century.* New York:

Burt Franklin, n.d.

———. *Religion and the Rise of Capitalism.* New York: The New American Library (Mentor Books), 1947.

Thomas, J. H. *Town Government in the Sixteenth Century.* London: George Allen & Unwin, Ltd., 1933.

Thomson, Gladys Scott. *Lords Lieutenants in the Sixteenth Century: A Study in Tudor Local Administration.* London: Longmans, Green & Co., 1923.

Trevelyan, George M. *History of England.* London: Longmans, Green & Co., 1927.

———. *Illustrated English Social History.* Vol. I: *Chaucer's England and the Early Tudors.* London: Longmans, Green & Co., 1949.

The Victoria History of the Counties of England. Vol. I: *London.* London: Constable and Co., Ltd., 1909.

———. Vol. III: *County of York.* London: Constable & Co., Ltd., 1913.

Webb, Sidney and Beatrice (Sidney James Webb Passfield). *English Local Government.* 11 vols. Hamden, Conn.: Shoe String Press, 1963.

Woodward, George William Otway. *The Dissolution of the Monasteries.* London: Blandford Press, 1966.

Index

201